Building ComMunity

Social Studies in the Middle School Years

EDITED BY

Mary Burke-Hengen

&

Tim Gillespie

HEINEMANN
Portsmouth, NH

HEINEMANN
A division of Reed Elsevier Inc.
361 Hanover Street
Portsmouth, NH 03801-3912
Offices and agents throughout the world

Every effort has been made to contact the copyright holders for permission to reprint borrowed material where necessary. We regret any oversights that may have occurred and would be happy to rectify them in future printings of this work.

The authors and publisher are grateful to the following for permission to reprint previously published material:

Figure 6-2 from *Preparing Citizens: Linking Authentic Assessment and Instruction in Civic/Law-Related Education*, edited by Barbara Miller (Boulder, CO: Social Science Education Consortium, forthcoming). Used by permission of the publisher.

Library of Congress Cataloging-in-Publication Data

Building community : social studies in the middle school years / Mary
    Burke-Hengen and Tim Gillespie, editors.
        p.   cm.
    Includes bibliographical references.
    ISBN 0-435-08904-8
    1. Social sciences—Study and teaching (Secondary)—United States.
2. Middle schools—United States.   I. Burke-Hengen, Mary.
II. Gillespie, Tim.
H62.B834   1995
300'.71'273—dc20   95-8643
                                                                              CIP

Editor: Carolyn Coman
Production: J. B. Tranchemontagne
Cover design: Catherine Hawkes
Cover art by Kari Sims, a former student of both Mary Burke-Hengen and Tim Gillespie.

Printed in the United States of America on acid-free paper
99 98 97 96 95   EB   7 6 5 4 3 2 1

To all our students—who have delighted us, confounded us, inspired us, challenged us, and taught us most of what we know about teaching.

Contents

Acknowledgments

We have been inspired and instructed over the years by countless teachers, students, friends, and colleagues. For their faith in us and their belief in the importance of what we do as teachers, we offer our heartfelt thanks. Mary would like to say a special thanks to Mary Bothwell, Linda Christensen, Jane Braunger, Lynne Shlom Ferguson and Ruth Hubbard for their leadership, innovation, and supportive nudges, and to Tim for his patience and his partnership. Tim would like to give special thanks to his family—wife Janet Giske Gillespie and sons Nathan and Joshua Gillespie—for their support, love, and laughter, and to Mary for her wisdom and partnership. And thanks to our editor, Carolyn Coman, for all of her encouragement, and to Jim Whitney, photographer and friend.

Introduction

"Create a community for learning," says the influential 1989 report of the Carnegie Council Task Force on Education of Young Adolescents, *Turning Points*. As teachers, we are firm believers in the report's first recommendation for improving our nation's middle schools: "The student should, upon entering middle grade school, join a small community in which people—students and adults—get to know each other well to create a climate for intellectual development. Students should feel that they are part of a community of shared educational purpose." (1989, p. 37)

That makes all the sense in the world to us.

And what makes sense for middle school students also makes sense for teachers. As we endeavor to create a community with our students, we also ought to consider the value of doing the same with other teachers. What we know young adolescents need—a sense of self-worth, meaningful work, larger purposes, intellectual and social engagement—is what we all need, and much of it can best be nurtured in a community of friends and colleagues. "Friendship," Henry Adams noted, "needs a certain parallelism of life, a community of thought." (1918, p. 312)

Thus, the theme of this book is *building community*. The discipline of social studies has at its heart the cultivation of community, by the sharing of the history and traditions that our students have inherited. In all the middle school social studies classrooms that the reader will visit in these pages, teachers are working hard to build communities of students deeply engaged in shared intellectual endeavor. And between the lines of these pages, the reader will find an argument for teachers to build their own communities. The book itself is the product of such a community collaboration, the work of a gathering of teachers in Portland, Oregon.

Here in Portland, as in many other places around the nation, the move toward middle schools began in earnest fifteen to twenty years ago. Old school buildings were remodeled, curriculum was restructured, schedules were reorganized for the special developmental needs of young adolescents, and the doors were flung open. Sixth, seventh, and eighth graders were put together in schools organized primarily like high schools with students moving around to different teachers for seven or eight periods.

As the years passed, many middle school teachers here were making the same discovery as their counterparts around the nation. Though we had abandoned the self-contained classrooms of elementary schools, there still seemed to be a need for more continuity in students' lives and more integration of curriculum than a diced-up six-period, six-subject day was providing. So, slowly, school by school, there has been a move back toward some sort of multiperiod block of time at the heart of every middle schooler's day. Most commonly in our neck of the woods, we call these kinds of arrangements "Core" classes, and most involve a two- or three-period chunk of time during which the teacher is responsible for multiple subject matters, usually social studies and language arts.

Some of the teachers who face this situation have been primarily social studies teachers; now they find themselves responsible for teaching reading and writing as well, without much training. Some teachers are longtime English and language arts teachers, now trying to figure out how to teach history. Some are high school teachers who have retooled for the middle years, and some are elementary-school teachers following their students up the grades. In other words, teachers are approaching these Core class assignments from many different directions. The group of teachers that wrote this book reflects those many directions—beginning with us, the editors.

In the 1991–1992 school year, the two of us managed to negotiate a joint teaching arrangement. We decided that we both wanted to try something new, and somehow we convinced the necessary authorities to let us job share an eighth grade teaching position at Beaumont Middle School in Portland. Mary was a longtime middle school teacher who was just coming off a research sabbatical; she had also taught high school social studies and special education. Tim was a language arts specialist in the Portland School District curriculum office who had taught elementary school and high school English and humanities.

For our job share, we split an assignment that would usually be covered by one classroom teacher. Tim taught the morning Eighth Grade Core class (three periods during which the district-stipulated social studies and language arts curricula were to be covered) in Room 220 at Beaumont Middle School and then went off to work in the district curriculum office. Mary spent her mornings at our shared desk in the basement of the curriculum office and then drove over to teach the afternoon Eighth Grade Core class in Room 220: two jobs split between the two of us.

At the start of the year, we vowed to meet in the classroom for lunch (the only time of the day when it wasn't packed with students) every Tuesday and Thursday, come hell, high water, or lack of lesson plans. Our goal was modest: to talk about our respective students and our work, to plan together when we could, to problem solve and use each other as a sounding board and sympathetic ear. Conversations that usually began with talk of specific students—their accomplishments and their challenges—often veered toward big pedagogical issues of content and method and meaning before they resettled on those energetic eighth graders.

In addition, we began an unplanned correspondence on a steno pad. These communications started out to be mostly about the logistics of sharing a classroom and curriculum—how long the films were checked out for, which desk kept getting marred with grafitti, and so forth—but they also became occasions for reflecting on our work at a deeper level. We filled many steno pads during the year.

What we were reminded of by this modest collaboration was the satisfaction of working with another teacher in a sustained way. Teaching can be such a solitary act, and little time is provided to most of us for continually and collaboratively reflecting on our work (in a way in which we usually cannot in rushed teacher lunchrooms or during tedious Monday afternoon staff meetings). As the year progressed, we realized what a gift we were giving ourselves by our commitment to this routine of chewing the pedagogical fat twice a week.

As we talked during those months, we found ourselves wishing there were more resources and accounts from other teachers who were faced with the engaging challenge of integrating social studies with other disciplines. As we talked, however, we also realized what a wealth of resources we had close at hand; plenty of middle school teacher friends of ours were undertaking exciting projects that wove history, civics, geography, literature, writing, and the arts together. Some of these teachers were at our school, Beaumont, and some were from other schools, teachers we knew from the Portland Writing Project and other situations. This book, then, grew from these seeds: our wish for more resources for middle school teachers, our belief that many fine teachers are engaged in practices that deserve celebration and sharing, and our desire to expand our conversation.

In these pages, a number of our teacher friends tell the stories of their efforts to teach social studies sensibly in integrated-curriculum middle school settings. The contributors constitute a gathering of friends, a community of professionals, each of whom has a particular contribution to make from his or her unique set of experiences.

With this group, we began a series of potluck dinners in Mary's condominium that overlooks Portland and the ridge of hills that runs behind the city. Not long after our first get-together, we ran across a description of a recent report by the federally funded Center for Research on the Context of Secondary School Teaching at Stanford University. The Center's recommendation to a congressional forum, based on a five-year study of effective teaching, was that national curriculum standards and assessment systems may not be the most significant factors in fostering effective teaching. The most effective teachers, the Center said, were those involved in professional networks that fostered teacher development and that combated teacher isolation. "Not one [of the teachers studied] who was able to develop sustained and challenging learning opportunities for students was in isolation. Each belonged to a professional learning community" (Rothman, 1993, p. 1). A cornerstone, thus, for our continued growth as teachers is to cultivate learning communities among ourselves, and this book bears witness to one such endeavor to do so.

Among us, members of our group represent a cross section of teachers. We have taught at many grade levels and in many settings. Most have taught in Portland, a public school system with many different kinds of schools serving a diverse urban population. Our schools are organized in different ways and have different kinds of student bodies. One of us is retired, some of us are veterans, and some of us are fairly new to the profession. We have different curricular backgrounds. Some of us are by temperament more single-discipline-bound, some more expansively interdisciplinary by nature. We teach in many different ways.

We do not believe we all need to teach in one way.

Our chapters are written in a spirit of collegial sharing, much as a teacher support group operates. We are not presenting teacher research, but rather teacher accounts, stories, curriculum ideas, classroom strategies, and reflections, offered in much the same way as we share them in our ongoing conversations about our work. The chapters are not all "how-to" pieces, though the reader will find much practical information in these pages. We are not all at the cutting edge of any movement, but we all write out of our classroom experience. We do not all feel extraordinary at every moment of every day; sometimes we're just tired and footsore and voice weary like any teachers. Sometimes we do things in class that flop, and sometimes it dawns on us that we have undertaken activities that seem to contradict our beliefs. We are teachers, fallible and hopeful, and we could be working down the hall from you.

Furthermore, though most of us share a general commitment to student-centered, process-oriented ways of teaching, we do not necessarily agree on all issues surrounding our work. We do not have one definitive point of view about integrated curriculum. What we *do* have in our small community is a willingness to share stories about what we've tried to do to connect social studies teaching with language arts and other disciplines. We want to be modest and do not presume to tell readers what they *ought* to be doing. We realize there are different approaches for different students, teachers, places, and times; we realize that children can learn and grow under many different kinds of conditions. What we mostly believe in is the importance and power of teachers involved in conversations with each other.

We have all experienced many delights, challenges, difficulties, and gratifications in finding our way along this path of change toward integrated social studies classes. Our stories express a range of responses to the challenges faced in teaching the social studies. We hope that you will find in these different teachers' accounts some useful insights, suggestions, classroom strategies, and provocations to further thought. We invite you to eavesdrop on our talk in the hope that it might stimulate conversations in your own teaching community.

BIBLIOGRAPHY

Adams, Henry. 1918. *The Education of Henry Adams: An Autobiography.* Boston: Houghton Mifflin.

Turning Points: Preparing American Youth for the 21st Century: The Report of the Task Force on Education of Young Adolescents. 1989. New York: Carnegie Council on Adolescent Development.

Rothman, Robert. 1993. "Study Urges 'Learning Communities' to Address the Isolation of Teachers." *Education Week.*

Part One
CONNECTING STORY AND HISTORY

Chapter 1
Once Upon A Time and Place: Stories of the Family

TONI KENNEDY

There's no magic quite like a good story. Once the tale begins, the listener spins through other times to explore land, culture, and people who miraculously have something to tell us about their past, the present, and our future. Much of my own fascination with stories has its source in the family-roots unit that my eighth graders and I do each year. From this community of writers, tales of courage, laughter, joy, suffering, and magnificent endurance have emerged. Together we learn from old documents, photographs, anecdotes, and lore. We keep faith with the memories by writing the stories, sharing the fruits of our research, and rejoicing as each of us becomes the storyteller for a new generation.

WEEK ONE: THE BEGINNING

Every year over a span of two months, for one period a day, my class gathers information about family history, keeping the following ideas in mind:

- The most difficult task is discovering that first story.
- Elders keep alive family stories.
- Family stories arise out of response to a question.
- We can understand our family scandals or "secrets" when we examine them in the light of history and geography.
- Family artifacts give a needed dimension to the research.
- Rituals are a grand source of stories.
- Young people play an invaluable role if they write and tell family history.

The first day on which I present the unit, the students are not at a loss for words.

"Family stories?"
"What are we doing this for?"
"My parents never talk to me about anything."
"Nothing exciting's ever happened to our family."

As they speak of their concerns and objections to seeking information, what surfaces is not the fear that they will find out too much about their family, but that they will discover the *too little,* or the insignificant. At the end of this first exchange, we discuss the importance of stories and talk about favorite myths, legends, and novels. Usually we can agree on these points: A story hooks the reader or listener when there is action, conflict, and characters to care about.

I assure them that with careful research they will find all these elements in their own family stories.

The Writing Journal

I lay out spiral notebooks of varying colors with a name label in the right hand corner. Each child chooses a notebook. This is my small gift to them for taking on the challenge of this journey through time. The journal is also my guarantee that every student starts on the same point.

What goes in this journal? Kernel ideas that I offer each day, their own brainstorming, the intriguing ideas of others, the stories they hear from family members, and their responses to these tales. Each night they try to discover at least one event, fact, or story. Sometimes this means examining old photos or checking on dates for a family tree; sometimes it means an interview and long distance call. Always it means a listening heart.

An Opener or Two or Three

The first few days set the tone for the rest of the unit. The subject matter of the opening sessions needs to be inviting, not intimidating. One opener has not failed me yet: I ask the students to complete, "My grandfather (or grandmother) told me about a time when . . ."

"He had to walk three miles in the snow to get to school."
"We only had black-and-white television."
"He bought his first car."
"She had to pick cotton."

Once a student speaks these first words, the interest of all is piqued.

"Where was that?"
"How much did he pay for it?" or "What kind was it?"
"My grandmother told me the same thing."

In my experience, that first story, no matter how brief, is the catalyst. Teacher, students, and the teller all know there is more to the story of that baby-blue Ford. "Was it a graduation gift or a Bingo prize? Did the driver mosey out once a year or *drag Main* every night of the week?"

To discover the *more* in our family stories remains the challenge for the next month.

The students wonder, "How do we know if what we're told is true?"

I tell them, "Don't worry now about what is *fact* or *make-believe*. Simply try to gain access to the story."

Family Sayings   Families pass down *words of wisdom* from one generation to the next. "We all have little sayings that our parents repeat in numerous ways. Sometimes this can be a riddle or a warning or a bit of advice. Chances are that the saying did not originate with your parents, but maybe with their parents or grandparents." I offer a personal example: "From the time we were small my parents would say, 'Open your hand and close your eyes and I'll give you something to make you wise.'"

What is important at this point is for the students to enjoy sharing these family words and that they begin to recognize that in every tidbit lies a story. In the example that I shared, my mother used those words when she handed my siblings and me birthday gifts; my father said those words whenever he returned from one of his business trips. The saying meant that my parents placed a surprise in my trusting, outstretched hand. I encourage the children to think of sayings of their own, to write them down, and to discover the context behind the sayings. By context, I mean the why, where, and with whom of the saying. Next, as a group, we brainstorm examples of family sayings so that I know for certain that every child in the room understands what to do. Their homework is to discover all that they can about one family saying.

The following day, the students share. Usually, the time period resembles an incantation or litany:

> "Don't advertise your ignorance."
> "When was the last time you took the garbage out?"
> "Take off your coat and stay awhile."
> "Wipe your feet!"
> "Can't you wait until Christmas?"
> "Eat your food. There are starving people in Africa."

It is important that every child shares a saying, even if it is a repeat of what others have said. If only a few children are willing to speak, the synergistic movement is lost, and a certain elitism takes over: Those whose families have a history, and those whose families don't. With enough encouragement, every child can offer something. While one student will simply know the phrase, others will know the context out of which it arose. Some will even dedicate themselves to passing on the tradition. Clarice's favorite saying has this little history:

> This summer when my family and I were staying at the beach house in Cape Cod, my cousin and I were bored, so we went into the living room to read the guest book. Everyone who stays there is supposed to sign their name, address and write a comment. My aunt's friend wrote 'Cool Beans!' in the comment section. Amanda and I liked it so whenever we see something nifty, we say 'Cool Beans!'

The *family sayings* class is usually a humorous time. Students discover phrases they've never heard before or applaud common sayings that cross ethnic and socioeconomic lines. The students give ideas and trigger memories for one another. This word game is an easy way for students. They begin to share those stories that give their family its uniqueness and its universality—two concepts that I'll deal with later in this essay.

Family Names   Just as the students find a history behind family sayings, so sometimes they have the same experience when they go to research family names. "What do we call people in our family, and how did they get these names? Is there logic behind the choice of our family name? Are there traditions behind the granting of names?"

One way in which I discover family history through names is by asking the students to first list the names of all brothers, sisters, aunts, uncles, parents, grandparents, great-grandparents. I encourage them to make some kind of diagram or tree. That way they have a visual representation of naming patterns and of the passage of time.

One child mentioned that the oldest male in his family had some form of the name John William. He traced this repetition back four generations! This, too, becomes the introduction to the elders in a family—those people who have lived beyond sixty years and who have seen so many events and fads come and go. There's never a time when someone doesn't say how old a grandparent or great-grandparent is. Always someone else tries to beat that record.

After Johntae had meticulously researched his family all the way to the early 1800s, he printed in black felt this sentence, starred and bold: "My oldest living relative is my great uncle who lives in Haynesville, Louisiana. He is ninety-nine years old. His name is Willie Ivory."

As the children examine their family trees, the interest at this point is not whether someone is a CEO or is suffering from Alzheimer's disease. The remarkable fact is that they have lived as long as they have. The students note the shadow people in their past, the unknowns with or without names, but those whose blood they share. LaShawna carefully wrote: "My grandfather's parents. These great grandparents I never met: Great grandfather: African, Blackfoot Indian. Great grandmother: African, Blackfoot Indian."

Adopted Children   When it is time to examine names, the teacher might be concerned about the adopted child. Over the years, the children have taught me a new perspective on what it means to have roots in more than one family. Blood connects a family, but so does a shared history. Adopted children have their origins in a family that gave them life and in a family whose bonds go beyond blood ties. Both families have helped to make the adopted children who they are. The stories and names of the ancestors are theirs as well. In fact, these children have more options than the others. One adopted child may choose to follow either family; another may choose to follow both.

Pets   Some say that if you want a good story, and grandpa's too tired, check out the hound dog. Children have many tales of adopting the stray cat or attending Fido's funeral. After brainstorming their own pet stories, I try to encourage my students to move beyond their own experience to that of someone older, to seek stories that go back in time, like the stray that found its way from Utah to Oregon or the dog who helped a blind grandfather or the parrot that crossed the Pacific. Mika tells this story:

> My great-great grandfather had a neat work dog. This dog was the milk churner. You have to churn the milk to make it into butter and cream. The dog's job was to walk around in circles for hours at a time churning the milk.

I can still see the glee in the faces of the students as they listened to the sound of the butter churner, a sound made possible by a dog's fidelity to a task. I suggest to the students that they discover a new way to put their pets' energy to work, but only after they write down a pet story from the past.

Sharing Time

Every day, the students listen to one another's stories, ideas, frustrations, and successes in their quest for family history. All the sharing times in this unit are in large groups, and the choice has always come from the students.

> "We don't want to miss anything."
> "If we're in small groups we don't get to hear everyone."

How then do we create a climate in which every child feels willing to share, even the smallest tidbit of family lore? I believe it is crucial to establish an atmosphere of trust among the students from the beginning, so that children are not teased or mocked and so that each person feels free to share and respond. Respect for one another is not negotiable. I have found that the clearer the rules, the more respectful the group. No one wants to tell a story, whether serious or humorous, when others are thoughtless or inattentive.

There are two ways in which the students share. One way is through daily discussion. The students discuss briefly what they've discovered or the questions they might have. The second sharing is a formal one, called "circle-up," which occurs every Friday for the first six weeks and every day during week seven.

"Circle-up" lasts longer than the informal daily discussions. Each child tells a longer story, or has the floor for a longer period of time. These are the sessions when the other students may ask the storyteller questions for clarification or for suggestions on how to make an interview better or on how to improve timing when approaching a parent or grandparent for information. The purpose of "circle-up" is to create a more intimate sharing time and to gradually teach the students storytelling skills by giving them a more intimate atmosphere and an audience response. I expect every child to participate verbally during this time, perhaps by telling family stories or by making affirming comments about the stories of others.

Keep the Daily Format Simple

Each class (approximately forty-five minutes) follows this same general pattern:

- a question or idea to ponder
- a teacher's personal example
- students' private brainstorming in their journal
- large-group sharing
- homework (finding a story that relates)
- end of the week: "circle-up"

WEEK TWO: NOW, FOR THE HARD PART

Going Back in Time: Listening

The primary focus of this *Family Stories* unit is not the here and now. Although I don't discourage a good contemporary story, I do stress that the students attempt to listen with new ears to a different time. "Parent stories are fine, but can you go back two or three generations?"

I usually sense relief with this preferred direction. Students know then that their research is not intended for the recent past—a past that seems to them boring or, often enough, riddled with divorce, failure, crime, and violence. The real purpose is to encounter the past, with its own ways of tasting, touching, hearing, smelling, and listening.

Taking the Time   The gracious art of spending time with someone is just that: an art. Most of the children have had the experience of listening to stories told by old people and the children's patience has been duly tried:

> "Grandma only remembers what happened long ago."
> "Grandpa has such good stories to tell. Mostly he talks about the war."
> "Once they get started, you can't shut them up."

Many of them, however, have had wonderful experiences with old people. The grandparents are the ones who really know what the children want for their birthday and are the ones who bake cookies hot from the oven, sticky with chocolate chips.

Mika's love for her grandparents resonates in the stories that she writes about them:

> There is a certain smell in my grandparents' house. I can't really describe it other than saying it is so comforting, I feel like I'm living in a mansion. It always makes me feel at home.

Elders are the bearers of the best tales. To learn to draw stories from old people is one of the main goals of this unit. When the students see the light in grandpa's eyes blaze and the chuckle from grandma escape, they experience the delight that comes from "taking the time."

With gentleness and patience the words and story come. With these words, grandparents usher young people into another era.

I'll Never Forget the Time . . .   One activity that helps students to understand the importance of older persons in the family is for students to catalog all that they remember about a grandparent. Mika had no difficulty at all in painting a vivid picture of her grandfather. The written portrait is both endearing and comic, the language of love:

> A couple more things about grandpa is that he is tall and has big ears. In the book, *The BFG,* by Roald Dahl, the BFG (big friendly giant) has big ears and since he is a giant, is very tall. If anyone ever makes a movie out of the book, grandpa is the perfect person to play the part.

Lashawna claimed her grandmother differently, as a friend and confidante:

> It was in 1983 or 1984 when I lived with my grandmother. We would play games, cards and talk to each other a lot about all the problems we had. She would show me all her letters from my grandfather and I would go to the store for her. She would help me with my homework. I can just see her now with her beautiful complexion and her nice brown eyes, hair such a brownish red color. Though she is a little overweight, she is still beautiful to me.

Just One   As soon as one student speaks with love about an older person, other students follow suit. This does not diminish the reality that some grandparents or great-aunts and -uncles are forgetful or in nursing homes, but the children remember the nurturing times. Through memories, letters, and photographs, young people can come to appreciate the old and what they have endured. They look at their family trees in a new way. The old are keepers of tales.

Breanna, blue-eyed, golden-haired, and fair-skinned, shared this story:

> When I talked with my other grandma she told me that there was an ancestor of ours that was an Indian princess. There was another relative that was also Indian. (My grandmother) said that her grandfather looked very Indian. He had coarse black hair.

I knew from Breanna's expression and response to questions asked of her that being German was no longer enough. She will trace this tiny footnote of her family history back to its source, all because of a few remarks spoken to her on a cold January day.

Young people enjoy this time travel, not only when it involves their own families, but also when it involves the families of other students. It's like being part of a grand drama—another, more intense experience of childhood dress-up times in dusty attic clothes.

Collecting Stories from Grandparents   Taking time to meet with older members of the family might be a walk down the block for some, or a ride across town. For others, this entails giving a call to another part of the country or writing a letter to Canada or South America. The first few times that I taught this lesson, I didn't think of timing. As a result, there was inconvenience as well as missed opportunities for some of my students. Now, I plan the unit far enough in advance so that students can interview relatives who come for Thanksgiving and Christmas.

WEEK THREE: ASKING GOOD QUESTIONS CAN MAKE A STORY LIVE

What's A Good Question?

The students and I have one guideline about asking questions: to get the person talking. Open-ended questions. Specific questions. We experiment to discover what works, and bring back our successes to the large group.

Superlatives   Some got the relative talking by asking, "What was the worst or best or scariest experience of your life?" Latrisha captured the terrifying experience of her grandmother in Alaska who was crossing a river with her husband.

> "Do you see that moose?" he asked her.
> "No," she said.
> "That black spot is a moose's ear!"
> The poor animal had fallen into the ice and was struggling to get out. That day my grandma was carrying her 30.06 and she walked behind the moose. There was no way she could save it because of how heavy and angry it was. So her husband told her to shoot it, to put it out of its misery. She shot it and the moose fell down into the ice under the river.

During the next week, the discussion rang with story after story of enduring physical and psychological traumas, such as the following rousing adventure. Clarice posed the question: Does anyone know about a travel adventure in our family? Her family deluged her with stories. This is one of the ones she wrote down:

> My great-great grandfather was named Theodore Henry Dean and was born January 2, 1850, in Chicago, Illinois. When he was sixteen, his cousin wrote to him wanting to know if he would come to New York City and they would take a trip to California together. They left about noon on February 2, 1866 on an iron steamship called the "Santiago do Cuba."
> Six days later, they reached the mouth of the San Juan River in Nicaragua. On the boat there were no beds so everyone had to sleep on the deck and whenever the steamer had to stop and "wood up," the passengers ran wild on the plantations, eating banana and shooting the monkeys. The Nicaraguans got mad. "No shooting monkeys. Superstitious!"
> Theodore and his cousin went up the Castilla Rapids where they had to transfer to other boats and go to Lake Nicaragua. Theodore then had to ride a mule eleven miles to the Pacific. The women and children got to ride ox carts with logs for wheels.
> At the Pacific they rode another big steamer, which they shared with a bunch of livestock. They arrived in San Francisco on the 17th of March at 1:00 A.M. . . .
> In 1871 he wanted to go back home again and received news that Chicago was in flames. An Irish woman's cow kicked over a lantern and set Chicago on fire

Open-ended Questions I worked with the students on these kinds of questions, then the students could add their own or keep what I had suggested. Michael kept the following list of questions. He also prepared his grandmother ahead of time so that she wouldn't be nervous. He wanted her to give him the longest answers possible!

What are the three most significant events in your life?

How have times changed since you were young; have the changes been for the better or the worse?

How have your friends and enemies made you a better person?

In your opinion, what are the best human qualities a person can have?

Learning from My Mistakes   Such questions move the children to a new level of listening, and it is important that they reflect on how they've changed because they listened to these stories. As I reread the responses of their grandparents, I realized that I didn't give time for the students to reflect aloud upon the wisdom so very evident: For example, Michael, Sarah, and Clarice, respectively, have these wonderful words in their keeping:

> The two best qualities to have are patience and not to be afraid.
>
> The three most significant things in my life are my marriage, children and grandchildren. All these things are important because they bring you more people to love.
>
> I think World War II was a significant event in my life. I had been puzzling for a long time about the meaning of my life, beyond being a dutiful family member. Finally I had it all boiled down to doing whatever I could to help others, and to try with all my might not to hurt anyone. I thought perhaps that cruelty was the only real sin!

What were the thoughts of these thirteen and fourteen-year-olds during and after the time they transcribed the words? What will their thoughts be thirty years from now when they reread these messages? I've made a promise to myself that next time I'll make sure they have time to add their own reflections.

There's No Such Thing as a Bad Question   Before I taught this unit and before I learned so much from the students, I used to think that the only good questions were *how* and *why* questions. I'm not so sure anymore. The students have had wonderful results with what was seemingly a *yes* or *no* question. Students do need help in framing thoughtful inquiries, but there is no single formula to follow, nor is there one definition that works for every person interviewed. What seems essential to the interview process is the willingness to take time to listen. If the grandparent being interviewed feels that his words are treasured, that her insights are valued, the stories flow easily, like water from the mountains in spring.

WEEK FOUR: SEEKING THE TRUTH

Whose Truth Are We Talking About?

In the research that the students do, there is a quest for a good story, but there is also a quest for truth. In this unit, I strive to make the students aware of the historical context of the stories they hear. There is no way that every tale will be actuality in the strict sense, for real stories are a hybrid of fact and fiction. Each story, however embellished with tragedy or triumph, takes place in a real world, with a specific set of mores and socioeconomic realities. Perhaps when a student interviews his grandmother from Cuba or Ireland, the harsh political realities that forced the immigration to the United States might no longer be part of the narrative. What grandmother remembers is her love for her native land and all the events that made this place home. The beauty is as real as the poverty or oppression. The present memory, even if it differs from a strictly historical fact, is her truth now and is valid in its own right.

Students come to the realization that everyone who experiences an event, and everyone who talks about that event, will put his own special marks on it. If a students grasps this interpretation of an event, he will understand the uniqueness of the family story. If a student seeks for historical accuracy, she will also recognize the universality that exists among us. Thus, while each teller of the tale has a special twist to a personal experience, we all are connected irrevocably.

Everybody Loves a Little Romance   One way to garner stories of truth and place is to try to connect them with the love stories in a family's history. Usually love stories are pleasant for people to tell. Zach's parents struggled to find time together. Zach's version of the story is this:

> After his graduation, my father was assigned to a destroyer that was participating in shore bombardment of Vietnam. My mother went to Hong Kong because my father's ship was supposed to go there. Instead, because one of the screws broke, his ship came to the Philippines. All of the officers' wives except for my mom decided to cancel their trips. My mom went to the Philippines instead to meet my dad, but there were no hotel rooms in Subic Bay. So they had to stay in a nice whorehouse.

Time makes the memories shine. The older the story, the greater the chance for embellishment; but those changes only add to the folklore and myth of a family. These revisions to stories are every bit as important as the strict facts that students document. Students learn of their parents meeting on a hayride in the Midwest or of their grandparents sipping a drink in a Boston soda fountain. Julia wrote a family story that reads as well as any gothic novel:

> My stepfather's grandparents lived in the Tetra Mountains in Czechoslovakia. His grandmother was a young woman from a wealthy family who owned a brewery. His grandfather was a young man from a poor family; he was in the Slovak army. The young girl's family did not approve of their relationship. They said he wasn't good enough for her. . . . She didn't listen. She married him.
> While in the army he was accused of killing an officer and had to leave the country suddenly to escape punishment. He told his young bride he had to go to the United States and that he would send for her someday.

Without a word between them for three years, he sent her a boat ticket to New York. On the day she arrived he was on the dock in New York waiting for her.

Chris tells about his grandparents, both marines stationed in Florida, who got married in a formal military wedding.

> In their hotel my grandpa had glued a giant poster to the ceiling. It said, "I love you." My grandma was in the room all day and never saw it. But as they were going to bed she looked up and saw it.
> After the war they moved to Portland and had two boys and two girls. My grandpa made up a poem. "I'm a marine, my wife's a marine and we have four submarines.'"

Everybody loves a little romance, and it seems only right that from stories students learn that their parents and grandparents did not just one day up and marry but had a history of courting: shining, youthful eyes and passion. Just as in the movies.

Seeking the Truth Can Be Painful   The Jewish and Catholic children whose relatives lived through the Holocaust have stories to move the heart. One of these is Talbot's:

> Both my grandparents, Henry and Frieda, lived in Poland. My grandfather was shipped off to the war. My grandmother, eight months pregnant, was put in a camp. My grandfather was caught by the Russians and imprisoned somewhere near the European/Russian border. When a friend of his appeared in the camp to do repair work, my grandfather escaped by helping him carry out a huge door. He hid in his friend's home and then went to search for Frieda. . . .
> He traveled a long time, eating hardly anything. When he found her in a camp along the Austrian border, he worked out a way for their escape. . . . On the way, my grandmother gave birth to a baby girl, but it died in the January cold, in a barren wheat field. Even though the child was dead, my grandmother wouldn't bury it. She treated it as if it were still alive. One night, while my grandmother slept, my grandfather slipped the baby away from her and buried it.
> When they finally arrived in Germany, they gathered their belongings once more and emigrated to Canada. They had four more children, my two aunts, my uncle and my mom.

Seeking the Truth Increases Our Knowledge of Place   To discover the truth about our families demands an understanding of geography and the part it played in the lives of our grandparents and great-grandparents. Many of the stories that the students bring are ones of families struggling economically. Sarah's story is different. This tale, filled with exquisite details, describes a middle-class joy ride across the country in a motorcar in the 1920s.

> In 1923, my grandmother, Helen Humpage, took a long trip to Pennsylvania with her parents, when she was four years old. The item I will tell you about is a water bag that was attached to the hood of the car, which was their home for their two-month trip. They went in their motor car which was a pretty new thing for people then.
>
> They traveled for months in their car to Pennsylvania, stopping to see the sights along the way. They had almost all the comforts of home built into their car. They had a fold down table top and three chairs so that they could sit down to dinner. They drank water kept cool in this canvas bag which really kept the water from leaking. They refilled it at towns they would pass through, and they would also replenish their water supply . . . They slept in a tent attached to their car.

Each time a student talks about a locale that is part of the story, we check our maps. "What was it like to live in this place during the twenties, thirties, and forties?" I cannot stress enough the importance of daily sharing, and one of its fruits can be seen in this lesson. Telling stories in specific locales gives credence to the story. The more students hear names of cities and countries, the more detailed their own stories become. No longer do they seem satisfied hearing, "It happened someplace in Europe or in a city on the East Coast."

Stories Are Not Isolated Events   As readers, writers, and students exploring American history, the children are called upon to be truth seekers, to realize that stories do not arise in a vacuum. They learn that people, their decisions, and the events of their lives are part of a specific socioeconomic and geographical context. Through an understanding of history, students can see how certain events came to pass. Breanna learned why her family came to America from Germany.

> My grandma told me that a lot of our family were poor and they came to the U.S. because they heard they could "be somebody" and nothing could stop them. When my great-great-grandfather was seventeen years old he came because his two older brothers were already here. They helped him get a job.

My African-American students learn about Black migration to the West after the Civil War. From research they learn about the Indians who called the African-Americans "Buffalo Soldiers" because of their courage and nappy hair. From their families they learn that people sometimes migrated to the North from Mississippi and Texas for the same reason that Europeans flooded into New York harbors: economic need. African-American grandparents remember well what occurred in World War II in our area. While Whites enlisted in the armed forces, huge job openings occurred on the Portland and Seattle docks.

During our discussions we explore the prejudice that immigrants faced. What happened to the Irish once they walked away from Ellis Island? What land could the Chinese possess when they immigrated to California? What happened to the workers—people of color and women, on the docks and in the factories after World War II ended?

As story after story unfolds, the students see more and more the common, yet fragile, thread that links one person's life with another's. Tara's great-grandparents came from China at the turn of the century. "They never talked much about China. I don't know why they left. I never thought much about it." Diane was in a similar situation. "My family were Russian Jews and they emigrated to Alaska in 1910, but I don't know why."

LaQuann's story of her great-grandmother's journeying with three small children from Texas to Portland parallels Julie's great-grandfather's waiting for his wife on the squalid New York docks. Both wanted a better life, something to hope for. There is, however, a uniqueness to their lives and to the specific horrors and joys, something that no one else shares or can share in the same way.

WEEK FIVE: THE FAMILY SECRET

From Scandals to Tales of Courage

Very closely linked to the discovery of truth is the acknowledgment of what I term the scandal, or the family secret. What students will discover if their research is both sensitive and meticulous is that events at one time considered shameful now have become powerful legends, parables that help to define a family. In no way is this part of the unit meant to violate a family's sense of propriety, or privacy. It is meant to look at past events in the light of history and to understand them in a new way. In stories of the family there can be the sensational, tell-all approach. Students gain nothing by listening to stories that another tells simply to shock an audience. Always the child needs to share his history with the utmost respect for those who endured. At the other extreme there is the secrecy approach: Some feel that only stories showing the family in the best possible light are worth retelling. In different ways, both of these approaches to history are a refusal to look at a story of the past in its complete context, not for the purpose of exploitation or concealment. I encourage the students, not to deny, but to understand their family tales of nobility, struggle, mistakes, and survival. **There's a Delicious Quality about Skeletons** Family secrets and scandals often enhance any oral or written history. Part of my task as a reading, writing, and social-studies teacher is to examine with the students how family scandals can give texture and depth to their poems, essays, legends, letters, and short stories. I begin this part of the unit by sharing the fact that my grandfather in 1907 sent my father, at the age of six, to an orphanage. Briefly, the class and I examine some of the reasons that this may have happened. As a class, we looked at the socioeconomic forces behind what might be considered today a heartless decision. I asked the students to discover similar stories and to look for the *whys*. Within the week, students brought to class stories gleaned from dinner-table and fireside discussions. **Each Generation Has Its Own Standards**   What the students find interesting is that times and society have changed. We do not seem to judge people as harshly as in the past. A student spoke of a great-grandmother who was *illegitimate* and of the shame this brought to the family. The class discussed why a child born out of wedlock was such a terrible thing. What did such an action do to the family reputation? What part did institutionalized religion play in judging a person and family? How has society changed? How has it remained the same?

During a discussion of the plight of Native Americans, at least one-fourth of the students in the class claimed Indian blood. When Alexis saw the response of the group, she shared this story.

> My great-great grandmother was Indian, but none of us knew that until just a little while ago. It makes me angry to think that we were so ashamed of her, the family burned all of her pictures and letters. They destroyed any thing that told us about her. Now that I want to know something about her, there's nothing! We were so ignorant to do that.

Over the next week, students had story after story of how family members were ostracized for one reason or another.

Tommy told how his great-aunt suffered: "[She] was a Catholic back in the 1920's. She got divorced and the family disowned her. She was driven out of the family, she and her two children."

When stories such as these arise, both teacher and students need to be more than passive listeners. This is the time to ask *why* from both family members, history books, and primary documents. All of us together as a society and as a community learn from one another. "Why would a family disown a woman who was divorced?" "Why would an Indian woman want to pass as a White?" Once the reasons are better understood, the shame of the past loses its power to keep the story from being told in the present. Often families maintain their silence and keep their secrets not because of the horrific, but because of the sadness. That dreams don't come true, that tragedies happen, that conflicts rise are the stuff of stories.

Not all parental responses to this particular section of the unit are identical. Some responses are more than enthusiastic, others see it as an intrusion.

"Ms. Kennedy, my mom said this was the best talk we've ever had."
"Ms. Kennedy, my dad told me to tell you that it's none of your business."

Although the story may be no teacher's business, it is the child's. So whether he decides to write it down or she shares it with the group is one thing. But after a certain age, children have a right to know their family history with its sides, whether bright, dark, or mundane.

Being Different   Some of the most inspiring *shame* stories are those that tell of great courage and strength of will. These are the tales of people coming new to our country, hoping for streets lined with gold, but finding a very different America. Zach wrote a story that holds within it the immigrant experience in all its humiliation and grandeur.

> My grandpa, Zenonas Vytautas Jasaitis, was born December 17, 1912, close to Kaunas, Lithuania. He emigrated to the United States in 1922 with his father and sister. When Zene first went to school in Baltimore at the age of ten, he was put in the first grade because he didn't speak English. . . . People teased him because he wore different clothes. He had also had his head shaved at Ellis Island so he looked different. He remembers kids asking him questions he didn't understand. He responded *Yes* or *No* to the questions at random and noticed the kids laughing at whatever he said.
>
> He eventually surmounted these challenges, and went on to receive his master's degree in chemistry from UCLA in 1937. From 1937 to 1943 he worked at Shell Development company helping to figure out industrial uses for ethyl alcohol, then a waste gas. From 1943–1944, he was picked because of his skills in chemistry and watch making to perform the experiments to determine the physical properties of plutonium.

The immigration theme in stories at first brings out the ethnic pride of the students. They can be quick to declare themselves *all* French or one hundred percent Spanish. A young African-American proclaimed that she had nothing in her but African until she discovered some Cherokee in her bloodlines. The real shock came when she told the class that there was a Mcguire in her family tree—an Irish great-grandfather. Situating this event in time, she came to understand why the two lovers, who met in Texas, never married. I teased her that with my *Kennedy* background and her Irish roots, the two of us could be relatives.

After the students rejoice in their own tales that captivate their classmates, they move to another phase in which they see, not just the uniqueness, but the commonalties of their histories. What seems to come of this research is an understanding that binds, rather than separates, the class. Each historical time has its own criteria for friends and enemies. Brutality that once divided a country dies, and in its place sit descendants listening to one another as friends. In a "circle-up" sharing that will probably happen only once in my lifetime, a child spoke of her great-grandparents' escape from Poland during the Nazi occupation. After a moment of silence, a boy spoke of his grandfather's involvement as an SS officer in Nazi Germany. These stories led to a discussion of the desperate economic conditions of the German people in the 1920s and of how Germans longed for a leader to give them power and dignity once again. The scandal of prejudice and cruelty cannot be removed by understanding, but our attitudes toward the shame or scandal can be tempered by knowledge.

No nation or family is free from the scandal. However, a great disservice, I believe, is rendered if students know the psychology of their stories but know nothing of the cultural and historical reality. Scandals have a place in our family stories, but these scandals do not drop out of the sky. They have a socioeconomic context and are part of a larger context that needs to be understood by the teller and the listener. These stories are too valuable not to be known or shared in some way. Unless they are told, they will die. Families will never know that members felt great hope and despair; they will never know of the choices that human beings had to make and then had to learn to live with; they will never know of the bonds that link ancestors to descendants. Compassion for our own families and the families of others is one of the gifts of searching for truth; and when we find the truth, we should not shudder or reject what we've learned but should accept the story in its own historical context.

WEEK SIX: TREASURES AND ARTIFACTS

Hands-on History

Up to this point, the students have shared and listened to stories told primarily through words. Sooner or later someone asks to bring a seashell, a teapot, a pipe, or a watch. Each of these heirlooms contains a richness that is unique to a family and open to the touch of others. The irony of this part of the research is that students, usually so enamored with the new and the unblemished, become fascinated with the worn and marred. One child said that when he held his grandfather's tobacco pouch he could feel the stories pulse through his hands. The search through the attic and grandmother's trunk begins. Artifacts are hands-on history—a powerful way to learn about families because what we keep tells others what we care about.

Show and Tell   Each day during the sixth week, students bring artifacts from home and we "circle-up" to hear letters read, to touch trophies from 1940, and to smell bookmarks made with crushed and fragile flowers. The classroom becomes the students' own museum and they tell the story behind each treasure. It is important to stress the fact that artifacts need not be exotic but should simply take us back in time and teach us about a family. Sometimes the artifact is so precious that parents do not want their children to bring it to school. That's just fine. They simply describe the treasure and share what they've written about it.

I usually bring my mother's wedding dress—a pleated, knee-length, silk and lace gown that is sixty years old. I tell the children of my parents' experiences during the Depression and of how it would have been impossible for my mother, a fashion designer, and for my father, struggling to pay his way through medical school, to have afforded a fancy ceremony. We discuss what they know of the Depression and the thirties. In the following days, the students come to class with additional information about this particular era.

The importance of the artifact is the visual, like a family crest that designates a particular time of victory or defeat, great sadness or joy. Best of all, someone in the family declared this item—however large or small, however impressive or diminutive—to be something worth keeping. The artifact captures a time when the family endured. Here are some of these stories of endurance.

Johntae brought a clothes brush that his grandfather had used as a porter for the Northern Pacific Railroad. Johntae described the way in which his grandfather brushed the clothes of the White passengers and the pride that his grandfather felt in wearing the uniform of the railroad and in being a trusted employee. He was proud of all his work on the Northern Pacific, and the brush was a symbol of his years of service to others. Such an artifact gives us a chance to explore the power of the railroad in the history of American transportation and the power of the people, like Johntae's grandfather, who helped make the railway system a success.

LaShawna's great-grandmother made things like sweaters, scarves, and afghans. Although LaShawna did not have the shawl, she shared her great grandmother's story and then wrote a response: "Well, she passed away a couple of years ago and she had plenty of things passed down. She passed one of her lovely afghans to my father because everyone in our family got at least one possession. I love you, Lizzy."

Michael's father has a gun that was given to him by his grandfather.

> My dad went back to Kansas to visit him when he was twelve and his grandfather thought that he should have it. It is the first Winchester 13 shot repeating pump action 22 rifle made. It was manufactured in 1906. His grandpa used it to hunt jackrabbits in Kansas. Someday my father will pass the gun on to me, and then I will give it to my son.

Mika struggled for three weeks trying to find one archive of her family. She greeted me each morning with soulful eyes and a weary expression, saying once again that there were no artifacts in her family history. As the days went by, however, and she saw the diversity of what people brought to the class, she realized that this didn't need to be the family silver or great-great-grandmother's wedding ring. So she told this lovely little story:

> It's just a small clock; it had a door that opens on the front so that you can wind it. It belonged to my great-grandmother, Edna Gibb. She was born on August 19, 1895. It has two holes on the inside where you have to wind them. There is a neat little key that you use. It is shaped strangely, but it works. The glass off the front is missing now. . . . Now it sits on our wall and is always chiming the wrong time of day. It usually says the wrong time, too.

Evan comes from a storytelling family and a family that treasures its history. He tells the story of his ancestors bringing fine silver from Ireland. They traveled by way of Panama and around the horn of South America and settled in San Francisco. When the Civil War broke out, the family moved to the South to fight with relatives against the Union Army.

> My great-great-grandfather became a Colonel. The Tuppers kept slaves while they were living in the South. I'm not proud of that at all, but they must have been very devoted slaves or also my ancestors treated them well. If you don't understand how that could be, read the next part of this story.
> When the Union Army came, . . The slaves took the silver and ran away with it into the woods. The Tuppers escaped capture. . . . When the Union threat had passed, the slaves went back into the woods. They dug up the silver they had buried and returned it to the Tuppers. . . . The colonel passed the silver on to his eldest son when he died. When the eldest son died he passed it on to his son, my father's father. Eventually it will be passed on to me. I'd be proud to own anything with that kind of legacy.

Aristotle speaks of knowledge coming only through the senses. A person truly knows what he can smell, hear, and taste. A person truly grasps what she can hear with her ears and touch with her fingertips. This is what the artifact week offers—namely, a time to hold in our hands what matters and to ask the memory keepers why it remains, generation after generation. So many family legacies lie in a dusty Bible or on the shelf. They remain faithfully present to the family, and the family returns that fidelity when the item is held and the story repeated.

WEEK SEVEN: TIME FOR RITUALS

Every Year at This Time

Family life is in itself a type of mantra—a rosary of the birth, life, death, and rebirth of persons, places, things. Because of this innate repetition, we might think of the family as constantly in ritual, joining in an initiation year after year, generation after generation. The students' views of ritual and tradition cover a variety of areas: annual Christmas-tree excursions and birthday celebrations, graduation parties and anniversaries, and so forth. My class, however, usually responds best to traditions centering on religion and food. For one week, we explore these family ceremonies and their mutuality—how, over the years, we help to create and shape rituals and how they create and shape us.

Religious Ceremonies   I found it surprising that as diverse as my students were in their formal participation in organized religion, most of them had experiences of religious rituals. Michael, a Christian, wrote about the Advent wreath.

> Advent means Christ's coming, so we celebrate Christ's coming into the world. Each Sunday we light a different candle until they are all lit. The first candle is the prophecy candle, the second is the shepherd's candle, the third is the Bethlehem candle and the fourth is the angel candle. The last we light on Christmas day to celebrate Christ's birth. We love to sit around the table after dinner in the candlelight and pray, sing, read Scripture and spend time with the family.

Some rituals prove memorable to students because of the combination of symbols and meals. Nick, a Jew, speaks of Rosh Hashana.

> We always go to my grandmother's house and we eat dinner there. We always have a tray, and this tray is very special. There's broccoli, a lamb's leg and parsley. You eat the parsley after you dip it in salt water, and there's a hard boiled egg. We have these crackers and grandpa used to hide one and which ever child finds it gets two dollars. You also eat the sauce with a special apple butter.

Zach waited until the end of the week to write about any tradition. He repeated that there were no rituals in his family because no one belonged to an institutionalized church. As the days passed and he listened to others, he wrote this about himself and his family:

> In fact, the only tradition we have is the celebration of Chanukah, an over commercialized, relatively non important Jewish holiday (and the only one we regularly celebrate).
> Starting with the first sundown of the holiday, we progressively light more candles according to how many days have passed. My brothers and I usually argue over who gets to light them. We also say prayers before we light the candles. Most of the time my dad says them. But sometimes my parents are able to persuade my brother or me to say them.

Other Ceremonies   If the children share on a regular basis during each phase of the unit, they discover that their family puts its own mark on a celebration or tradition that seems common to many. Martin took center stage when he told the students how it was only on the twelfth of December that his family went Christmas-tree shopping. No other day of the week would do. Each step of the way, the child sees, "Yes, I'm the same, but I'm different." Histories are unique and universal.

There needs to be a place for all children to tell stories during this week. The traditions can be those of parents reading to the children at nighttime or being tucked in or kissed before they head for school. The traditions can take the form of going to favorite vacation spots, the same person's carving the turkey, or placing binoculars in a special drawer. Opening our minds to repeated acts that occur in the family are what rituals are all about.

For some of my students there is the tradition of never celebrating holidays or events. That in itself is a ritual passed down through a community, and the fact that the family holds fast in its refusal shapes a history. There are also children from agnostic or atheistic backgrounds.

For all participants to listen without judgment is liberating to the shy or hesitant storyteller. I've been fortunate to teach children from diverse ethnic, religious, and socioeconomic backgrounds. Everyone learns by listening, and the children's horizons of compassion and understanding broaden.

Family Recipes Keep the Stories Alive   Perhaps because food brings with it thoughts of comfort and happiness, the students receive this final part of the unit enthusiastically. The kitchen seems to be a welcome place for stories to begin and end.

I ask the students to list their favorite recipes and to discover not only their own experience of the food but also experiences of their family members. Their goal, then, is to discover the ingredients, how far back in time the recipe goes, and whether there are any stories about the recipes worth keeping. For one week, we listen to ways of making pasta and fruit drinks or how best to use garlic or mushrooms.

In Martin's story, we discovered that food helped a love affair blossom.

> My dad called my mom and asked her out on a date. After that a week later my mom prepared dinner and invited my dad over to her house. They had barbecued ribs, potato salad, greens, punch, bread and pork and beans. My mom put onions in the food but my dad didn't like onions. They started inviting each other over to eat. They became good friends. One day they were talking and my dad kissed my mom and that's when they became girlfriend and boyfriend.

The class got the impression from Martin that his parents still had that meal on special occasions, helping to keep the memory of first love alive. He was not the only one in the class to talk about repeated meals. What I found so remarkable was the number of recipes that had been in families over the years, passed down from one generation to the next. Most of the students had helped make the food they wrote about.

The kinesthetic element, that storytelling ability to create a sense of taste and touch, dominated the stories. Mika spoke of vanilla milk when someone is sick, chantilly fudge at Christmas time. "It smells so wonderful. You can hear it boiling on the stove and mom's wooden spoon stirring and stirring. When I pour the fudge into the pan I love to watch it slither into place."

There were many stories dealing with stoves. I forgot to follow up on the history of these appliances. Sarah created a large mug, colored it to perfection, and then shared her recipe and the story behind its special nature:

> Stir some vanilla and a half teaspoon of sugar into a mug of milk. Heat and stir until warm. My grandma used to make vanilla milk for her children a lot. She made chocolate milk, too, but not as often as vanilla milk. It was very comforting to the children, especially when they were sick. In our family now, our mother makes it for us. She makes it when we're sick or staying up late to finish homework. It is comforting for us, too.

Stories from the kitchen, stories when we're cold or sick or hungry from romping in the woods, stories about hot dogs roasting over the fire, stories bursting from that recipe box on the second shelf in the kitchen—this is what the students explore. They discover that food is not simply something fast for the here and now, but that meat and flour, sugar and butter go back into time where they've nourished another child in a shack or mansion, along a railroad track or in a one-room schoolhouse. The history of their food is part of them, and the stories coming from these meals is as rich as any chocolate fudge.

WEEK EIGHT: BECOMING THE STORYTELLER

Whose Story Is It Now?

In this final week of the unit, the entire focus is on the child as keeper of the story and as the one responsible to share the tales in an oral and written fashion. I try to help them by assigning simple performance tasks. These tasks serve to strengthen their skills and to summarize what they've learned during the unit.

Geographical Storytellers   The students peruse their writing journals to check on family sayings, names, migrations, scandals, artifacts, rituals, and recipes. Next to the stories they place geographical names relating directly to their family history. I have two large maps, one of the world and the other of the United States. I give them sticky dots, the number depending on how many geographical places they've found in their writings. They print their names on the dots, and one by one go up to the maps, placing their dots on countries and states. Each child tells his family story and its relationship to geographical places.

Of All the Stories, This One Is My Favorite   Over the past six weeks, the students have listened to one another and to members of their families.

They have researched old documents and have held tools and treasures in their hands. Now comes the time for them to choose their favorite story to tell. Magic happens this week. The scholar turns storyteller, and all the units of labor are put to the test. It is a moment when the student ceases taking down verbatim the words of another and begins to claim the words as her own. The story can now be his.

When Evan told about his grandfather in World War II, he spoke of the knives that his grandfather made when he was stationed in the Aleutian Islands and of how he'd watch the planes sometimes crash while they were returning from maneuvers. His grandfather would salvage the Plexiglas from the cockpit and the aluminum from the plane's body. With the knife in his hand, Evan told how his grandfather used the bayonet heads, the aluminum, and the Plexiglas to make the knives. "This was like his hobby during one of the most hated periods of his life. He made two knives this way. One is in his room at his house. The other is in my room. He gave it to me when I asked about this story."

Just as the knife is Evan's, so is the story. He has earned the tale that was his grandfather's simply by asking.

The students discover that when they really listen, the stories come back in their own unique version, but a transformation does take place. The child takes on the voice and cadence of the person being interviewed, capturing the words and phrases of another time. Fourteen-year-old Clarice, of the MTV generation, told this story of her grandmother. We are transported back in time. Listen to how Clarice listened.

> In 1937 at Otterbein College, my grandpa, James Joseph Keating, was starting school on a football scholarship. My grandmother, Dorothy Beck, was working on the college newspaper. Some said she could have been the Barbara Walters of the thirties. She had her eye on my grandpa, Jim. That is why she was so excited when she was chosen to interview him for the school newspaper.
>
> After the interview she had reasons to love him. She loved the way he dressed, like Cary Grant with starched white collars on his shirts. She loved his hair, the widow's peak on his forehead. He could really dance and the way he took a puff on his cigarette was so suave and sophisticated.

Not all the stories the children choose to call their *favorite* are happy or humorous ones. The following example is the storyteller Michael united with past suffering.

> When my grandma was a little girl growing up in Oklahoma, they lived with an aunt and were quite poor. They later moved into a little three-room shack. It was very dirty and they had to give it a good cleaning There was an old mattress and her dad took it outside to burn it and it burned for days.
>
> Fay, my grandma's little sister, went out to play in the yard. Before my grandma could stop her she was running and jumping on the mattress. . . .

Fay started screaming and yelling. She tripped on one of the springs and fell down. The mattress was still hot and my grandma couldn't see her under the ashes. Her dad ran over and pulled her out. The burns on her body were so bad that she died. There wasn't enough money to buy medicine for her. My grandma missed her sister very much.

My grandma tells me to always value my time with my brothers and sisters and I try to remember that.

Michael's promise to remember the words of his grandmother are at the heart of this unit. In his own telling, he has the opportunity now to integrate the values of elders, to capture their courage and endurance, to be proud of the bright and shadowed group that is family.

I do not wish this project to be a mere collection of photographs or only deeds of glory. My hopes are grander ones: that the students come to know and love their family tales enough to write them down; that they are proud to share the stories of what makes them who they are; that they possess new eyes to see and new ears to hear the power of history; and that they experience themselves as storytellers of the present and the future, the ones destined to keep alive family fact, myth, and folklore.

I hope that the tales of my students endure in written form, so that fifty or a hundred years from now, on an exploration through the attic, a new storyteller will find one of these classroom journals, open it and discover another dimension of a family history. Through the children, a story can become an archive of the heart, promising that a family's ecstasy and sorrow, courage and endurance will live on generation after generation.

Chapter 2
Our Stories, Our History, Our Memories

TIM GILLESPIE

When I first set out to teach U.S. History to eighth graders at Beaumont Middle School, the Portland school district had just purchased new textbooks. On the second day of September, each student picked up a copy. The textbooks were bound with a striking silver cover and were lavishly illustrated, well written, thought provoking, and *heavy*, many pounds' worth of narrative, facts, time lines, and questions. I was excited and thought my students would be, too. We'd be experiencing together the sweep of our shared national history in the crackle of those new pages, I figured.

I gave the students a few minutes to make butcher-paper covers to protect the beautiful textbooks. As they were folding and taping, many opened the books and flipped through, checking out the year's curriculum ahead. A small rumbling started in one corner of the room, and spread. This was the general tune:

"Explorers . . . again?"

"Geez, we read all this stuff before."

"Didn't we do this in fifth grade?"

"What's the point, anyway? This is all past."

"Yeah, that was then, this is now."

Oh yeah, I thought as I eavesdropped. I've forgotten to address the first issue of any curriculum: What's the point? Or, in this case, What's history for? What's the purpose of studying it? The new book was an enticement, but not a rationale; meaning and purpose aren't intrinsic in educational materials, no matter how beautiful. My students and I needed to think and talk about *reasons* for studying history. I had what I thought was a great bunch of activities ready for beginning the year, but I decided it might be better to hold these off for a few days. A prior issue needed to be addressed: *Why are we doing this?*

I mulled over the question that night. How would we approach it? The well-worn words of the Spanish-American philosopher George Santayana floated into my mind. Of course. I wrote on a big piece of butcher paper his famous quote, as I remembered it:

"Those Who Do Not Know History Are Condemned To Repeat It."

The next morning, I thumbtacked my sign above the chalkboard and asked the students to write a short response in their new social-studies logs. Nearly every response was a minor variation on the quotation. Then we had a discussion. It lasted about three minutes. Everyone agreed with Santayana's pronouncement. Okay. Ho hum. So now, I wondered, are we ready to start reading Chapter one? Have I done my job of helping my students establish a reason for studying history? Is that it?

Maybe, I considered, I need to draw other sources of authority into this, to broaden the discussion. The Santayana quotation is remote and abstract, seemingly infallible in its assertion. Perhaps, I thought, I should counter it with a different thesis, set up a dialogue with a notion like Aldous Huxley's that the only real lesson of history is that humans generally ignore the lessons of history. But that would be another abstraction, I thought, worth only a couple of minutes more of conversation. If, as I believe, education's best first question is "What's the purpose?" the answer can't be something glibly offered in just a few minutes' time to justify nine months of classroom study. I wanted a way to shake off Santayana's dusty aphorism, to bring the idea to life.

As a writer, I've often followed this principle: *When in doubt, look more closely: Study a detail, search for the specific, tell a story, find a telling fact.* As Theseus says in *Midsummer Night's Dream*, the writer's job is to "give to airy nothing a local habitation and a name." That's what I needed. To bring to life this airy abstract rationale for the study of history, I needed to figure out a way to help my students find actual history—a story, a detail, a name, a local habitation, a specificity—in which the truism might be embodied. Walking in my Portland city neighborhood that evening, looking at the sidewalks imprinted "1924" and the rings for tying up horses that are still attached to some of the curbs, I could not help but think how close and specific history really is to each of us. My neighbor waved a greeting with her garden hose, and I thought of her stories about her parents immigrating to the United States from Russia, fleeing persecution as Jews. Then, just as I tripped on the uneven old sidewalk, an idea for my classroom came to me.

So, the next day, I gave my first history homework assignment. I asked students to interview someone over thirty years old, preferably a parent or relative, but it could be a neighbor, teacher, whomever. Here were the questions to ask: What events have happened in *your* lifetime that you hope future generations will *never* forget? Why is it important for people not to forget these things? (Reader, I would strongly suggest that you stop reading at this point, take a few moments, and answer the questions for yourself. You might enjoy comparing your responses to others.)

By asking these questions, I thought that we might come up with a rationale for the study of history rooted in family or community memory and beliefs and that such a rationale might have more sticking power for the students. I hoped that my students' parents would be willing to give specific instances to their children of why they thought history was important to study, in this way giving Santayana's airy observation a "local habitation and a name."

Three days later, I had an "In" box stuffed with responses. Many parents got involved in answering the questions, including a notable number of fathers. Some students said they'd heard new stories or learned new things about their parents, and many spoke of family conversations, provoked by the assignment, about issues and events of recent history. The range of responses from my diverse urban families was remarkable. We made a chart: The event most often mentioned was the Vietnam War, and the second most mentioned was the assassination of JFK. Other important historic events that parents wanted future generations to remember included World War II, the Holocaust, the Cuban Missile Crisis, the Civil Rights Movement, the countercultural "Summer of Love" in San Francisco in 1967, the shootings at Kent State University, the murder of Black Panther Fred Hampton, the Women's Movement, the discovery of a hole in the ozone layer, the Exxon Valdez oil spill in Alaska, the dismantling of the Berlin Wall, the decline of Communism, contemporary problems in cities and schools, and much more.

Here are a few brief excerpts from parent interviews:

I would like future generations to understand about the blacks in South Africa, and never let it happen again.

The dissolution of the Soviet Union and the resultant freedoms that the residents of the independent states are enjoying . . . sets an example for the whole world to decentralize and reduce government influence on the people. . . . The good of the individual must always be top priority over the good of the group.

The events that happened in my lifetime I hope future generations never forget were the social changes of the 60's; for example, the women's and civil rights movements, because I want people to remember that we can change society for the better if we work together.

The Vietnam War should never be forgotten, because a whole generation of men was slaughtered in a war that was illegal and immoral. Our government fought a war that was political and based on money, and tried to tell the people that it was a war against Communism and that Communism would take over the world if we didn't fight the war. No one won the war because there was nothing to win. . . . The events in Russia prove Communism isn't taking over anything. We need to be careful of what we believe about what our government says.

Landing on the moon . . . showed what people can do when they work together using all their talents toward a common goal.

These responses provoked discussion, debates about the lessons that different adults drew from their experiences, and many questions about the events themselves. (Not all, it should be noted, were covered in the textbook.)

Best of all, however, was the way in which this simple family-interview idea that I stumbled upon provided us with a home base for much of our year's study of U.S. history. For a few days, I wondered if the interviews might have unintentionally conveyed to the students the idea that only recent history, history that resides in the memory of living people, is worth studying. But, I discovered, when we looked at *any* historical period, I could use variations on those interview questions as an entry point: Why might this be important to learn about? Why do you suppose the historians who wrote this textbook want future generations to remember this? What lessons can be drawn for today? Do you see any parallels or connections to events that your parents talked about? Those touchstone questions brought us closer, I believe, to that healthy sense that the past is never past, but always with us.

Furthermore, as the months rolled by, I realized how many important notions about the *teaching* of history were confirmed for me by that interview.

For example, the historical events that parents shared with their children were often brought to life by the personal stories in which they were embodied:

Where I was when I heard John Kennedy had been shot.

The civil rights demonstration your father and I marched in.

How it felt when I was your age and my family decided we better make a temporary fallout shelter in the basement during the Cuban Missile Crisis, but when we went to the grocery store the shelves were nearly emptied of canned foods.

The students' fascination with these bits of personal lore reminded me again of the power of stories. A criticism of school history has been the way in which it has been offered in some textbooks and some teaching as a tedious spinning out of facts: "Dull data dumps," a colleague said. If the textbook or school resources don't offer compellingly told stories to supplement the data, we had better find some, whether accounts of family members, oral interviews on file at the local historical society, well-written history, or credible historical fiction. During my year, I had students read or I read aloud from sources such as Lewis and Clark's journals, Scott O'Dell's Sacajawea novel *Streams to the River, River to the Sea* (1986), Oregon Trail diaries, and Michael Shaara's Gettysburg novel, *The Killer Angel,* (1974), all for the motivating effect of the stories in which they present history.

Motivation is not the only power of stories. Those fascinating parent interviews reminded me of the importance of putting human faces on historical events. A danger of teaching history is allowing it to become a recitation of statistics or events or an account that becomes mere stereotype, melodrama, myth, or bit of nostalgia. An antidote to these dangers would be stories that reveal the effect of large sociohistorical forces on singular humans. We must teach our students about the millions killed by the Nazis, but we must also try to bring those awful numbers into close focus, an important reason for sharing Anne Frank's diary. The complex historical facts behind the war in Bosnia may seem bewildering, but one important manifestation of its significance is found in the words of Zlata Filipovic, the young girl of mixed ethnic heritage who kept a diary of her horrifying life in war-ravaged Sarajevo before she was evacuated (1994). History is not just dates and the names of prominent actors on the historical stage; it is also the effect on folks like us. The family stories unearthed by our interviews confirmed that sense of the local and personal effect of large historical forces and events.

Finally, I liked the way in which our family interviews and the resulting discussions offered a wide range of opinion and response. One possible way out of the thicket of current cultural arguments about history—who controls it, who owns it, who writes it, whose story is it, and what is left out?—is to offer a wide diversity of voices and stories. Niels Bohr, the Dutch Jewish physicist who barely escaped Nazi-occupied Denmark (he was spirited off to England in the bomb bay of an airplane, just one step ahead of the Gestapo), said he found some important philosophical insights in his studies of atoms and particles. Most important, he said, was the idea he labeled "complementarity." This is his notion that even the best scientific claims we can make are always partial and incomplete, and "only by entertaining multiple and mutually limiting points of view, building up a composite picture, can we approach the real richness of the world" (Rhodes, 1992). Bohr applied this idea to his study of physics and to his analysis of history, including a critique of the cultural superiority claimed by the Nazis.

One of the best current examples that I know of this kind of composite picturing is a remarkable little book that I only discovered recently, Bill McCloud's (1989) *What Should We Tell Our Children About Vietnam?* McCloud, a junior-high-school social-studies teacher from Oklahoma and a Vietnam vet, decided in 1987 to teach a unit on the Vietnam War. However, he could find few appropriate resources for middle schoolers, and he didn't have much of a sense of direction about the historical lessons of that war that he felt he might fairly share with his students. He decided to write letters to people who had been involved—decision makers who had been in the government, prominent journalists, public figures who had supported the war and those who had opposed it, combat veterans, and others—asking them all that simple question, "What should we tell our children about Vietnam?" He received over a hundred responses, with widely varying views and voices, from the likes of George Bush, Jimmy Carter, Geraldine Ferraro, Barry Goldwater, Alexander Haig, Tom Hayden, Henry Kissinger, Robert McNamara, Tim O'Brien, Arthur Schlesinger, Pete Seeger, Oliver Stone, Garry Trudeau, Kurt Vonnegut, and William Westmoreland. The book is a great resource, but also an example of the kind of varied human tapestry that history truly is. In his afterword, McCloud attempts to find points of agreement or any lessons commonly held among all those disputatious voices. This effort of a fellow middle-school social-studies teacher inspired me; he demonstrates what I think is an honorable stance for a history teacher, an acknowledgment of diversity and disagreement coupled with a quest for wisdom and hope.

The point here is that we can involve students in our classrooms in this exercise of seeking complementarity by the sharing of their voices and the collecting of their family testimonies about the lessons of history. History is part of a society's attempt to structure a self-image and communicate a common identity. In our current debates about whose history and identity is valued and whose is marginalized, one contribution that we can make as teachers is to encourage our students to join in, adding their voices, opinions, experiences, and family stories to the classroom history collection. In this way, we honor the pluralism in our own community; we enter different cultures, hear of different experiences, listen to different perspectives and conclusions drawn from the same historical events. But because we are in one classroom together, in one community, in one nation, we can also work to ferret out values, characteristics, traditions, ideals, and hopes that we share in common. In our classroom community, we have a grand laboratory for Bohr's experimental framework, the using of multiple points of view to build a composite picture that reflects the real richness of the world. This is in the best democratic American tradition; take a coin out of your pocket and find "E pluribus unum": "Out of many, one."

Thus, I was happy to have students get this big message through their parents' involvement in the interview: You have a stake in the past and in the future because your story is part of the larger story of history, and history is an amalgam of the stories of people like you.

All year long, then, we returned to this theme again and again. What follows is the final assignment of the school year for my students, the culminating activity in June for our study of U.S. history

YOUR PLACE IN HISTORY

History is the story that humans tell about their past, and we are each part of that story. What happens to you today is the material of tomorrow's history textbooks. However, there may come a time when your children and grandchildren say to you, "Who cares about what happened in the 'good old days?' We're tired of hearing about all that old stuff!" So what will you tell them about your place in history, and theirs, and why it is important?

Write a paper answering these questions:

- If you were writing a history textbook for middle-school students thirty or forty years from now, what would you say about these times we are currently living in?
- Of all the events of the last thirteen or fourteen years, which do you think are so important that no one should ever forget them?
- What has happened during your lifetime that people *must* remember? Why?
- What lessons need to be learned from these events by future generations, in your opinion?

To help the students write their papers, we made a classroom time line of events that had happened each year since most of them had been born (using almanacs, *World Book* yearbooks, the history textbook, and our collective memories). This gave them a chronological collection of happenings from which to draw for their essays.

The final papers were colorful and varied, more scraps for our classroom history quilt. The most commonly mentioned events were the Gulf War against Iraq and the Rodney King beating and trial and subsequent riots in Los Angeles. The following events were also mentioned numerous times:

- Fall of the Berlin Wall
- Various environmental depredations (cutting of rain forests, depletion of the ozone layer, overpopulation, logging old-growth forests, generation of smog, and so on).

- Explosion of the space shuttle Challenger
- AIDS epidemic
- Eruption of Mt. St. Helens (a high-impact event in Portland, since it happened so close by and most of the students remembered the city being sprinkled with volcanic ash in their preschool years).

Also mentioned were:

- End of the Cold War
- Animal rights movement
- Proliferation of hate crimes
- Tienamen Square massacre in China
- Freeing of Nelson Mandela from prison in South Africa
- Five-hundreth anniversary of Columbus's voyage to the Americas
- Erection of the Vietnam Veterans' Memorial in Washington, D.C.
- Growth of gangs and urban crime
- Federal budget deficit
- Trip into space of first female astronaut Sally Ride and first African-American astronaut Guion Bluford
- Important historical fact that the Portland Trailblazers' basketball team had made it to the National Basketball Association championship finals twice in recent years!

I could never have offered as comprehensive an overview of the history of the last decade.

Here are some brief excerpts from student papers (Note the great difference of opinion between Katie and Meghan about the lessons of the Persian Gulf War. In such difference is authentic historical inquiry and debate born):

Something people must remember in the future is the L.A. riots. It shows that every system fails sometime, in this case the judicial system. It also shows that violence is not an answer.

—Sean

The Rodney King incident affected me in that it was mind-boggling that the police officers who beat King weren't found guilty, even with the videotape. . . . The incident affected me because police are supposed to *protect* us from that kind of violence, aren't they? If the judicial system can't find men (who are obviously and undeniably bludgeoning someone) guilty, something is wrong. I think the Rodney King incident and the L.A. riots that went with it shouldn't be forgotten. I think this partly because people need to know that the government isn't always as wholesome as it says it is. In my opinion, a lesson to be learned from this is that justice isn't always brought to someone, and when it isn't brought by the government, the people may want to take things in their own hands.

—Brian

When I'm as old as my parents or as old as my grandparents, I'll want the children of tomorrow to remember President George Bush's term as President, the way he led the nation headfirst into 'Desert Storm.' He took men and women away from their families and friends, just so America got a steady supply of oil.

—Katie

In 1991, we had a war against the Iraqi leader. I thought it was for a good cause. . . . People talk about world peace. I feel that helping other countries in need is world peace.

—Meghan

There are some days I'd say my life was wonderful, the best time in history a person could live. Other days I'd say I'm altogether confused. There are times I think the things we do are ignorant and stupid, but other times I'd say we have learned from our mistakes and have broadened our minds. Every day we live is history, but history is not always good and it's not always bad. It's just advances and mistakes and memories.

—Sarah

May all our students start the year with something even more important than beautiful new textbooks. May they all be able to see that our history includes the advances, mistakes, and memories of us all.

BIBLIOGRAPHY

Flipovic, Zlata. 1994. *Zlata's Diary: A Child's Life in Sarajevo.* New York: Viking/Penguin.

McCloud, Bill. 1989. *What Should We Tell Our Children About Vietnam?* New York: Berkley Press.

O'Dell, Scott. 1986. *Streams to the River, River to the Sea.* New York: Fawcett Juniper.

Rhodes, Richard. 1992. "The Philosopher Physicist." *New York Times Book Review,* 26 January, 3.

Shaara, Michael. 1974. *The Killer Angels.* New York: Random House.

Shakespeare, William. 1600. *Midsummer Night's Dream.* London: Globe Publishing.

Chapter 3
Telling Points: Teaching Social Studies with Literature

MARY BURKE-HENGEN

The barn is cold, colder even than the unheated loft above the kitchen where they both sleep. The milk steams as it hits the bottom of their pails. The cows' udders warm the hands of the two children. At first, as they milk, Lawrence and Stella carefully practice the English they will not be able to use once they finish their milking and return to the house for the night. Soon, however, Lawrence reverts to speaking in his native French Canadian, even though the teacher he will have to face tomorrow and the day after tomorrow will forbid its use. He tells Stella about his desire for a bicycle because of his fear that the horse on which he rides the eight miles between their farm and the school will die before he finishes his elementary degree. It is very dark when they finish their milking, and they eat quietly and go to bed. They are too tired to complete the written homework that the teacher assigned for them that day.

These two children were my father and his older sister. Their struggles around the uses of language eventually resulted in lives of hard physical work for them and an ambivalence toward literacy that became part of my inheritance. This story has helped me understand my father's distrust for the schools that demanded such a high price for achieving an education. The family and local school conflicts over language that they experienced went on in many places in the United States in the early 1900s. They were not uncommon in this period of intense immigration. They were part of a national conflict about the meaning of the word *American*.

LITERATURE: PATHWAY INTO THE SOCIAL STUDIES

I begin *My Brother Sam Is Dead*, a fictional accounting by Christopher and James Collier of conflicts in a family and community during the Revolutionary War, by reading the first part of the book to my integrated literature, language arts, and social studies classes. As I read, my beginning mental pictures of the story come from my images of my father and his sister and their Minnesota barn. Shortly after the Collier book begins, there is a scene in the family barn between the two Meeker brothers: Tim and Sam. Old Pru, the family cow, and the family horse furnish warming comfort and an opportunity for the brothers to talk as they consider their own ideas and feelings about the war and their parents and community's responses to it.

Sam, the older brother, is all for freedom, so much so that he is willing to steal his father's gun and leave college in order to fight the British. He knows that his father does not agree with his position and that if he takes the gun and fights, it is likely that he will be cut off from his family and community. For Sam, the gun means freedom.

I was reminded of my own freedom symbol—namely, books, and the conflicts that I experienced in my family as I sought to attain a level of literacy higher than what they were comfortable with. I believe that this personal and emotional connection to the reading deepened and enriched my understanding of the conflict in the Collier book.

When I finished reading that day, I asked my students to write in their class journals about freedom and *My Brother Sam Is Dead*. One of my students, Aaron, wrote this: "Americans don't know what war is until it is fought in their homes. . . . I think that all is lost until it is won. . . . Freedom, the goal of life, is rarely attained. WHY?"

Aaron's images and ideas about freedom and mine were quite different. So were the ideas of the other members of our class. Students were surprised when I told them that only one out of three Americans actively supported the American Revolution. Another one out of three Americans stayed loyal to the British, and one out of three were neutral. We talked about the Revolution in much the same way in which I remember talking about the Vietnam War, and we raised as many questions as conclusions. We were equals in this discussion, and though I guided the flow of ideas, there were students with a great deal of information to share and some with strong convictions to express.

Literature promotes empathy because of the ties that readers make between themselves and characters in stories and in history. I believe that when I encourage my students to find connections between their experiences, the thoughts and feelings that they have about them, and the experiences of people in books or in history, their understandings of events and ideas are more likely to be empathetic and more likely to be remembered and applied to new situations. This is the concept that guides me as I choose readings (often with my students) and plan activities for my classes.

In the Colliers' book (1985), older brother Sam is a debater at Yale. He explains the thrill of scoring telling points to Tim. My students, most of whom are the age of the narrator, Tim, listen as I explain that telling points are logical constructs, ideas that are based on thoughts as well as on feelings. They are developed through reasoning about facts and information and are used as ways to convince others of a particular point of view. I tell them that skilled debaters can take any side of an argument and develop telling points for that side even if they don't personally believe in a point of view. Later in the year, we will refer to telling points as we stage class debates and mock trials.

Telling points can be used as a way to think about many things. For example, there needs to be several sound and persuasive reasons in answer to the questions: Why use one particular piece of writing rather than another piece with a particular class, small group, or individual? Why use literature at all in the social studies? In this chapter, I will offer several telling points to these questions and give suggestions for ways to incorporate literature into social studies. I will also discuss how the teacher's role might change by using this approach. At the end of the chapter, you will find a list of books that could be used in an integrated middle-school curriculum.

Teachers have long known the benefits of story in their teaching as well as in their own lives. Stories can help us learn about ideas and facts that our minds might otherwise resist as unrelated to us and perhaps uninteresting. Identification with characters in a story can affirm us and can help us to create a climate of respect for all kinds of people. The projecting of self onto a character in a story, along with opportunities to discuss ideas about the character's actions and options, is sometimes the only time that self-conscious students will risk revealing their ideas. For most of us, reading and hearing stories is an experience that liberates ideas that otherwise might not surface. This truth about stories may be as old as the awareness of self, society, and action that set in motion the telling and retelling of life's events.

I think that literature is history. It was, after all, only a few generations ago that we first embraced a belief in scientific objectivity. We hoped to isolate facts, to eliminate feelings and attitudes so that we could find what we hoped would be truth. But what we have learned instead is that there is little understanding of history or literature without consideration of feelings and attitudes. We find wisdom as well as understanding in stories. They offer a view of life led in a total sense of the word *living*. We are alive and our culture is evolving, never fixed at such and such a time. Discovery is ongoing, and authoritative-sounding words in history textbooks are false promises of certainty in an uncertain and evolving world.

Although one of the primary reflections of any culture is its literature, until recently literature was rarely included in a social studies curriculum or text of the social studies. Other reflections of culture—art, music, dance, theater, and movies—were also rarely seen as parts of a study of history or culture. Incorporated or integrated into the curriculum, however, literature and these other cultural means can help to provide the most comprehensive forms of knowing and understanding. Story and all of our rich subjective responses to it can be the most valuable part of what have been traditionally taught as objective subjects.

For several years, during sabbatical and vacation times, I have made a study of a Pacific Northwest native culture known as the Nuuchahnulth. When I began this study, I read what several Western anthropologists had to say about the culture, but soon I could see conflicting ideas and notions depending on who was doing the observing and recording. I wondered how I could learn or understand any truths about these people and their history and culture. At first, I thought that there wasn't a recorded history, except by outsiders to the culture, and that although these outsiders agreed on the basic facts of Nuuchahnulth history, they didn't agree on meanings or on interpretations of events. After some initial confusion, I saw the obvious: This culture was carried on by its owners through their oral literature. Their stories contained their history and their sociology, and their literature was their pedagogy, entertainment, and religion.

These stories strike me at many levels. They are often entertaining. They teach a profound wisdom. I enjoy the stories of Raven and Mink while I learn the taboos and the customs of the culture. I learn a new perspective about history through a reviewing of the first European encounters with America. One story handed down in oral literature reports that native observers on the west coast of Vancouver Island thought that English sailors were huge dog salmon.

We call some of these accounts oral history, and we call some story or theater; but to the people whose stories they are, these differences do not have meaning. These stories are unselfconscious; they are collective tales. They are told by the people themselves, a view of an insider looking out, and it is for listeners and readers to understand what they can and will. I believe we can best understand a culture by reading its literature, for its stories contain the dreams and the realities. Literature is the record of people's prejudices, triumphs, and moral underpinnings.

When I think about integrating the curriculum, I respond in ways similar to the idea of using stories. I think we are now reappreciating an older way of learning and responding: stories. When we look at cultures that have survived long time spans and listen to and read their stories, we begin to understand the values of those cultures as well as their knowledge, and we become more able, I think, to examine our own culture. Through stories, we can examine more fully our history, and, perhaps thus, we can better shape our futures.

In the course of reading *My Brother Sam Is Dead*, my students and I learn about the American Revolution at several levels. We learn about the language and terms of that time and what was contributed to our language during the Revolution: *Lobsterback, Minutemen, Rebels, Continentals, Patriots, Tories, Loyalists,* and *Brown Bess* (a gun named after Queen Elizabeth and brown in color). We gain some perspective on the customs of the time and the places where historical events were happening: Lexington and Concord, Long Island, New York City, Stratford, Danbury, Redding, New Haven, Bunker Hill, and White Plains, N.Y. Mention of Benedict Arnold, Louisbourg, and Fort Ticonderoga in the reading are opportunites for us to discuss aspects of the war and what led up to the war. Hunger and loyalty become more than terms as we experience them through the lives of the characters.

During our reading, we are presented with many opportunities for discussion and writing. Elements of fate and choice are unraveled as we read, discuss, and write. War is considered and even understood as an outcome of conflict and as an opportunity for change as we respond to the characters and events in the story. We ponder the effect on history of one decision versus another as we view life for a while through the thoughts and actions of others. Was the Revolutionary War inevitable? How about other wars that the United States has fought? What can we do to avoid war now? We consider these questions as we read about the reasons for the Revolutionary War through their characters. We look through their eyes and consider what else we know from nonfiction background materials and our own reasoning as we try to answer these questions (see Figure 3–1).

Through our reading and the meanings that we construct because of it and the accompanying activities we engage in, we develop ideas that might otherwise seem abstract and unrelated, ideas like *freedom, war, choice, integrity,* and *victory.* Using literature in this way might be best described as the difference between asking middle-school students to write an essay on an abstract topic like democracy and asking them to write a paper on the ways in which Sam Meeker lived his beliefs about government and what you think about his choices. The first format gives students little clue as to where to begin or how to give structure to their thoughts. In the second, there is a path to follow that is more likely to help students define their own particular thinking about an otherwise abstract subject.

Playing the role of characters in a story orally lends a certain passion to the words and an immediacy to the the telling of a story. I often use *Readers Theatre* (1985), whose author discusses a technique whereby the *he said's* and

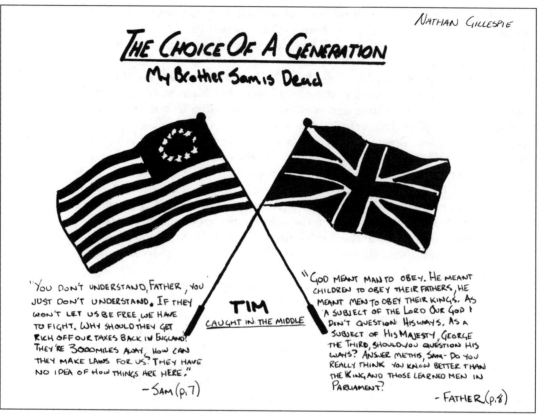

Figure 3-1

she said's are left out and students take the roles of narrator and characters and read the story as if it were a play. When my classes and I do this with *My Brother Sam Is Dead,* we are much more likely to feel the effects of war and to be better able to define freedom. We can more easily feel a part of the Revolution and understand why it took place: the telling points of the war.

After a *Readers Theatre* participation and the discussion that followed it, Brandon wrote this about victory:

> Victory was a big and vicious word to the English. Victory was a sign of bravery and boldness. The definition of victory is the final and complete defeat of the enemy in a military engagement. Another definition you might be familiar with is any successful struggle against an opponent or obstacle. In the Revolutionary War, the Tories lost and gave up at Yorktown. . . . After the war, the damage was done. The costs were high, and many people went bankrupt. Everybody wanted to be victorious after the war so they could get whatever they were fighting for, and that hurt a lot of people in different ways.

Sometimes while reading this and other stories, my classes and I write interior monologues (thoughts and feelings that are not expressed out loud) as characters. At other times, we compare the actions and thoughts of the characters to our own experiences and consider what we could learn that would affect our lives. We contrast then and now and think about and discuss the problems that we face as a country and what we have or haven't learned from the decisions of the past.

MIDDLE SCHOOLS AND WISH-LIST TEACHING

Much is asked of middle school teachers:

- Plan teaching with the growth needs and issues of young adolescents in mind.
- Be vigilant about drug use, gang and violence involvement.
- Watch for signs of grief, depression, suicidal thoughts, and eating disorders.
- Use cooperative learning techniques that students will need for today's jobs and that provide opportunities for individual creative expression and discovery of abilities and leadership.
- Introduce students to the technology that will help them now in their schoolwork and that will also help to prepare them for the careers that they will have in a yet-to-be-created society.
- Include only materials that show respect for all people, and exclude what is offensive to the families and communities within which we work.
- Know the policies of the school and district; use currently popular professional techniques.
- Be knowledgeable about textbooks, films and other visual aids, including television, *and* produce students who are successful at completing the work of our classes and who are competent in the skills and understanding of our courses.

To this list, I would add:

- Possess a wide-ranging working knowledge of books, fiction and non-fiction, that are appropriate for class, small-group, and individual use.

I believe that this knowledge of books, rather than being an additional demand, is just what we need to help us deal with the other items on this list. Separating the items into separate tasks to be done, in addition to designing a curriculum, results in an impossible wish list—a formula that,

I think, results in disgruntled and overwhelmed teachers. If we read widely ourselves, structure assignments so that students talk and write about books, meet with other teachers and share reading titles and ideas, and use media specialists and others to introduce and help us with new books, our work can be joyful. It can also help us locate and match the resources that we need to address adolescent concerns.

Rather than an extra job for us to do, reading is a way for us to enjoy our shared culture with our students. We can learn from stories the truths and details of the lives of some individuals and some groups. We can also examine and think about themes of life, like love, friendship, justice, and authority, and topics of real concern, like the environment, violence, drugs, and peer pressure. It is our stories that unify us with our students and with each other and that help us to be increasingly more effective in what we offer to students and to ourselves in the way of solutions to societal issues. In a story, there is often just the right amount of closeness to character and distance from our own lives to help us look at what we're doing and examine other options than the ones we're using. Stories are a way in which we all participate in the great American drama that we create and that recreates us as people.

READING GROUPS IN AN INTEGRATED CURRICULUM

I begin the year with a novel that the whole class will experience. I want the class to become a community of learners, and I want to model many of the techniques that we will use during the year. Alternating silent reading with teacher and student oral readings keeps the book satisfactorily paced for most class members while large- and small-group discussions and dramatic portrayals help hold interest. During this time, we establish that there are no right and wrong answers and that each person's ideas are to be treated with respect. By the end of this first novel, students are able to work more independently; it is time for small, self-chosen reading groups.

At the time of the following student writings, students had chosen their books, met, and set a timetable for their reading. There were six groups, five of them reading a novel, and the sixth a book of historical accounts. All of the selections related to our study of westward expansion, and we had just about concluded the reading of our books. The prompt questions I gave were three: What is conflict? What conflicts are presented in the book you are reading? How do those conflicts apply to our world today? Fred had joined a group that was reading *Streams to the River, River to the Sea*, a Scott O'Dell historical fiction story about Sacajawea and the Lewis and Clark expedition to the Northwest.

This is what Fred had to say that day in his reading journal:

Conflict is a disagreement between two parties. Conflict plays an important role in the way things work and probably will work. If it weren't for conflict, there would be no negotiating and that would totally halt everything. For instance, in the making of our Constitution, there was a conflict on the amount of people representing each individual state. Since there was a conflict, negotiation occurred and we formed the House of Representatives and all the parts of Congress were agreed upon.

I would like to think that things like what happened to the natives in *Streams to the River, River to the Sea* don't happen any more, but I know I am wrong. There are still false trials where the innocent are found guilty.

Fred then compared a few examples of injustices in our judicial system today with the treatment of native people in his reading. He traveled back and forth in his mind between past and present and developed his own ideas on these topics. The tie between ideas that Fred made was unique to him and yet showed an understanding of our common history and connections to our collective present.

Another student, Kellie, chose to read Louis L'Amour's classic *Comstock Lode* as part of her reading on westward expansion. About halfway through the book, however, she began to show up for reading time with a different book.

In her journal, she wrote:

I decided to read *Dances with Wolves*. I couldn't wait. I had to read it now. I have often wondered what it would be like to be on the frontier, so quiet and peaceful. And what it would be like to see an Indian standing right in front of you. I would probably be a little frightened, but it would be wonderful at the same time I would think.

What I am reading about now is how John and the Indians are communicating and finding things out about the others' lifestyles. It's interesting to hear how women dealt with their husband's dying. They go out and cut themselves and some even commit suicide. And their fathers tell them how long they will be mourning.

John Dunbar was walking around naked at Fort Sedgewick. That is something I would personally never do, especially if people could see me.

In my response to Kellie, I decided to ask her why she thought John was naked and what his nakedness meant in the story.

In her next entry, Kellie first wrote about the story and then responded to my question:

Kicking Bird was put in charge of the White Man. So he decided to get Stands With A Fist, who is white, to try and remember the *White Man's words*. But Stands With A Fist is afraid to talk with the white man, afraid they will take her away from the Comanches.

I would think it would be great to go to an Indian village or whatever and see the way they do things. Seeing them actually there before you. But not disturbing them.

About Dunbar being naked. He had to wash his clothes so he decided to wash the ones he had on, too.

Kellie continued to work with her reading group and to read on her own. Her group decided on a project presentation of *Comstock Lode* in which they discussed the role of women in westward expansion and how other people, including writers, saw that role. Meantime, Kellie continued her own explorative questions about *Dances with Wolves*.

In a journal entry to a classmate, she said:

> I am reading *Dances with Wolves*. It seems that talking a different language would be easy but reading this made me think how difficult it would be because Stands With A Fist has a lot of trouble speaking English and she knows the language but she's just so used to speaking Indian that she has trouble pronouncing the words.

Kellie finished the book just as school was ending. In one of her final entries, she wrote:

> I finished *Dances with Wolves*. It was like the movie mostly but some parts were different. Michael Blake must have done a lot of research on Comanche Indians. I learned a lot about the Comanche ways. It was interesting how they accepted a white man to be a Comanche.
>
> It was sad how they killed Two Sox. That Wolf sounded sweet. It was a good book, not as good as other books I have read but okay.

Both Fred and Kellie made connections between what they already knew and were thinking and wondering about and what they were reading. I believe that Kellie could more fully appreciate the research aspects of writing because she and a friend had been researching AIDS for most of the school year and had written both a research paper and a short novel regarding the topic. Fred brought knowledge and awareness about the law to his reading. Not surprisingly, he noticed justice and the lack of it in the book that he chose to read.

Although both Kellie and Fred liked to read from a wide variety of choices, Kellie often looked for Jack London stories to read. She also liked romances and other young adult books. She read and wrote poetry. She was thoughtful about her reading, willing to learn from it. Fred especially enjoyed a genre of books that combined adventure, fantasy, and the Middle Ages. He wrote so enthusiastically and descriptively about Susan Cooper's series that I was convinced to read one myself and asked him for a recommendation of *Best of Series*. Kellie and Fred had enjoyment as their strongest motive for reading. They were typical of their classmates. Although they were willing to discuss elements of plot, theme, setting, and characterization in their reading journals, their primary motive in reading was not literary analysis nor the learning of history and geography. They liked to read for fun, for exploring ideas and places, and for the chance to identify with characters who might or might not be like themselves.

SELECTING QUALITY READING MATERIALS

In our moves toward integrating the middle school curriculum, it is important for us to remember that although the motives for reading are numerous and complex, the main reasons that students want to read are enjoyment and self-paced, self-controlled learning. Motivation can sometimes be fanned into life by our sharing of ideas about books or by making reading assignments, but the reader-learner must also want to read. Our students seek stories, seek to be in control of their own explorations, just as my father and aunt escaped to the barn to speak new words and ideas and, many years later, I found trees to climb and closets to hide me so that I could read about people and places that were not part of my immediate world. I believe that a primary goal of teachers is to promote that seeking, to provide many opportunities for bonding with books.

It is important for us to suggest to students places to look for good reading on particular topics that we think will be of interest to them and to hold students accountable for their use and misuse of time. There are many books and shorter selections we know that past students have learned from and enjoyed; but if reading is constantly assigned rather than chosen and is treated as something primarily existing for pragmatic use, we will defeat our larger purposes. We may accomplish the short-term goals of specific content learning at the price of a longer, more important goal of helping students develop a loving connection to books.

Finding and selecting good reading materials for an integrated language arts and social studies curriculum starts with reflecting on our reasons for the use of those materials. In the beginning enthusiasm of this curricular change, it may seem important to find readings whose settings or time periods are the same as some area or time period that we're studying. There is a tendency at this point to forgive a lot in the way of asking for a well-researched background for the book. Later, we may find that the connection that we were so enthusiastic about is shallow, that the actions that took place in the story could have happened anywhere to anyone, and that there is nothing unique connecting the setting, the characters, and the plot. The book may turn out to be even inaccurate in some of its facts and ideas. When that does happen, I don't feel that anything is lost. Rather, it may be part of the road to defining and finding the truly good works of literature that have strong and truthful cultural portrayals and connectedness to contemporary themes. When I find books of this last kind, I am as delighted as an archeologist who has just found the buried door to a previously un-known pyramid.

Recent examples of books that I think are contemporary in theme and that portray an informative and accurate cultural and historical back-ground are Linda Crew's *Children of the River,* Omar Castaneda's *Among the Volcanoes,* Katherine Patterson's *Lyddie,* Mingfong Ho's *Rice Without Rain* and *The Clay Marble,* and Luis Rodriquez's *Always Running.* Each of these books contains an informative background as well as a powerful story, and each would be the right book for some students.

Sometimes, we find a piece that contains a story that we're sure our stu-dents will love, but it presents a stereotyped view of women or minority groups, or it may be slanted with expressions of intolerance for old people, people of a particular religion, or homosexuals. I think that there are times to read these pieces. They may be historical records of other times and places. The caution I feel about this is that literature, like film, provides models, especially for young people. If we select certain readings, it may well seem as if we agree with the interpretations of reality presented. We may choose certain pieces to use as examples of bias, but we ought to care-fully seek out quality literature: that which portrays respect for all people.

There are some hard questions for teachers to ask regarding these issues. I do not think it makes any sense to live our teaching lives in fear of criti-cism for one of the thousands of decisions that we make over time. I do think we need to be prepared to explain our literature choices and to han-dle any controversy or strong responses that might arise from them. Ways of avoiding confrontations that might compromise our use of certain books are to use small literature groups rather than whole-class readings so that there are several choices and to supplement whole-class readings with other pieces of literature that present other information or points of view.

Good literature conveys joy, fear, longing, and individual quest in ways that are honest whether the story told contains an actual historical account of a time or place or is totally imagined by the writer. I remember the awe with which I read *Giants in the Earth,* a pioneer immigrant story about the area where I was born and raised and one of the first books that hooked me on reading historical fiction as a way to enjoy myself while learning history I would remember.

I know that writing from the view outside of a culture is the most likely to be inaccurate or flawed by omissions of relevant cultural material. When I look for books about another culture, I first look for ones written by a member of the cultural group that the book addresses. An example of this idea is the book *Fool's Crow,* by James Welch. At first, I found it a hard book to read, and then I realized that Welch's writing perspective for this book was tribal rather than individual. He wrote as though he were the voice of many people. Knowing that culturally this is a far more accurate book of Native-American life than most of what has been published about Native Americans, I continued my reading and developed a real love of the book. This reading experience richly changed my understanding of the word *tribal* because, though I knew the definition of the word, I did not understand how feeling and thinking would be affected by the perspective of considering yourself as many people rather than as one person.

PRESENTING AND PAYING FOR READING MATERIALS

Before asking students to select a book as part of small-group or individualized study, either you, a student, or the media specialist might do a book talk so that students can learn about the books in a general way. Enough information needs to be given so that students can know the setting, genre of book (historical fiction, romance, mystery, adventure, fantasy), the type of book (novel, poetry, short stories, or essay collection), and the characters' ages, sexes, and cultural backgrounds if a novel is being read.

The media specialist might not only be of help in locating appropriate books and in giving book talks, but may also have ideas for locating the four to six copies needed for small reading groups. Administrators may have funds that are no longer needed for textbooks and workbooks or may have film resources that can be diverted in order to purchase the needed four to six copies of each title. Parent organizations and small district grants for innovative programming can also provide the needed budget. Using paperbacks rather than hardcover books allows for the purchase of more books and for the opportunity to update selections more frequently.

ACTIVITIES TO LAUNCH LITERATURE READINGS

Whether you're chosen to ask students to read a literature selection as a whole class, as individuals with personally chosen selections, or in small study groups, a common experience base is needed in order to develop a thematic core for later thinking and discussion. What is the common denominator between students, the books they are about to read, and curriculum? How can ideas be isolated that will develop focus and community during the reading?

I cannot know ahead of class discussions or journal entries the issues that may emerge for students as a result of their reading, but I can, and do, involve students in the selection of reading materials by using their statements of interests, concerns, and past favorite reading choices. If I'm looking for books or groups of books to use as part of integrated social studies and language arts classes, I start by thinking about why an individual book might be better than another. If choice relates to topic, like the American Revolution, Africa, the Middle Ages, or Ecology, I try to associate the topic with a theme that I believe to be common to the time, place, or era that is part of our course focus and relevant to the lives of my students. For example, conflict and the study of war is an easy connection with many books; Africa works well with change, challenge, returning, continuity, and blessings; environmental issues go well with most of the themes, although I favor utopia or returning, depending on whether I want the focus to be on how society could handle environmental concerns or on the cyclical nature of most of the natural world. Changes, choices, challenges, courage, conflict and conflict resolution, Utopia, focus, leadership, cooperation, continuity, character, creativity, and glory are themes that mesh well with adolescent growth issues. These themes can stand alone, can be expressed in phrases like *beginnings and endings,* and can be paired with topics, as in *Civil War/Challenge* or *Conflict/The American Revolution.* In this way, a bridge can be built between students' lives and another time and place.

We can help students find parallels between their own experiences and the experiences of people who lived in another time or place by first asking them to look in their own lives and to share their own stories. Using a theme like continuity, I ask students to make lists of the traditions, things, and people that have been constant in their lives. We either share some of these lists in the class or we choose one aspect to write about and develop a description of it and what it means to us. I say *us* because whenever possible, I write with the students and share what I write, just as I ask students to do. As we read our pieces to the class, a list begins to emerge of words that we use for describing experiences common to most of us. This is the class bridge to understanding how we share experiences with people in other times and places.

Another way to launch a book or books is to ask a question that relates to our lives and to what we value. In an important scene from *Upon the Head of a Goat,* Piri, the main character, hands over the back fence her phonograph, which she knows she will soon not be able to use. Later that morning, she and her family are given a few minutes time to gather necessities and mementos for their trip into the Polish ghetto of World War II. What would we give as a gift if we were about to leave behind all the familiar objects in our lives? What would we take along to sustain ourselves on a long journey? What photographs, letters, and other keepsakes would we choose to carry? What book or two might we bring? Choosing objects, bringing them into class, and describing why these objects are special makes this experience even more meaningful. Making lists or taking photographs and posting them during the reading of the book gives a constant reminder of the tie between the people in the book and ourselves, and the reading and thinking about the book take on increased importance.

A fun way to get into a book is to list the names of the book's characters on the board or overhead, give a short description of each character, and then put descriptions of the characters on note cards with the names of the characters on the other side. Pin the cards on everyone's backs so that the person wearing the card cannot read it and ask the students to mingle and talk with each other until all characters have been identified. The goal is for the students to identify the names of the characters that they are wearing. They may ask as many questions of other class members as they like, but the other person can only answer *yes* or *no*.

Names of the characters can also be put on cards and drawn randomly. Students are not to reveal the name of the characters that they have drawn. After descriptions of the characters are given in the same way as noted above, make hats out of paper and other art supplies. The hats should be worn during a mingling-talking time during which students attempt to identify the characters that would match the hats. Names of characters are left posted, and only yes and no answers are given by the person wearing the hat. The people in the book become like old friends, and students have a familiarity basis with which to begin their reading.

This introductory experience can be extended by making paper or cardboard cut-out figures of characters or figures of the time and place in the book's setting. Students can make and keep a diary as one of the characters during the reading. All of these activities usually work successfully whether my students and I are reading the same book or are reading several books with a unifying theme or topic. Another of the advantages I find in doing these activities is that some students may become motivated to read two or three books when more than one title is available.

ACTIVITIES FOR CONTINUED EXPLORATION

For some students, reading the same book with a classmate and having opportunities to discuss the book in class conversations and in dialogue journals can build enthusiasm about other activities surrounding the book or unit. Having opportunities to share thoughts one to one with a peer in a directed way helps some students expand their thoughts and make connections with books. Pairing also allows for a natural kind of conversation about books and opens up more possibilities for ideas and responses about a book.

Broad-based but focused questions are often helpful to the reading process, especially if a teacher is clustering ideas around a theme being developed with students. If conflict is the theme, questions during the reading of *Brother Sam* might vary from "What are the ways in which the members of the Meeker family solve conflicts?" to "How are the ways in which the Meeker family solves conflicts typical of the times in which they lived?" or "How do the ways in which the Meeker family solves conflicts relate to you?"

Whether I have selected and organized books around themes like conflict, choice, or justice, or I have used topics like historical periods or geographical areas, my choice of activities is affected by the goals that I hope to achieve. Some activities that I have found to work well in addition to journal and essay writing in developing and expanding topics and themes are mock trials; murals and other drawings; interpretative presentations of scenes from the book; writing a short play around character, theme, or events in the book; interior monologues; informational films; oral character interviews; character diaries; human sculptures; art of the time or place; nonfiction cultural and historical readings; studies of the land, landforms, vegetation, and animal life that are part of the book; storytelling and story writing; and debates.

Sometimes, I choose a particular approach because I haven't used it with a particular class before, and I'm seeking variety in classroom techniques. Once I have introduced a few ways to develop the content and themes in books that we're reading, some students start creating their own ideas for book projects. I am often delighted, challenged, and enriched by their innovations. I learn new ways of looking at things, and I gain a wider perspective as well as a bigger repertoire of ideas for future use.

Murals lend themselves well for use with books in which the landscape is important. When I think of *The Endless Steppe,* I think of pictures of land that is both desolate and sheltering. *Among the Volcanoes* and *The Land I Lost* are other works that portray people and places that might be best interpreted through illustrations. Students can work in pairs as well as small groups to develop murals. They can pretend that their paper is a wall where people leave messages for each other through drawings and paintings. What is the message? A student can be a character in the book being read and can be challenged to portray an event from the book through a drawing. Again, once you have defined an outcome, the students display incredible creativity in their interpretations.

When I ask small groups of students to choose a scene from a reading and to present an interpretation of it (sometimes based on criteria that we have developed in class, sometimes on their own ideas), students often respond in ways that initially surprise me. Students who are quiet in class discussions often find it easier to talk as a character in a book. Writing a short play or story based on key ideas of a book are other, similar kinds of activities.

An activity that takes less time than those listed above and yet can be very productive in literature interpretation is to give students a short period of time, five to ten minutes, to form human sculptures that illustrate what they believe to be the theme or primary meaning of a book. Three or four people make a group, and they arrange their bodies to portray conflict, greed, jealousy, yearning for love, and so forth.

CHANGES IN THE TEACHER AND IN THE STUDENTS

It has been several years now since the day I took the writers' stool and read the poem that I had written about the death of my youngest sister. It told a story that was central to my life, and I believed that I had to be willing to be as vulnerable as I was asking my students to be if we were to explore themes of real meaning and significance. My voice cracked in places and then got soft. They strained to hear my words.

We were each to write a piece about a loss in our lives so that we could better understand the characters in our reading-group novels who faced many losses in war. Still, I found it hard to risk the loss of self-control, to put down my teacher mask of calm equanimity and take up a position within the class as one of many looking for meanings in literature and in my experiences. I don't remember now what my escape plan was to be if the students didn't respond with sensitivity—but I didn't need one.

In the days and weeks that followed, many people read their stories of loss. I was surprised at the depth of their experiences and at how vividly they wrote about: a grandparent's death, a dog run over, a friend who moved away, a parent moving out, moving away from a place they loved, a move from the honor roll to barely making it, a cat who ran away, and romance gone sour. We shared experiences, compared our feelings and thoughts about them with each other and with book characters. We became a community of mutual learners, and I was excited to go to work each day and hear more about their ideas.

I learned that for most students personal and family stories were what was most interesting to them and that if I wanted to lead the students into abstract ideas or even historical facts I could do so by tying our stories to ideas in history and literature. We could see connections to themes of heroism by our telling stories about how dad got the car out of the mud on the mountain or how mom killed the diseased cat that threatened to hurt her children. We could more easily view courage, injustice, and conflict as connected to us and could better understand the people and events that we read about in class. I could better understand and share parts of my own history.

Understandings about the connections that each of us has to other people, times, and places can come from many avenues. Storytelling is a powerful avenue. Debate can be another.

It is initially difficult for many middle-school students to examine their own worldviews, to think about what other people have thought and to think differently than they previously have. I remind students of the telling points of *My Brother Sam Is Dead* and use this concept as a way of trying to nudge them past the notion of argumentation as purely emotional venting or persuasion. I want them to see the world as external enough to themselves that they can understand someone who thinks and does things differently.

After we have decided a debate topic and who will be on which side and in which order of speaking, I model the *telling-point* concept for them by teaching them how to score debates: For each reason given by the speaker that is informative and convincing of their point of view, I award a point. After a while, I cease to model, and the students score the debate.

In a broad view of teaching and learning, I am hoping that students will learn to view the world with more wonder and less judgment. I want my students to strongly consider that all people probably have reasons for what they do and that these reasons may be just as valid for those people as our own reasons are for us.

I am not trying to teach cultural relativity; rather, I want to foster cultural respect. I want students to move past the attitude of "It is so because I think it or feel it" to a place of curiosity about the mystery we all are to each other. I want them to think in terms of what they have in common with an Aleut or a Tongan as well as the person sitting next to them.

It is in isolating what is familar and individual to us and in finding and embracing what is *other* and perhaps initially strange that we come to know ourselves and to connect ourselves in our minds with the present and the past. I am in that barn with the Meekers and with my father and my aunt. My students and I are part of the experience of the American Revolution and all the other events and ideas that we study. In participating together in a lively quest for the telling points of our lives, we are studying what we most need to study: the world

I have been changed by the readings and activities that I have participated in with students. I have been changed by knowing more about their lives. When I think about my interest in the environment, I think of Heather and all the other students who taught me about holes in the sky and chlorofluorocarbons. I think of Adrienne and her speech about homosexuals and their need for acceptance. I think of Mujib, Loris, and Soloman. I remember how badly I felt when I realized how ineffective the curriculum that I had to offer these students at the time I taught them really was, and I wish they were all back in the classroom with me so we could begin again.

I now know that there is literature that can help us understand our history and our society as well as our places in it.

BIBLIOGRAPHY AND SUGGESTED
MIDDLE SCHOOL TITLES

Achebe, Chinua. 1988. *Things Fall Apart*. London: Heinemann.

Angelou, Maya. 1971. *I Know Why the Caged Bird Sings*. New York: Bantam Books.

Babbit, Natalie. 1987. *Tuck Everlasting*. New York: Farrar, Straus & Giroux.

Barry, Lynda. 1991. *The Good Times Are Killing Me*. New York: HarperCollins.

Bierhorst, John, ed. 1987. *In the Trail of the Wind: American Indian Poems and Ritual Orations*. New York: Farrar, Straus & Giroux.

Blake, Michael. 1991. *Dances with Wolves*. New York: Newmarket Press.

Bode, Janet. 1991. *New Kids in Town: Oral Histories of Immigrant Teens*. New York: Scholastic.

Borton, Elizabeth de Trevino. 1965. *I, Juan de Pareja*. New York: Farrar, Straus & Giroux.

Brown, Dee. 1972. *Bury My Heart at Wounded Knee*. New York: Bantam Books.

Burgos-Debray, Elisabeth, ed. 1984. *I, Rigoberta Menchú*. London: Verso.

Calvert, Patricia. 1982. *Snowbird*. New York: New American Library.

Campbell, Bebe Moore. 1992. *Your Blues Ain't Like Mine*. New York: G. P. Putnam's Sons.

Castaneda, Omar S. 1993. *Among the Volcanoes*. New York: Dell.

Childress, Alice. 1989. *Those Other People*. New York: G. P. Putnam's Sons.

Cisneros, Sandra. 1991. *The House on Mango Street*. New York: Vintage.

Clark, Ann Nolan. 1952. *Secret of the Andes*. New York: Viking Books.

Collier, Christopher, and James Collier. 1985. *My Brother Sam Is Dead*. New York: Scholastic.

———. 1987. *Jump Ship to Freedom*. New York: Dell.

Coman, Carolyn. 1993. *Tell Me Everything*. New York: Farrar, Straus & Giroux.

Crew, Linda. 1991. *Children of the River*. New York: Dell.

Dickinson, Peter. 1990. *Eva*. New York: Dell.

———. 1994. *AK*. New York: Dell.

Douglass, Frederick. 1973. *Narrative of the Life of Frederick Douglass*. New York: Doubleday.

Eckert, Allan. 1987. *Incident at Hawk's Hill*. New York: Bantam Books.

Frank, Anne. 1958. *The Diary of a Young Girl*. New York: Pocket Books.

Gaines, Ernest. 1974. *Autobiography of Miss Jane Pittman*. New York: Caedman.

———. 1993. *A Lesson Before Dying*. New York: Knopf.

Gordon, Sheila. 1987. *Waiting for the Rain*. New York: Bantam Books.

———. 1992. *The Middle of Somewhere: The Story of South Africa*. New York: Bantam Books.

Goss, Linda, and Marian E. Barnes, eds. 1989. *Talk That Talk: An Anthology of African-American Storytelling*. New York: Simon & Schuster.

Hale, Janet Campbell. 1991. *The Owl's Song*. New York: Bantam Books.

———. 1993. *Bloodlines: Odyssey of a Native Daughter*. New York: Harper Perennial.

Hautzig, Esther. 1987. *The Endless Steppe*. New York: HarperCollins.

Hernandez, Irene. 1989. *Across the Great River*. Houston: Arte Publico Press.

Hersey, John. 1968. *Hiroshima*. New York: Bantam Books.

Higa, Tomiko. 1992. *The Girl with the White Flag*. New York: Dell.

Ho, Minfong. 1990. *Rice Without Rain*. New York: Morrow.

———. 1991. *The Clay Marble*. New York: Farrar, Straus & Giroux.

Houston, James D., and Jeanne Wakatsuki. 1973. *Farewell to Manzanar*. Boston: Houghton Mifflin.

Howard, Ellen. 1985. *When Daylight Comes*. New York: MacMillan.

Hubert, Cam. 1978. *Dreamspeaker*. New York: Avon Books.

Ishikawa, Yoshimi. 1991. *Strawberry Road*. New York: Kodansha International.

Kadohata, Cynthia. 1989. *Floating World*. New York: Penguin Books.

Keith, Harold. 1987. *Rifles for Watie*. New York: HarperCollins.

Kheridian, David. 1979. *The Road from Home: The Story of an Armenian Girl*. New York: Greenwillow Books.

Kincaid, Jamaica. 1986. *Annie John*. New York: Penguin Books.

Koningsburg, Elaine. 1973. *A Proud Taste for Scarlet and Miniver*. New York: Dell.

Kroeber, Theodora. 1981. *Ishi, Last of His Tribe*. New York: Bantam Books.

Krumgold, Joseph. 1953. *And Now Miguel*. New York: Harper & Row.

L'Amour, Louis. 1981. *Comstock Lode*. New York: Bantam Books.

Lamb, Wendy, ed. 1992. *Ten out of Ten*. New York: Delacorte.

Lee, Harper. 1960. *To Kill a Mockingbird*. New York: Warner Books.

Lesley, Craig, ed. 1991. *Talking Leaves: Contemporary Native American Short Stories*. New York: Dell.

Lester, Julius. 1968. *To Be a Slave*. New York: Scholastic.

Lord, Bette Bao. 1990. *Legacies: A Chinese Mosaic*. New York: Knopf.

Maalouf, Amin. 1988. *Leo the African*. New York: Norton.

McCunn, Ruthanne Lum. 1988. *A Thousand Pieces of Gold*. Boston: Beacon Press.

Myers, Walter Dean. 1988. *Fast Sam, Cool Clyde, and Stuff*. New York: Puffin Books.

———. 1989. *Fallen Angels*. New York: Scholastic.

———. 1990. *Scorpions*. New York: Harper & Row.

Naidoo, Beverly. 1986. *Journey to Jo'burg*. New York: HarperCollins.

———. 1993. *Chain of Fire.* New York: HarperCollins.

O'Dell, Scott. 1970. *Sing Down the Moon.* New York: Dell.

———. 1977. *Black Pearl.* New York: Dell.

———. 1977. *Carlota.* New York: Dell.

———. 1978. *Zia.* New York: Dell.

———. 1987. *Island of the Blue Dolphin.* New York: Dell.

———. 1991. *Streams to the River, River to the Sea.* New York: Ballantine Books.

———. 1980. *Sarah Bishop.* New York: Scholastic.

Patterson, Katherine. 1987. *Bridge to Terabithia.* New York: Harper & Row.

———. 1988. *Park's Quest.* New York: Trumpet Club.

———. 1991. *Lyddie.* New York: Dutton Children's Books.

Pitcher, Diana. 1981. *Tokoloshi: African Folk Tales Retold.* Millbrae, CA: Celestial Arts.

Quang Nhuong, Huynh. 1986. *The Land I Lost: Adventures of a Boy in Vietnam.* New York: HarperCollins.

Rodriguez, Luis J. 1993. *Always Running.* New York: Curbstone.

Robinson, Margaret. 1992. *A Woman of Her Tribe.* New York: Ballantine Books.

Rölvaag, O. E. *Giants in the Earth.* 1929. New York: Blue Ribbon Books.

Siegal, Aranka. 1983. *Upon the Head of the Goat: A Childhood in Hungary, 1939–1944.* New York: Farrar, Straus & Giroux.

Soto, Gary. 1990. *A Summer Life.* New York: Dell.

Taylor, Mildred D. 1990. *The Road to Memphis.* New York: Puffin Books.

———. 1991. *Let the Circle Be Unbroken.* New York: Puffin Books.

———. 1991. *Roll of Thunder, Hear My Cry.* New York: Puffin Books.

Tsuchiya, Yukio. 1988. *Faithful Elephants: A True Story of Animals, People, and War.* New York: Houghton Mifflin.

Uchida, Yokhiko. 1985. *Journey to Topaz.* New York: Creative Arts.

———. 1992. *Journey Home.* New York: MacMillan.

Watkins, Yoko Kawashima. 1987. *So Far from the Bamboo Grove.* New York: Puffin Books.

Webb, Sheyann, and Rachel West Nelson. 1980. *Selma, Lord, Selma: Girlhood Memories of the Civil Rights Days.* New York: Morrow.

Welch, James. 1986. *Fool's Crow.* New York: Viking.

Yep, Lawrence. 1990. *Child of the Owl.* New York: HarperCollins.

———. 1977. *Dragonwings.* New York: Harper & Row.

TEACHER RESOURCES

Bowe, Bert, Jim Lobdell, and Lee Swenson. 1994. *History Alive: Engaging All Learners in the Diverse Classroom.* Menlo Park, CA: Addison-Wesley.

Hubbard, Ruth. 1989. *Authors of Pictures, Draughtsmen of Words.* Portsmouth, NH: Heinemann Educational Books.

Murphy, Richard. 1974. *Imaginary Worlds: Notes on a New Curriculum.* New York: Teachers & Writers Collaborative.

Rief, Linda. 1992. *Seeking Diversity.* Portsmouth, NH: Heinemann Educational Books.

Rosen, Betty. 1988. *And None of It Was Nonsense.* Portsmouth, NH: Heinemann Educational Books.

Simons, Elizabeth Radin. 1990. *Student Worlds, Student Words: Teaching Writing Through Folklore.* Portsmouth, NH: Boynton/Cook.

Tanner, Fran Averett. 1987. *Readers Theatre.* Caldwell, ID: Clark.

Part Two

CREATING INTERDISCIPLINARY CLASSROOMS

Chapter 4
Call of the Wild

JACKIE O'CONNOR

> My name is Iptuk. I am thirty-eight years old, and I have lived in the Yukon all of my life. My ancestors are said to have come here from Asia by means of a land bridge over the Bering Sea.
>
> There are many names for my people, including Yukip, Igulik and Inuit, each of which means *The People*. The word *Eskimo* means 'eater of raw meat' and was given to us by outsiders like yourselves.
>
> The reason I've asked you to come into my home today is to teach you about my people, so you can journey back home with the knowledge of another culture.

As I tell Iptuk's story, interweaving facts about daily life with Inuit folktales, my sixth graders surround me in a large circle which resembles the shape of an igloo. The classroom has been darkened as much as possible. In the center is an oil lamp, which is our only illumination. It is light enough to see, but dark enough to allow us to get caught up in the magic of make-believe.

A few days later, two teachers are in my classroom, observing. They hear several students refer to "getting into the igloo." They look around, unsure where the igloo is. One teacher asks a boy. He looks at her, not understanding why she asks, points to the back of the room, and says, "It's right there, of course." The way the igloo had been talked about made her think it was a *real* object—and to the students it was. The teacher still laughs when she tells the story.

If you were to observe our classroom from November through December, you would hear students putting final touches on totem-pole stories and getting ready for a potlatch. You would see a variety of well-packed dog sleds with groups of characters traveling to the Yukon looking for

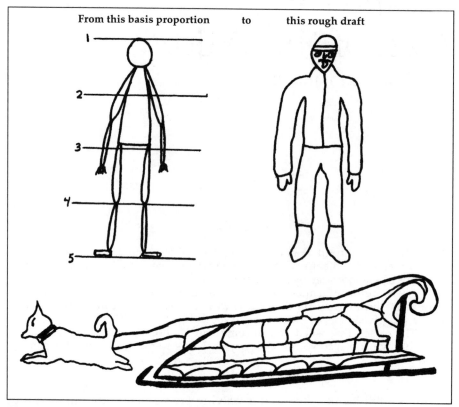

From this basis proportion   to   this rough draft

Figure 4–1

gold, their journeys penciled on maps. You would feel an excitement in the air, and you might well get caught up in it.

What we are doing is an adapted version of the "Scottish Storyline"—a content-based, unfolding story that links subject areas together in a meaningful way for students at all ability levels. Students are actively participating in producing their own visual texts, reading, writing, learning history, solving problems, and working with cooperative groups. From this, a strong sense of ownership and success occurs. The "Scottish Storyline" originated in Scotland, and it is a teaching technique used by many Oregon teachers.

Because our sixth-grade curriculum includes Canada, because all the sixth graders in our school are to do a research report on animals, and because I love the Jack London novel *Call of the Wild*, I have put together with my students a "Storyline" centered on the land and people of Northern Canada and the historical period at the end of the nineteenth century when the Klondike Gold Rush brought two cultures into contact, the Sourdough gold miners and the Inuit natives of the region. This "Storyline" is a perfect way for my students to immerse themselves in another culture. Through this activity, they meet new friends and ideas. They learn the ways of other individuals through the stories and characters they develop. With the stories, they can capture political, social, and personal issues of the past and the present and can even project into the future.

CONSTRUCTION

Part of the fun of the "Storyline" is constructing your physical "text"—in this case, a dog sled. We read about and look at pictures of dog sleds. We discuss which dogs are best for pulling sleds (although every year I see at least one poodle hard at work pulling a huge sled). The students are then put into "Dog Sled Groups," and each group constructs one three-dimensional dog sled and dog. Then the students decide on necessary supplies and fill their sleds. Each individual constructs a character, complete with a biography, who will be going north to hunt for gold (see Figure 4–1).

WRITING

Writing plays an important role. Each character keeps a journal, and through the journals you hear your students' stories of the North. The journal is a great assessment tool, an interesting way to discover what students are learning. Because the writing comes out of an invented character's mind, it allows students a great deal of freedom of expression. Even reluctant writers usually have fun telling someone else's stories.

Here are a few journal excerpts of letters written home by various students' characters:

Dear Alder,

I'm in the Yukon now. As you know, I'm with John and I also have another partner. I met her on the train to the trading post. The three of us bought a team of dogs.

Dear Edmond,

Your sweet, wonderful sister isn't so sweet anymore. A few weeks ago, Jacob, John and I struck it rich. The bank teller says we have at least one million dollars worth of gold. But gold isn't all the glory and heaven that it is told to be. In fact, it is full of hate and wickedness. Unfortunately, I have a lot of hate and wickedness hidden in my heart, just like everyone else. That is what caused me to do what I did.

Dear Mark,

    I'm sure all of the family is wondering where I am. The truth is I don't really know where I am, just somewhere in the Yukon. You're probably mad at me for not telling you where I was going, but I had to be safe and keep all doors closed to Mother finding out. She would tell me hunting for gold is not a ladylike thing to do and that I should learn more fancy stitches and how to manage my maids better.

Working on vocabulary from the North, here are examples of Yukon ABC poems:

ARE YOU LIKE BUCK?

Alex

Are you like
Buck? He's one
Courageous
Dog. He pulls the sled until the bitter
End. He pushes on,
Fighting through the snow,
Gasping for breath, past
High mountains covered with
Ice,
Jumping, running, pulling through. He
Killed Spitz to gain
Leadership of the pack. Traded from
Master to master,
Never slowing down, must press
On.
People shouting,
Quarreling over gold,
Ready to kill for it,
Slowly
Transforming Buck into a savage
Untamed beast,
Visions of ancestors dancing in the fire.
What will become of Buck? A
Xylophone-like sound chimes out, awakening Buck—
Yearning to see the figures again,
Zig-zagging through time, hearing the call of the wild.

THE YUKON

Karen

Almost instantly a
Bushel of people
Came streaming into the Yukon,
Doctors and lawyers and people of all kinds
Everyone hoped for a better future, but
For many it would mean loss.
Gold fever

Had broken out.
It wasn't really a fever,
Just a greed that
Killed many people. The
Loss of these
Many people was tragic, but death did
Not stop the gold rush.
Once beautiful land was turned to towns,
People bursting at every side.
Quick as that, sleds were
Running all over the Yukon,
Sleds that were meant to carry back gold, meant
To help a man make his fortune. People
Used to being pampered were
Venturing out to
Watery graves under breaking ice.
X-ray these people's brains, they have no knowledge of the
Yukon, just the hope to
Zap some yellow dust into their purses.

GOLD

Melissabeth

A giant sled comes
Bounding down the glittering snow. People have good
Cause for
Doing this. It's a gold rush in Canada. People say there's
Enough for everyone in the world to have a handful of
Gold. Gold is also bad. It
Has made many people go
Insane. Causing them not to think
Justly, but causing them to
Kill.
Lust for gold has caused
Many families to leave families that they once were
Nurtured by.
Once I saw a man kill for his gold. Everyone said he was
Possessed. I
Quoted this in my journal and
Ran from the area.
Sometimes people didn't make it to a mine on
Time. Then,
Unfortunately their gold mines
Vanished,
Without a trace of gold left. People became
Xtremely vain,
Yearning for more gold, acting like they belonged in a
Zoo.

These ABC poems captured the times. The students used vocabulary appropriate to the North and researched their verbs and adjectives. Through all this, they created visual, emotional pieces. Reading these, you can tell that they understand!

We also wrote poems using *Northern Lullaby,* by Nancy White Carlstrom, as a starting point. Here are a few of our poems:

> Good night Sister Owl,
> in darkness you fly.
> Under your wing,
> Hold tight to the sky.
> > Gwynedd

> Good night Mother Grouse,
> protecting your youth,
> snug in your nest,
> you lie under the massive
> patch of blackberries.
> > Ryan

> Shine down Mama Moon
> on the newly fallen snow,
> cast light on the shadows
> of the dark night.
> > Gillian

> Good night Sister Owl,
> wrapped in old feathers,
> hunting among darkness and
> shadows for old Deer Mouse
> hidden in the pale, cold snow.
> > Scott

Because I am captured by visuals and am convinced that children of all ages can be successful at art, my students create pictures to go with their pieces, using the medium of watercolor. The softness of the watercolors and the softness of the words make great companions.

STORYTELLING

Iptuk, *my* character in this classroom experience, shares many stories from the past. I also read to the students some of my favorite Inuit folktales. Some excellent examples are *Northern Lullaby,* by Nancy White Carlstrom; *A Promise Is a Promise,* by Robert Munsch; *Ka-ha-si and the Loon,* by Terri Cohlene; and *Song of Sedna,* by Robert D. San Souci. These books share both wonderful stories and beautiful illustrations.

An important historical part of the Inuit culture is the carving of totem poles. They share the poles and the stories that go with them at a potlatch. Why not do it in class, too?

The assignment that I give my students is purposely nonspecific. All I say is that they have to construct a group totem pole and be ready with its story for our potlatch. Their pole might illustrate a folktale or it could be about their dog-sled team's journey. Here is an example of a folktale for a totem pole that one group created:

How the Eagle Got Its Feathers

John Hammer flew across the
ravine. He wondered what he did
wrong to make his sled fall apart.
His dogs cried unmercifully as
they tried to escape from the
binding sled that pulled them over
the deep ravine that seemed to go
on forever. As John hit the other
side, he grabbed onto an icy rock.
He started a silent prayer to the
God of Creation. Suddenly, John
slipped and started into a dive.
Then John and his dogs started
shaking. John slowly transformed
into a bare bald eagle. The dogs
rammed into his naked body,
forming thousands of feathers. He
then flew off in silence. That is
how the eagle got its feathers.

Sarah, Gillian, Sam, and Scott

ART

Art and visual materials are great assessment tools. One way to tell if students are understanding the Gold Rush times is to have them draw scenes. I ask them to include at least five vocabulary words in visual form. Any child at any level can do a beautiful job. Another art project possibility is the diorama. Each group makes a scene from *Call of the Wild*, using a large box. They can't tell anyone what scene they are working on. Students then walk around and write down which scene they feel is illustrated in each box. It's fun to watch them suddenly get it, as they really look at the details.

Because *Call of the Wild* is written so visually, there are many art ideas you can create. How about making a reward poster for Buck? How about illustrating your poems? You get the idea.

READING

Through all this, we are reading *Call of the Wild*. It's a difficult book for many sixth graders because of the vocabulary that is new to them (and was to me, too, the first time that I read it). However, it is a rare child who doesn't eventually get hooked by the novel. The characters come alive, and students have trouble remembering who is a dog and who is human. I read the book aloud. Some scenes I can hardly read because I get all choked up, and you can hear my students clearing their throats. I once stopped in the middle of the moose scene because it was lunch time, and my class got angry. We went late to lunch that day. A substitute teacher once remarked, "It was so quiet while I was reading that you could hear every page being turned." I hear remarks about the book all year, such as, "Remember when Buck . . .?" This is a novel that engages students!

After we read the book, we watch the movie. Many students are not happy with it. They want to know why some of the scenes in the book were excluded. They don't understand why a woman had to be in it. "I liked the book better," is a constant refrain. Many go on to read Jack London's *White Fang*, and we also see that movie later on. I laugh because it never fails to get my students all excited when a dog named Buck appears. You hear the murmer of voices and "Look, there's Buck. I didn't know Buck was going to be in this movie."

We read more than just *Call of the Wild*. We read all about the Sourdoughs and then compare their culture to the Inuits. We read about Northern Canada in our social studies book. We read factual accounts of the times from Michael Cooper's excellent history, *Klondike Fever: The Famous Gold Rush of 1898*. We read all about hunting for gold. The students write down and illustrate the steps in this process. I find articles from the newspaper and magazines. Reading never stops.

RESEARCH

Because research means to search and investigate, it's something we do throughout. The students are always searching for information. They use maps to follow Buck's journey and to figure out climates. They search for information and come up with lists of necessary items to take on their own journeys. They look up information about totem poles and potlatches. We watch movies and videos and learn new facts. The students are continually searching out new information.

EVALUATION

The *Call of the Wild* exercise has many nontraditional ways of assessing students. Evaluation occurs throughout. Some of my assessments are through letter writing. For example, each student's character writes a three-page letter home telling about meeting Iptuk. Because I want to know how much information the students retained about the Inuit culture, the majority of the letter needs to be content based.

Here are excerpts of letters written home:

> *Dear Susie,*
>
> Well, my partners and I are in the Yukon, in an Eskimo village. The Eskimos like to be called *The People*. They have warm clothes made out of seal and walrus fur. The boots they wear are made out of a thick material and sometimes when it's cold they wear two or three pairs at a time.
>
> *The People* stay very warm when they sleep because they sleep in igloos. They make their igloos from the inside out and make them out of ice and snow. They cut the snow from the ground with an ivory knife, made out of walrus tusks.
>
> Now that we are in the village, *The People* have made us a cozy igloo with a wonderful window.
>
> *The People* have legends that they tell late at night. There are many of them, but my favorite one is about how there was a sun. . . .
>
> I love you and miss you a lot. Kick my brother for me.
>
> *Love, Alex*

> *Dear Sam,*
>
> How are you? I'm fine. You wouldn't believe all the amazing sights there are to see around here. I am staying with a family who belong to the Nanook tribe. They are Eskimos, but prefer to be called *The People*. The father of the family that I am staying with is named Iptuk. He is the most talented craftsman I have ever met or heard of. Iptuk can make a knife out of a walrus tusk which will be useful for almost every task of his day. Sam, you wouldn't believe what I saw today. . . . *The People* have wonderful stories to tell about themselves and their environment. My favorite tale is about how the animals came to be. . . .
>
> We sleep in igloos. Sam, you would love it. Ours is about six feet high and eight feet long; of course it's round. Iptuk and his family built this igloo from the inside out. . . .
>
> *The People* have no written laws, but they do have consequences. . . .
>
> I really love it here, but I miss you and Mom and Dad. I'll see you in a few months.
>
> *Hugs and kisses, Sarah*

The students do a character analysis on each character, including the dogs, in the novel. They write down descriptive words or phrases and have to back up these characterizations with sentences from the novel. If a student writes that John Thornton loved dogs, an example of a sentence from the book that would back it up might be, "'If you strike that dog again, I'll kill you,' he at last managed to say in a choking voice."

Their artwork tells you what students understand. Remembering scenes from the diorama tells you if they are remembering the novel. I listen to group and class responses. What kinds of questions and answers do they have? Do they complete their assignments? I look at their maps of Canada. I sometimes use worksheets from the textbook. I always do self and group assessment. I also do a final exam, using mostly short answers.

The ways to evaluate are endless.

Doing the *Call of the Wild* exercise is a big commitment of not only time, but space. Student work goes all over the walls. No matter where you look in my classroom during this time, you will see something from the North. It takes about two months, and it's a priority over anything else we might need to do. All sixth graders in our school do a research report on an animal. During one year, our class was scheduled into the media center right in the middle of the *Call of the Wild* exercise. There was nothing I could do about the timing. That was one year in which we as a class struggled with both. I honestly think neither project was very successful. Timing is very important!

During the course of a school year, I do two "Storyline" projects. The main reason that I use this method is that it motivates and educates my students. If you, the teacher, set the stage by your own enthusiasm, if you are well organized and prepared, if you can be flexible to fit your own class needs, you can do a "Storyline" that will have your class in the palm of your hand. The students will have a blast! Over the years, I've heard comments like, "When are we going to do social studies?" If we skip a day and do something different, students want to know when they get to go into their "Dog Sled Groups" again.

The students enjoy the *Call of the Wild* exercise, and so do I. Because I also play roles, I'm right in the center of it all. I get to be Iptuk and come in costume and play his role. I get to tell stories, invite the students into my igloo, see them having fun, see them coming together as a group, watch their successes, be a resource if they get stuck, and learn new things from them. I am having fun, too!

BIBLIOGRAPHY

Carlstrom, Nancy White. 1992. *Northern Lullaby.* New York: Philomel Books.
Cohlene, Terri. 1990. *Ka-ha-si and the Loon.* Mahwah, NJ: Watermille Press.

Cooper, Michael. 1989. *Klondike Fever: The Famous Gold Rush of 1898*. New York: Clarion Books.

DePoncins, Gontran. 1941. *Kabloona*. Alexandria, VA: Time-Life Books.

London, Jack. 1903. *Call of the Wild*. New York: Washington Square Press.

Munsch, Robert. 1988. *A Promise Is a Promise*. Canada: Firefly Books.

Newman, Shirlee. 1993. *The Inuits*. New York: Franklin Watts.

Ray, Delia. 1989. *Gold! The Klondike Adventure*. New York: Lodestar Books.

San Souci, Robert D. 1981. *Song of Sedna*. New York: Doubleday.

Tolboom, Wanda. 1956. *People of the Snow*. New York: Coward-McCann.

Chapter 5
Show, Don't Tell:
Role Plays and
Social Imagination

BILL BIGELOW

My lecture had put kids to sleep. As I looked out over the classroom, students' faces had that droopy, how-many-minutes-'til-the-bell-rings look. "But how can this be boring?" I silently protested. "We're talking about the Vietnam War." As students filed out of the classroom, I shook my head and pledged to find a way to ignite their interest. I was just a first-year teacher, but I knew there had to be a better approach.

Over the years, I've concluded that lectures have their place—but only when directly linked to activities that draw students into the intimacy of social dynamics. For me, the teaching strategy that most consistently enlightens and brings students to life is the role play. There are all kinds of role plays, but the best of these raise critical questions that require student initiative and creativity. At times students may roam the classroom, building alliances with other groups in a strike or debating whether the U.S. government should recognize the independence of a united Vietnam at the end of World War II or discussing whether logging should be allowed in old-growth forests. A good role play invites students to enter the personas of contemporary or historical social groups to learn about issues in their characters' lives from the inside out.

I start with a controversial contemporary or historical problem: Should the United States Constitution abolish slavery and the slave trade? Should the federal government build the Dalles Dam on the Columbia River? What is the ethical response to the war with Mexico in 1846? Should there be a Palestinian state? Should nuclear weapons be banned? Who is to blame for the 1968 massacre at My Lai?

And role plays aren't only for social studies classes. In a music class, students could debate whether rock'n'roll and rap should be regulated by the government. In an English class, students might represent different community groups debating whether Standard English should be spoken at all times in school. In a science class, students might examine the ecological complexities of logging old-growth forests by role playing the interests of timber companies, loggers, and environmental activists, as well as the salmon, owls, rivers, and trees themselves. Each group could propose answers to the question: Should logging be restricted?

Now, before I proceed, a disclaimer: I teach high school, not middle school. However, I have engaged middle school students, and also fifth graders, in role plays with good success. My friend, Karen Miller, who teaches at Kellogg Middle School in Portland, has adapted a number of my role plays for her eighth graders and designs others of her own. (See her article, "Tapping into Feelings of Fairness," in Christensen et al., *Rethinking Our Classrooms: Teaching for Equity and Justice,* 1994.) I steal her ideas to use with my high school juniors. They may have somewhat different reading levels, but students at middle and high school levels share a fondness for *doing* instead of hearing about and a hunger for talking about big ideas. I trust that the examples I include here will be of use to middle school teachers.

DEVELOPING A ROLE PLAY

Stage one is conceiving substantive questions like those described above. Stage two entails selecting groups that will give voice to a range of perspectives on a particular issue. For example, a role play on land reform in Central America divides students into five groups: tenant farmers, the managers of an instant-coffee factory owned by a U.S. company, landless peasants, urban unemployed workers, and coffee planters. In the role play, each group has a somewhat different perspective on whether there should be land reform, how much land should be involved, and who should receive it. As in real life, strategic alliances between certain groups are possible; and in the course of the role play, students usually discover these alliances and work together. The vitality of a role play depends on insuring that actual social conflicts come to life in the classroom.

In a mock U.S. Constitutional Convention, I include roles for groups that weren't represented at the real convention. So instead of only lawyers, financiers, and plantation owners in attendance, I also invite poor farmers, workers, and enslaved African Americans. Students debate questions from each group's standpoint: whether to abolish slavery and/or the slave trade, whether to allow debt relief to farmers by permitting payment "in kind," and how political leaders should be chosen. This more-representative assembly allows students to experience some of the underlying conflicts that were suppressed in the actual Constitutional Convention.

But a role play wouldn't work, or at least wouldn't work as well, if I simply said to students, "You play a poor farmer; you play a plantation owner." They'd have nothing to go on beyond their own preconceptions, often stereotypical, of farmers and plantation owners. So I have to do some research in order to provide students with information on the circumstances in different social groups' lives—circumstances that would contribute to shaping these groups' attitudes on a given issue (for examples, see the roles provided below). Students can do some of this work, of course, but my experience is that they need a base to work from. This is especially true because many of the groups that I want to include in a role play are missing from traditional history books. For instance, it's not that easy to find information in a high school library on the problems of farmers after the American Revolution or about the Unemployed Councils of the 1930s (Bigelow and Diamond, 1988, pp. 74–77). That said, involving students in researching different groups can sometimes create greater empathy for their characters and, hence, can make them more engaged in the role play.

ROLE PLAYS AND LEARNING

Amidst the deal making, arguing, and oratory of the role play, students absorb a tremendous amount of information. But they absorb it in a way that reveals underlying social conflict and solidarity and thus can make sense of that information. In large measure, the process itself is the product. To be effective, the results of a role play need not repeat history. Indeed, some of our best debriefing sessions concentrate on discussing why students didn't make the same choices as the actual social groups they portrayed. Role plays allow students to see that history is not inevitable and that events might have turned out very differently if people understood their interests more clearly or had overcome prejudices that kept them from making alliances. I want students to see themselves as social actors, to realize that what they do in the world matters—they are not simply objects to be thrown about by some remote process called History. When they succeed, role plays can help chip away at students' sense of predetermination, their sense of powerlessness.

In the Cherokee/Seminole Removal role play below, I include roles for plantation owners and farmers, missionaries and Northern reformers,

Black Seminoles, the Andrew Jackson administration, and the Cherokee. In this, as in other role plays, the intent is never to suggest that all points of view are equally valid. Andrew Jackson and land-hungry Southern plantation owners and farmers can't propose stripping the Cherokee and other Southeastern Indian nations of their territory without resorting to racist arguments. The role play allows students to see that. It's essential that key interests in a particular issue be represented, not necessarily so students can hear "all points of view," but so they can dissect the relationship between people's social conditions and their ideas—and recognize, for example, contexts that breed racism.

A caution: A role play aims at nurturing students' appreciation of why people in history and the world today think and behave as they do. But I never want students to sympathize with individuals who behaved in hurtful or exploitative ways—that is, I never want students to have emotional identification or agreement with these people. In my experience, students are able to make the distinction. This is especially so when, in follow-up discussion, we critique positions espoused by various groups in a role play. It is possible to *understand*, but not *agree with*.

Indeed, role plays offer students a way of thinking about some of the sharp divisions that have characterized and continue to characterize life in the United States—and, for that matter, in societies the world over. An important new study of major U.S. history textbooks (Loewen, 1995) has shown that these texts fail to alert students to social-class—and even, surprisingly, racial—divisions in the United States. Almost uniformly, these texts portray government officials and the powerful as the "good guys"—then and now. It is elitist history that masqerades as *our* history. In his book *A People's History of the United States*, Howard Zinn (1980) critiques this traditional flag-waving approach that our students absorb: "Nations are not communities and never have been. The history of any country, presented as the history of a family, conceals fierce conflicts of interest (sometimes exploding, most often repressed) between conquerors and conquered, masters and slaves, capitalists and workers, dominators and dominated in race and sex. And in such a world of conflict, a world of victims and executioners, it is the job of thinking people, as Albert Camus suggested, not to be on the side of the executioners" (pp. 9–10). Role plays should bring that world of conflict to life in the classroom and allow students to explore the underlying premises of arguments and to decide: What do *I* think is right?

ROLE PLAYS: SOME GUIDELINES

1. Introduce the role play and give students a sense of why the class is participating and what the general guidelines will be. Break students

into groups, roughly equal in size. It's vital that the question(s) that each group will address are clear and understood by all.

2. Allow students to connect with the roles they've been assigned. You might encourage students to read their roles aloud in their small groups. I usually ask students to answer questions in writing based on their role: "How do you make your living? Why do you put up with such rotten working conditions?" Or I might ask them to write interior monologues—their inner thoughts—about hopes and fears. Students can read these to each other in the small groups. Have each group make a placard so they can see who's who. You might interview students in front of the class or even bait them in devil's-advocate fashion: "How do you really feel about that poor farmer in that group over there?" As mentioned earlier, be sure that students' roles are not too prescriptive. I've seen many role plays in which students are told exactly who they are and what they think. What's left for the kids? Likewise, some role plays don't give students enough information to participate thoughtfully: "You are a Mexican farmer." That's not much to go on. Moreover, try not to mix up roles by making some roles economic and some moral, for example, steelworkers and liberals: Steelworkers may be liberals.

3. It's the students' show, but the teacher's participation is vital. I circulate in the classroom, making sure that students understand their roles. I help them think of groups they might want to ally with. I also instigate turmoil: "Do you know what those middle-class people are saying about you immigrants?" It makes for more lively exchanges.

4. Each role should include at least some information that other groups don't have. This requires that students teach and persuade one another. So they need an opportunity to meet. After they have read and considered their roles and positions on issues, I tell students to choose half of their group to be "traveling negotiators." The travelers may only meet and "wheel and deal" with nontravelers, to insure that the whole class is involved at any given time.

5. It's important that students have an opportunity to present their points of view and hear from other groups. I often structure these gatherings as "community meetings," assembled to discuss the burning issue under consideration. As with the small-group negotiation sessions, I encourage students to use the information in their roles in their presentations to teach others. I usually play a role myself, sometimes as a partisan. For example, in a role play on whether an imaginary "Mother Country" will grant independence to its Asian colony, "Laguna," I play the colonial governor and chair the assembly. I know that some teachers will disagree, but in my experience, it hasn't

been a great idea to have students actually run the meetings, since discussion is often heated and students will jump on each other for seeming to play favorites in whom they call on. However, at times I'll conduct a meeting with a simplified version of Roberts' Rules of Order, which offers students a good deal of say-so in the pacing of discussion. In some role plays, a major aim is to give students practice in making decisions without the presence of an authority figure. For example, a role play on the 1912 textile strike in Lawrence, Massachusetts, asks students in a large-group format to confront strategic and tactical issues on their own: "With thousands of workers out on strike, how will we make decisions? Should our commissaries feed nonstriking workers?" In this role play, students simulate the euphoria and frustration that accompanies grassroots democracy (Bigelow and Diamond, 1988, pp. 57–64).

6. It's essential to debrief. No activity stands on its own. Before we discuss, I usually encourage people to step out of their roles by asking them to write for a few minutes. I might ask them to speculate on what actually happened in history. Sometimes I'll urge them to critique their own positions to give them permission to distance themselves from the points of view that they espoused in the role play debates.

THE CHEROKEE/SEMINOLE REMOVAL ROLE PLAY

In her book *A Century of Dishonor,* published in 1881, Helen Hunt Jackson wrote, "There will come a time in the remote future when, to the student of American history [the Cherokee removal] will seem well-nigh incredible." (Filler and Guttmann, 1962, p. 98). I wrote my first version of this role play on the Cherokee and Seminole removal exactly one hundred years after Jackson's words were published. And she was right: Students had a hard time believing that the Cherokees could have been uprooted and marched at bayonet point almost a thousand miles from Georgia to Oklahoma during what came to be called the "Trail of Tears." The government passed a law just kicking them out of their homes forever? Incredible. Perhaps 1981 was a slightly less cynical time than the one we live in today, but most of my students thought that the Indians' removal couldn't be typical of the U.S. government's conduct throughout history. Horrible, yes. Typical, no.

The students' response underscores one of the challenges of teaching American history. Knowledge of past injustice can at times make students complacent about today's society and can blind them to today's injustices: "I sure am glad I wasn't around back then." Our curricula should not encourage a self-righteousness about contemporary society. How can we ensure that this complacency doesn't happen? One way is by inviting students to look for *patterns* throughout history—patterns that continue into our own time. My own reading of history leads me to conclude that far from being the exception, the "Trail of Tears" exemplifies fundamental aspects of the nature of U.S. expansion and foreign policy more broadly, not only in the early nineteenth century but also throughout U.S. history: economic interests paramount, race as a key factor, legality flaunted, the use of violence to enforce U.S. will, a language of justification thick with democratic and humanitarian platitudes. The U.S. war with Mexico, the Spanish-American War, Vietnam, support of the Contras in Nicaragua, and the Gulf War come readily to mind. These are my conclusions; they needn't be my students'. Our task as teachers is not to tell students what to think but to encourage them to search for the links between past and present.

In previous years of teaching this role play I did not include a "Missionaries and Northern Reformers" role. The omission of a sympathetic White role left students with the misleading impression that all White people in the country were united in the quest to forcibly move Indian tribes and nations off their lands. In fact, White people as diverse as the abolitionist William Lloyd Garrison and the Tennessee frontiersman-turned-congressman Davy Crockett opposed the Indian removal bill. The vote in the U.S. House of Representatives in favor of removal was 102 to 97—an underwhelming majority. Nonetheless, it's important that students recognize the racial and cultural biases of even those who considered themselves the Indians' friends and allies. As indicated in their role, missionaries described Cherokee families as "having risen to a level with the White people of the United States." Thus, as we seek to inform students of important currents of social reform in U.S. history, we need to do so with a critical eye.

Materials Needed   Construction or other stiff paper for placards; crayons or markers.

Suggested Procedure

1. First, a suggestion to you on how to read these lesson procedures. Rather than reading all these in one-two-three order, it may be more clear if you review the student readings in the order in which they are mentioned in these instructions. This will help you to imagine the role play more easily and to encounter it as students might.

Read with students "Cherokee/Seminole Removal Role Play: Problems to Consider" [see page 82.] Show them on a map how far it is from Georgia and Florida to Oklahoma. Tell them that each of them will be in a group representing one of five roles: Cherokees, the Andrew Jackson Administration, Plantation Owners and Farmers, Missionaries and Northern Reformers, and Black Seminoles. All of them are invited to a hearing to discuss the Indian Removal Bill before Congress. They should consider the resolution, and in their presentations, they should be sure to respond to the following: whether they support the bill, what questions they have of other groups, and how they will react if the bill passes or fails. This last hypothetical situation encourages students to see that people will not necessarily passively accept a decision by Congress.

(*Note:* The teacher plays the congressman—they were all men back then, but the teacher needn't be a man to play this role!—who runs the hearing, but an option is to select a few students to join you or to run the meeting on their own. This choice has the advantage of giving students a group of peers as an audience for their presentations. The disadvantage is that those who will run the hearing have little to do during the session of negotiation between groups, and, as mentioned above, they sometimes become targets for other students' ire if they manifest the slightest inconsistency in calling on people to speak.)

2. Have students count off into five groups. Students from each respective group should cluster together in small circles throughout the classroom. They should begin by reading their assigned role. As in other role plays, you can urge students into their characters by asking them to write interior monologues about their concerns in 1830. They might invent a more detailed persona—give themselves a name, a place of birth, family, friends, and so forth. This is especially valuable for students in those groups (plantation owner/farmers, missionaries and Northern reformers) that include people in somewhat different circumstances. Students in each group might read these to one another. You can interview a few individuals from different groups so that others in the class can hear.

3. Distribute placards and markers to students and ask them to write their group name and display it so that everyone can see who they represent.

4. In each group, students should discuss their ideas on the questions that they will be addressing at the congressional hearing. Remind them that an important question to consider is what they will do if Congress decides against them. Will they resist? If so, how? If not, what might happen to them? When it seems that students have come to some tentative conclusions, ask them to choose half their group to be traveling negotiators. These people will meet with people in the other groups to share ideas, argue, and build alliances. Remind students that each of their roles includes different information and that this is an opportunity to teach each other. (Remind them that travelers may not meet with other travelers, but only with seated members of other groups. Travelers may travel together or separately.)

5. Begin the teaching/negotiating/alliance-building session. These discussions should last until students seem to be repeating themselves—perhaps fifteen or twenty minutes, depending on the class. During this period, I circulate to different groups and occasionally butt in to raise questions or point out contradictions. Don't skip this step: It's the time during which students are perhaps most engaged in their roles and with one another.

6. Students should return to their groups to prepare the presentations they'll make at the congressional hearing. My experience is that if they write these out, they think more clearly and raise more provocative points. Encourage them to use the information in their role sheet, not merely to copy it.

7. The class should form a large circle, students sitting with their respective groups. I structure the hearing by allowing one group to make its complete presentation. Then either I or the students who are running the hearing raise a few questions. After this, members of other groups may question or rebut points made by the presenting group. This process continues until all groups have been heard from. The more cross-group dialogue, the more interesting and exciting the meeting.

8. As a follow-up writing assignment, you might ask students to stay in their roles and comment on the congressional hearing—whose remarks most angered or troubled them? At what points did they feel most satisfied with the deliberations? Or you could ask them to speculate on what happened in real life and why. Some discussion or writing questions include:

- What do you think actually happened to the Cherokees and the Seminoles?
- Might there have been tensions between the Cherokees and Seminoles? Why?
- Which group might have been in a better position to resist removal? Why?
- What reasons did some groups offer for moving the Cherokees and Seminoles? What were their real motives?
- Why were the Seminoles such a threat to the Southern plantation owners? Do you remember some of the laws that were passed to keep Indians and Blacks divided in early America?
- In real life, a slim majority of U.S. representatives and senators voted to remove the Cherokees and Seminoles. What arguments might they have found most persuasive?
- Do you think that all those congressmen who voted against Cherokee/Seminole removal did so because they cared about the Indians? Can you think of other reasons that congressmen from Northern states wouldn't want the Southern states to expand into Indian territory?
- Do you think the missionaries would have been as sympathetic toward the Seminoles as they were toward the Cherokees? Why or why not?
- Do you seen any similarities in the situations faced by the Cherokees and Seminoles and situations faced by any other groups in U.S. history? in our society today? in other parts of the world?

9. After discussion, assign students to do some research to see what actually happened to the Cherokees and Seminoles.

Cherokee/Seminole Removal Role Play: Problems To Consider   The year is 1830. There is a bill before the U.S. Congress that would provide funds ($500,000) to move all Indians now living east of the Mississippi River to "Indian Territory" (Oklahoma) west of the Mississippi River. The Indians would be given permanent title to this land. The money would pay the Indians for any improvements made on the land in the East where they are now living. It would also cover the expenses of their transportation and living expenses for a year in "Indian Territory."

The U. S. Congress has decided to hold hearings on this bill, and you are invited to give testimony and to question other individuals who will give testimony. Remember, the main question for discussion is:

> Should all Indians living east of the Mississippi River be moved, by force if necessary, west of the Mississippi River to Indian Territory?

Questions for each group to consider in planning your presentation are:

1. Do you support the Indian Removal Bill? Why or why not?
2. What questions do you have for members of the other groups who will be in attendance?
3. What will you do if Congress passes this bill? What will you do if Congress does not pass this bill?

CHEROKEES

Your people have lived for centuries in the area that the Whites call "Georgia." This is your land. At times you've had to fight to keep it.

You've had a hard time with Whites. Ever since they began settling in Georgia, they have continued to push westward, plowing the land, growing their cotton and other crops. Long ago, as early as 1785, the Cherokee nation secured the right to their land by a treaty with the U.S. government. The United States recognized the Cherokee people as part of an independent country, not subject to the laws of the United States. After the U.S. Constitution was approved, the U.S. government signed another treaty with the Cherokee nation—in 1791, when George Washington was president. Article Seven of the Hopewell treaty said, "The United States solemnly guaranty to the Cherokee nation all their lands not hereby ceded."

In other words, the government agreed not to push the Cherokee out of the land where they were living.

But now the U.S. government is about to break its own treaty and steal your land. Many Whites have already bribed and tricked lots of your people out of their land. The Whites say they need the land to grow their cotton and other crops, and miners have been trespassing in the foothills looking for, and finding, gold. These Whites say you have no right to the land, that you're savages. Last year, in December 1829, the state of Georgia passed a law saying that you are under *their* control and must obey their laws, their wishes. This new law forbids anyone with any Cherokee blood from testifying in court or protesting the plans to move you out of your land. But you didn't vote for this Georgia government, and besides, you have a treaty with the federal government that says you are citizens of an independent country. When the U.S. government made a treaty with you, that proved you *are* a nation.

The Cherokees are one of the five "civilized tribes." Much of this "civilization" was taught to you by the Whites. You have well-cultivated farms. By 1826, members of your Cherokee nation owned 22,000 cattle, 7,600 horses, 3,000 plows, 2,500 spinning wheels, 10 saw mills, and 18 schools. And like Southern Whites, some of you also owned Black slaves. In 1821, Sequoya, a brilliant Cherokee, invented an eighty-five character alphabet, and now most of the Cherokees can read and write. It's said that more Cherokees are literate than are Whites in Georgia. You even have a regular newspaper, the Cherokee *Phoenix*. You've adopted a written Constitution for your nation very similar to that of the United States. Many of your leaders have attended White schools in the East. Even by the White man's standards you're as "civilized" as they are, if not more so. But still they want to kick you off your land and move you to a place west of the Mississippi River—a place you've never even seen. You must continue to argue your case if you are to survive as a people.

ANDREW JACKSON ADMINISTRATION

You're the president of the United States. You must deal with a serious problem in the state of Georgia. This past December 1829, the state government said that all land belonging to the Cherokee nation would from then on belong to Georgia. The Cherokee would have no title to their land, and anyone with Cherokee blood wouldn't even have the right to testify in court. The Georgians want the Cherokee moved, by force if necessary, west of the Mississippi River. They support the Indian Removal Act, now before Congress. There is a place called "Oklahoma" set aside for all the Indians in the East, including the Cherokee. Personally, you agree that Georgia has a

BILL BIGELOW

right to make whatever laws they want, but the Cherokee do have treaties signed by the U.S. government that guarantee them their land forever. Of course, you personally never signed any of those treaties.

You're getting a lot of pressure on this one. On the one hand, there are White missionaries and lots of northerners who say that Georgia is violating the rights of the Cherokees. The supporters of the Cherokees point out that the Indians have done everything they can to become like civilized White people: They invented an alphabet, started a newspaper, wrote a constitution, started farms, and even wear White people's clothes. Many church groups supported your election in 1828. On the other hand, there are a lot of farmers and plantation owners who would like to get on that good Cherokee land. Recently, gold was discovered on Cherokee territory, and gold seekers are already starting to sneak onto their land. Your main support was in the South, especially from poor and medium-sized farmers.

From your standpoint, you have to look after the welfare of the whole country. The main crop in the South is cotton—it is a crucial crop to the prosperity of the slave-owning South and to the new cloth factories of the North. Cotton, grown with slave labor, brings in tremendous profits to slave owners and—you're a slave owner yourself, so you understand their concerns. There is excellent land taken up by the Cherokees, as well as by some of the other Indian tribes in the region—the Creek, Choctaw, Chickasaw, and Seminole—though some of these have already moved west. This land could be used to grow cotton for the world. The exports of cotton to England and other countries are vital to the health of the economy. Cotton sent North is building up young industries, and you can see that there is great potential for manufacturing in the North.

The Seminoles, who live in Florida, represent a special problem. For years, they have taken in escaped slaves from Southern plantations. Sometimes, they've even raided plantations to free slaves. They are a threat to the whole plantation system in the South. A number of years ago, you ordered an attack on the Seminoles in Florida and had their farms burned. The proposed removal act would get rid of the Seminoles forever by moving them to "Indian Territory." The escaped slaves living with them would then be taken away from them and sold.

PLANTATION OWNERS AND FARMERS

All I ask in this creation
Is a pretty little wife and a big plantation
Way up yonder in the Cherokee Nation.

That's part of a song people like you sing as you wait for the Cherokee people to be kicked out of Georgia. Then you and your family can move in.

Some of you are poor farmers. You live on the worst land in Georgia and other parts of the South. The big plantation owners with all their cotton and slaves take up the best land and leave you the scraps. You've heard that the Cherokee land in Georgia is some of the most fertile land in the country. Best yet, the government of Georgia is having a lottery so that even poor farmers like you will have an equal shot at getting good land. One of the reasons you voted for Andrew Jackson for president is because you knew he was an Indian fighter who beat the Creeks in a war and then took their land away from them. That's your kind of president. The Cherokees are farmers too. They grow corn, wheat, and cotton. If you're lucky, you'll be able to move onto land with the crops already planted and the farmhouse already built. Others of you aren't quite as poor; you have some land, and grow corn and raise hogs—but you, too, would like to move onto better land.

Some of you are plantation owners, who grow cotton on your land and own many slaves. You live in Georgia near the coast. The problem you have is that cotton exhausts the soil, so that after a number of years, your land is not as productive as it once was. You need new land with soil that hasn't been used to grow cotton for years and years. As of now, the Cherokees are living on the land that rightfully belongs to the state of Georgia. The Georgia legislature recently voted to take over that land and divide it up so that Whites like yourself could move onto it. That's a great law, but some people in Congress and around the country want to stop you from taking this territory from the Cherokees. What's the problem? There is a place set aside for the Cherokees and other Indians west of the Mississippi River. They belong with their own kind, right? Remember, the whole country—no, the whole world—depends on cotton. Your plantation and plantations like yours are what keep this country strong and productive.

But you have another major problem. In Florida, many escaped slaves live side by side with the Seminoles. Slaves throughout the South know about this haven for runaways. In fact, sometimes the Seminoles and escaped slaves raid plantations, burn them down, and free the slaves. You won't stand for this. The Seminole communities must be destroyed and the Seminoles shipped off to "Indian Territory" along with the Cherokees. As for the escaped slaves who live with the Seminoles, they need to be recaptured and either returned to their rightful owners or put up for sale. There's also some good land in Florida that you might want to move onto once the Seminoles are gone.

MISSIONARIES AND NORTHERN REFORMERS

Some of you are White Christian missionaries who either live amongst the Cherokee people or once did. You are not plantation owners, gold prospectors, bankers, or military people. You are simply individuals who want to preach the word of God and do what's right. At great sacrifice, you moved away from the comfort of civilization to go live in much more difficult conditions.

You believe that the Cherokee people have made great progress in advancing toward civilization. According to a resolution that your missionary group recently passed, some Cherokee families have "risen to a level with the White people of the United States." Most Cherokees now wear clothes like White people and have given up their original Indian dress. Women wear decent gowns, that cover their bodies from neck to feet. Formerly, the women had to do the hard work of tending the corn by using hoes. Now, the men do the farming with plows. They are a much more industrious people and own more property and better houses than in the past. Slowly, some of them are becoming Christians and—thankfully—are forgetting their old superstitions. As your resolution points out, "Ancient traditions are fading from memory, and can scarcely be collected." The Cherokees were in a "purely savage state" when the Whites came upon them. But this is no longer the case. Many Indians and Whites are beginning to mix. Surely this is a good thing since it brings in closer contact with civilization.

You don't know of a single Cherokee who wants to leave home and go westward across the Mississippi River. As your resolution states, there is "an overwhelming torrent of national feeling in opposition to removal." And you ought to know: You live with these people. You are reluctant to take sides in political arguments, but you do have to bear witness to what you see and hear.

Those of you who live in the North have read the writings of the missionaries who live amongst the Cherokees. They don't want to steal the Cherokees' land, so they have no reason to lie. Senator Theodore Frelinghuysen from New Jersey has spoken eloquently about the Cherokee situation in Congress. He calls the Cherokees, "the first lords of the soil." The senator puts himself in the Cherokees' position and asks, "If I use my land for hunting, may another take it because he needs it for agriculture?"

It's true that the richest Cherokees—about ten percent or so—own some Black slaves. Some of you are abolitionists, who want all slavery to end and don't approve of this. However, almost everyone who ever traveled in Cherokee territory agrees that the Cherokees do not treat their slaves as harshly as the Whites treat theirs. Most slaves in Cherokee country have some rights, and individuals in families are almost never sold away from each other. But slavery is slavery, and some of you don't approve of *any* slavery.

BLACK SEMINOLES

You are Black and you are Indian, a member of the Seminole people in Florida. You are descended from enslaved Africans who ran away from British plantations in Georgia over a hundred years ago and came to settle with Indians who left their lands farther north. This was before the United States was even a country. You are a free person. Some of the Black people who live in Seminole communities ran away from slavery in the last few years. Others were bought from White slave owners by Seminoles. These people are still called slaves, but are not treated as slaves. They can marry anyone, can't be sold away from their families, can travel where they want, have their own land, carry guns, and so forth. But every year they must pay part of their crops to other Seminoles as a kind of tax.

The Indian Removal Act of 1830 is now being considered by the U.S. Congress. It calls for all Indians east of the Mississippi River to be forced off their lands and moved to a place called "Indian Territory" west of the Mississippi River. Full-blooded Seminoles would be moved. But you, a *Black* Seminole, would become a slave and would be sold in one of the Southern slave markets. You would be forever separated from your community, your friends, your family. You will never allow this to happen.

The White plantation owners in Georgia and throughout the South are very threatened by the thought that the Indians, free African Americans, and escaped slaves live peacefully side by side. They know that *their* slaves hear about these Seminole communities and want to run away to join them. The Seminole communities are a kind of symbol of freedom to enslaved Black people throughout the South. In the past, your people have attacked plantations, freed the slaves on those plantations, and brought the slaves to Florida to live with you and become Seminoles. Whites also want to steal your land so that they can grow their cotton with slave labor.

President Andrew Jackson is one of the biggest slaveholders in Tennessee. Some years ago, when he was a general in the army, he ordered his troops to attack your people and destroy your farms and homes. You know that in this debate about Indian removal he is not on your side.

He also wants to move the other Indian nations in the Southeast, especially the Cherokees. You don't have much to do with the Cherokees. You know that they own large numbers of Black slaves, though they say they treat them better than do the White plantation owners. But if this law passes, the government will try to move them, too.

The U.S. government and the White plantation owners call the Seminoles "savages." But you have farms and raise horses, cattle, hogs, and chickens. And, unlike White plantation owners, you know what freedom means. What is "civilized"? What is "savage"?

FINAL THOUGHTS

Not all students appreciate role plays. I remember Missy, a painfully shy girl who took my Global Studies and U.S. History courses in back-to-back years. At the end of year two, in big block letters, she wrote on her final class evaluation: "DEATH TO ROLE PLAYS." I guess that was better than writing: "DEATH TO MR. BIGELOW." But it was less than the ringing endorsement I would have preferred. No teaching strategy will succeed with all students at all times, and I need to remind myself of that. But I'd be willing to bet that for every Missy there are ten Kamillahs or Jeremys whose minds and voices fire to life in each role play. And even Missy would admit that although she didn't like to speak before the entire class—OK, she *hated* to speak before the entire class—she nonetheless learned lots from participating in small-group discussions, watching the role play dynamics develop, and post-activity writing and discussion.

Role plays are a "show, don't tell" strategy. They democratize learning as social conflicts unfold in the classroom and students can join in at their own levels of ability and knowledge. As in the "Cherokee/Seminole Removal" role play included here as an example, everyone is challenged and no one is held back. And role plays invite empathy. Along with other first-person teaching strategies, role plays remind students that we're studying real human beings and the choices they've made—and might have made differently. Simply put, role plays help put the *social* back into social studies.

WORKS CITED AND ROLE PLAY
BACKGROUND REFERENCES

Bigelow, Bill, and Norm Diamond. 1988. *The Power in Our Hands: A Curriculum on the History of Work and Workers in the United States.* New York: Monthly Review Press.

Ehle, John. 1988. *Trail of Tears: The Rise and Fall of the Cherokee Nation.* New York: Doubleday.

Filler, Louis, and Allen Guttmann, eds. 1962. *The Removal of the Cherokee Nation: Manifest Destiny or National Dishonor?* Lexington, MA: Heath.

Katz, William Loren. 1986. *Black Indians: A Hidden Heritage.* New York: Atheneum. See especially Chapters 4, 5, and 6.

Loewen, James. 1995. *Lies My Teacher Told Me: Everything Your U.S. History Textbook Got Wrong.* New York: New Press.

Meltzer, Milton. 1972. *Hunted Like a Wolf: The Story of the Seminole War.* New York: Farrar, Straus & Giroux.

Miller, Karen. 1994. "Tapping into Feelings of Fairness." *Rethinking Our Classrooms: Teaching for Equity and Justice,* ed. Linda Christensen, Bill Bigelow, Stan Karp, Barbara Miner, and Bob Peterson. Milwaukee, WI: Rethinking Schools.

Wright, Ronald. 1992. *Stolen Continents: The "New World" Through Indian Eyes Since 1492.* New York: Viking.

Zinn, Howard. 1980. *A People's History of the United States.* New York: Harper-Collins. See especially Chapter 7.

Chapter 6
Teaching Citizenship Through Mock Trials: Blending Social Studies and Language Arts

THERESA R. MURRAY

Your honor, my name is Eric Linne, the Prosecutor representing the People of Oregon in this action. Martin Mann is currently a student at Westdale High School with a 3.11 G.P.A. He plays football and is also on the spring track team. He gets along with everybody and has no police or school record.

We will prove Martin Mann was brutally attacked with a two-by-four by Brad Stevens for no apparent reason. We will be calling four witnesses to the stand and asking for their testimony.

Martin Mann will tell us that Brad Stevens attacked him with a two-by-four for no reason. Connie Cook will also testify what she witnessed on the night of June 4th. We'll also call Richard Cervantes, the video arcade manager, who was there that night and witnessed the assault. Finally, we'll call Dr. Chen who was the emergency room doctor on June 4th. He will testify that Martin's condition that night was nearly fatal.

After hearing this evidence, we're sure you will reach the decision that Brad Stevens was out of control and brutally attacked Martin Mann for no reason. We ask that you find Brad Stevens guilty of assault and award Martin Mann $20,000 for his medical costs and lost wages. Thank you.

A scene from Perry Mason? Hardly! This is the prepared opening statement from my eighth-grade students performing a mock trial. A mock trial is an enactment of a modified court trial in which students play the roles of persons in a court hearing. Through an adversary procedure, a judge and jury are called upon to decide the facts of a case and to match laws to the issues raised during the trial. Students gain a better understanding of the judicial system in a *learn-by-doing* environment. Although not identical to an actual trial, a mock trial procedure closely resembles the real thing, and students go through every major step of a criminal or civil trial. Mock trials involve students in active research, cooperative learning, and critical thinking. Students get excited and involved because these activities are more like real life to them than reading about our court system in a book.

Mock trials in the classroom require students to use all the language arts of reading, writing, speaking, and listening and give them a chance to experience social studies' themes of citizenship. Students critically read the facts of the dispute as well as sworn-witness statements to determine the points of their case. They are involved in writing questions to bring out the main points of their case or questions to cast doubt during cross-examination of the opposing side. The witnesses and attorneys practice good speaking skills in the course of performing the trial. And all students sharpen listening skills as they play the role of jurors, or even of attorneys. Students must listen to all testimony in order to effectively portray their case and to find holes in the opposing side's case.

Mock trials initially come into my classroom as a culminating project for the study of the Constitution in American History. Once students learn the process, trials can be chosen from any period in history or about any issue that interests the students. For example, in one school year, a class experienced in mock trials prepared a trial for the Scottsboro Nine (a 1931 trial of nine young African-American males accused of rape that tested the Constitutional promise of due process as it applies to minorities), stemming from their own fascination with the facts of this case. This mock trial was totally student initiated, coached, and prepared.

One of the reasons that most of these mock trials have been successful is the match between the trial and the students. It is important for the teacher to choose a trial appropriate to the age, grade, and level of maturity of the students. There are trials for children in third grade (like a trial of Goldilocks for trespassing) through high school, and many resources are available for teachers with trials for classroom use. The first trial in the school year involves an issue that my students can easily relate to so that they can become proficient in the trial process. I typically start with an assault case involving two teenagers at a video arcade. My students can relate to the issues that lead to the escalation of the argument between Brad Stevens and Martin Mann and become passionate in their defense or prosecution of the defendant (see *People v. Stevens* reference in bibliography). In other years, we begin our unit with a simple fairy tale, such as the "Three Little Pigs" or "Jack and the Beanstalk." Subsequent trials are more relevant to American history themes, such as *Scott, a man of color, v. Emerson* (the Dred Scott decision) or *Brown v. Board of Education*. In one year, my students studied the *New York Times v. United States* as a culmination study of the Bill of Rights and the gray areas of the First Amendment. *Law in American History* (1983) or *Great Trials in American History* (1985) contain classic examples easily used in the classroom.

A teacher does not need to be a lawyer to coach students through a mock trial. The object is not to replicate an exact legal model but rather to inform students about the general process and give them practice in the language arts and group processes mentioned above.

We begin by brainstorming the roles and vocabulary of the courtroom. Most students have observed enough television to identify many of the roles involved. As each role is identified, we discuss what part it plays in the process. I make sure that students describe the judge, prosecutor, defendant, defense attorney, witnesses, victim (in criminal cases) or plaintiff (in civil cases), court reporter, court artist, bailiff (state and local courts) or marshal (federal courts), clerk, jury, the public, and the press. There are many jobs that cover many skill levels, from the court reporter who tape records the proceedings to the attorneys, so that all students can find a comfortable role.

We then brainstorm together the order of events in a typical court proceeding. I use the following list to guide this discussion:

1. Court is called to order.
2. Judge states the charges against the defendant(s).
3. Plaintiff/prosecution delivers its opening statement.
4. Defense may open now or when plaintiff/prosecution is done presenting their case.
5. Plaintiff/prosecution calls its witnesses and conducts direct examination.
6. Defense may cross-examine each witness.
7. Plaintiff/prosecution rests.
8. Defense may deliver opening statement now.
9. Defense calls its witnesses and conducts direct examination.
10. Plaintiff/prosecution may cross-examine each witness.
11. Defense rests.
12. Plaintiff/prosecution delivers closing statements.
13. Defense delivers closing statements.
14. Plaintiff/prosecution may give rebuttal closing. (Because the burden of proof is on the plaintiff/prosecution, they always get the last word.)

15. Jury deliberates.

16. Judge calls for the verdict, and it is announced.

17. Defendant is released or sentenced.

Charting both these brainstorming sessions to display during the unit is very helpful. At the conclusion of that first day, I explain that every person will play a role in the trial, and students should begin thinking what role they would like to play.

The next day, we begin class with a review of the charts from the previous class. Then, we discuss the differences between civil cases and criminal cases. I make sure that students understand that civil cases involve disagreements between individuals while criminal cases involve a crime that has been committed. In a civil case, an individual citizen accuses another citizen of wronging them, and a judge or jury must reach a decision from a *preponderance of the evidence*. In a criminal case, an individual is accused of breaking a law, and a judge or jury must decide if the prosecution has proven *beyond a reasonable doubt* that the defendant did commit the crime.

When students have a clear understanding of civil versus criminal trials, I distribute a fact sheet of the case that we will be doing. Students read the case, and we extrapolate the main facts for each side as a whole group. Students are asked to define what each side might emphasize to get the facts of its case across. We compile a list of the witnesses, noting whether they are prosecution or defense witnesses. Using this list and the roles brainstormed on the previous day, students write down a first, second, and third choice for a role they would like to play. It is useful at the middle school level to assign three attorneys for each side to work together as a team: one to concentrate on opening and closing statements, one to conduct direct examination of their own witnesses (getting the main facts out for their side), and one to cross-examine the opposing witnesses (breaking down the opposing side's facts).

That evening, I consider their choice preferences and assign roles. Alternatives to this process are to have students apply for a role, giving reasons why they should be given that role, or to have them draw names out of a hat for particular roles. If roles are drawn out of a hat, then let students have the choice to switch and trade with classmates, giving a commitment to a role by the time they leave the classroom that day.

When students arrive in class on the next day, I hand out role assignments and more details to students about their roles. We spend some time discussing the criteria that will be used to assess their involvement and performance. The class divides into three groups to begin preparing for the trial. All defense attorneys meet with defense witnesses as a team, prosecution attorneys meet with their witnesses; and the jury, bailiff, court reporter, and other court officials meet together to improve listening skills. (Linda Rickes and Sally Ackerly have written a useful book with these kinds of activities entitled *Conflict, Courts, and Trials,* 1991). I move from group to group, assisting with any problems that arise. Attorneys are busy writing questions that will bring out the facts of the case during the trial and coaching their witnesses on important facts to remember during testimony. Witnesses are learning their roles and the parts that they will play in the trial. The teams must work cooperatively to be successful. There is a lot of discussion in the prosecution and defense teams about what facts to emphasize and about how to effectively get points across.

There are some guidelines to assist students in writing appropriate questions for witnesses while on the stand. One is that no question should ever ask for more than one fact at a time. Another is that it may take several questions to bring out the necessary information on some matters of fact. Students should begin by outlining the points of the case from the sworn statements. Once they have a list, they should determine whether each fact is relevant to their side of the case and whether each fact will help or hinder their case. Then students should arrange the topics in some order that seems logical to them, usually the chronological order of events in the case. Finally, students are ready to write questions that will elicit the facts and responses that they want.

Cross-examination questions can be formed in a similar fashion. The student attorney with cross-examination as an assignment can outline the facts of the case and look for holes in the opposite side's witnesses' statements. What can you bring out or emphasize that will cast doubt in the jury or judge's mind? Write questions that mostly require a *yes* or *no* answer, and don't allow the witnesses to elaborate. An example of cross-examination questions, written by one of my students, Tawan, from the assault case discussed in the first paragraph, are the following:

> Mr. Mann, did you or did you not threaten Brad Stevens?
> Did you or did you not call Mr. Stevens by a foul name?
> Did you push Mr. Stevens?
> Did Mr. Stevens walk away from you at this point?
> Were you pulling an object from your pocket?
> What you are telling me is that you pushed a young gentleman, spraining his wrist. Then you called him a name and charged at him, while pulling a foreign object out of your back pocket. And you expected him not to react?

Students usually need two, three, or more days of class time to prepare. I invite a local attorney to assist teams in their preparation, looking over their questions and offering suggestions. It is important to brief the attorney about the level of expectation that you have for the trial and to encourage the attorney to discuss presentation skills. (Contact your state bar association and ask for their law-related education program for names of attorneys.) I also make sure that students write down questions they have about their case prior to the attorney's visit. Students learn a great deal from these sessions and this experience gives them much pride in their work. Another resource is to visit your local courthouse to observe the trial process in action. This also helps set a tone for your trial in the classroom as students see the manner and decorum of a real courtroom.

As the teams become ready for the trial, set a day for the trial, and include a skeletal rehearsal on the day before, which will help students see how the room will be set up, where they walk to and from the witness stand, and how to place the jury so that they can observe and hear the witnesses adequately (see Figure 6–1). It makes the trial special if I can arrange

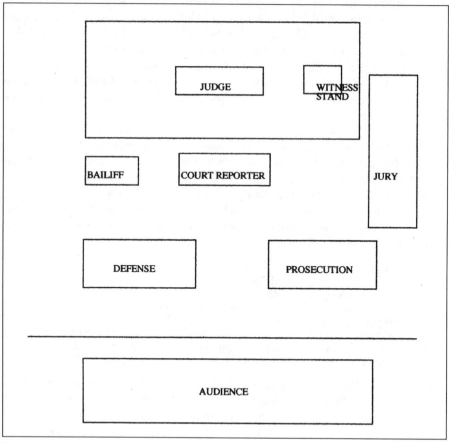

Figure 6–1

for an attorney, judge, parent, or my building administrator to be the judge. Students view these individuals as impartial. Their demeanor is much more serious through the trial with an outsider as judge.

I emphasize appropriate courtroom demeanor during performance of the trial. I take the students on a field trip to our county courthouse to observe the tone in a courtroom, and I expect them to behave in the same manner. Many students will dress formally on the day of the trial if they are playing the role of a student attorney. The judge is always "Your Honor," and I have the students practice at rehearsal saying, "Yes, Your Honor" or "No, Your Honor" when addressing the judge. I stress that judges are all-powerful in their courtrooms and must be respected no matter how right or wrong they may be.

I usually allow two class periods (ninety minutes) per trial. The students perform their roles by calling witnesses and presenting their case. It is important to maintain a respectful atmosphere while allowing the students room to breathe. Many may get nervous at trial time, even though they have practiced. If possible, videotape the proceedings. The students are proud of their performance and enjoy watching it later, while the tape also provides an excellent tool for assessment. You can view it later to analyze the roles or can view it with the group, stopping the tape periodically for comments or suggestions to improve the case.

During the trial, jury members are required to take notes; and when deliberating, jury members complete a tally sheet with reasons for their decision. While the jury is deliberating, it is a good time for the judge to give comments to the attorneys and witnesses, thus evaluating the ways in which they carried out their roles. When the jury returns, a foreman reads the decision; and I either ask each juror to explain, or I collect the tally sheets and read the comments anonymously. Sometimes jurors will ask questions on their decision sheets that are helpful in analyzing how the jury voted. For example, one juror for the Brad Stevens assault case wrote, "I think that he isn't guilty because he was just looking out for himself. I also want to know why Mr. Mann pulled out his wallet when he didn't need to." This led to a discussion of holes in testimony that remain when attorneys are so familiar with the case that they leave out important details for the jury.

Moreover, I have developed a tool to assess the performance of the individuals involved in performing the trial. This form is easily scored while watching, especially if you use someone from outside your classroom to be the judge (see Figure 6–2). Or you can view the videotape of the performance and have students assess their own performance with the criteria in front of them.

When the trial is done, it is important to allow time for all participants to express opinions on the process of the trial, on how they felt in their role,

MOCK TRIAL SCORING RUBRIC

Opening Statement

Does the opening statement include a summary of what happened, a summary of the applicable law, a summary of the witnesses to be called and their importance to the case, and an explanation of what you want the jury/judge to decide at the conclusion of the trial? The opening statement includes

    3—all of the above characteristics

    2—most of the above with omissions

    1—only one or two of the above characteristics

Does the opening statement include an introduction of the attorney/student and incorporate appropriate legal language? The opening statement includes

    3—all of the above

    2—most of the above

    1—only one of the above

Does the opening statement incorporate good public-speaking skills? The speaker

    3—talks clearly and at an appropriate pace and uses voice inflection, and effective eye contact

    2—has most of the above characteristics with omissions.

    1—cannot be understood, has little eye contact, and speaks too slow or too fast

Direct Examination

Regarding the introduction of the witness, the attorney

    3—effectively asks the witness to provide all of his background information

    2—provides background information with omissions

    1—omits key background information and/or leads the witness

Questions are clear, relevant, and asked in a logical sequence

    3—most of the time

    2—some of the time

    1—none of the time

Regarding the attorney's establishment of an effective rapport with the witness, some or most of the attorney's questions demonstrate

    3—work with the witness

    2—lack of preparation

    1—a lack of team effort

Regarding questions to the witness, the team's overall strategy outlined in the opening statement is supported by

    3—most of the questions

    2—some of the questions

    1—none of the questions

Regarding good public-speaking skills during direct examination, the attorney

    3—speaks clearly and at an appropriate pace and uses voice inflection and effective eye contact

    2—includes most of the above characteristics with omissions

    1—cannot be understood, has little eye contact, and speaks too slow or too fast

Figure 6–2

Regarding appropriate objections, the opposing counsel

> 3—objects in a timely and appropriate manner when there has been a violation of rules of evidence and is able to state his reasons
>
> 2—objects effectively at times but misses other key opportunities to object
>
> 1—rarely objects when it is appropriate to, or objects in an untimely, inappropriate manner and is unable to state her reasons

Cross-examination

Regarding effective use, the attorney asks questions that

> 3—are related to direct examination, that contain or suggest the answers, that are short and simple, and that do not badger the witness
>
> 2—are sometimes effective
>
> 1—require narrative responses and would be more appropriate as direct examination

Regarding overall team strategy, the questions

> 3—attack the credibility of the witness, require agreement, and support the team strategy outlined in opening statement
>
> 2—sometimes meet the qualifications above
>
> 1—do not attack credibility, allow the witness to explain herself, and do not relate to the team strategy

Regarding good public-speaking skills during cross-examination, the attorney

> 3—speaks clearly and at an appropriate pace and uses voice inflection and effective eye contact
>
> 2—includes most of the above characteristics with omissions
>
> 1—cannot be understood, has little eye contact, and speaks too slow or too fast

Regarding appropriate objections, the opposing counsel

> 3—objects in a timely and appropriate manner when there has been a violation of rules of evidence and is able to state his reasons
>
> 2—objects effectively at times but misses other key opportunities to object
>
> 1—rarely objects when it is appropriate to, or objects in an untimely, inappropriate manner and is unable to state their reasons

Witness

Regarding effective presentation in direct examination, the witness

> 3—convincingly tells the story and is responsive to questions asked without being narrative
>
> 2—knows the story but sounds rehearsed and not original
>
> 1—is unclear on the facts, unconvincing, and not responsive

Regarding good public-speaking skills, the witness

> 3—speaks clearly and at an appropriate pace and uses voice inflection and effective eye contact as well as appropriate gestures and facial expressions
>
> 2—includes most of the above characteristics with omissions
>
> 1—cannot be understood, has little eye contact, and speaks too slow or too fast, with few gestures or facial expressions

Figure 6–2 (cont.)

Regarding effective presentation in cross-examination, the witness

3—remains calm, unshaken, and consistent in her story
2—has some difficulty handling questions in character
1—gets confused and is unable to stay in character

Closing Argument
Does the closing argument highlight the key facts brought out through witness testimony during the trial? The attorney

3—makes reference to key testimony from both sides
2—makes reference to some key facts but omits others
1—misses the opportunity to highlight key testimony

Does the closing argument integrate key testimony with the applicable law and articulate what you want and support why you want the jury/judge to decide in your favor? The attorney

3—demonstrates a clear and accurate relationship between the key testimony and the applicable law and convincingly states his team's position
2—attempts to integrate key testimony with the law and is barely convincing
1—fails to integrate facts with the law and does not convincingly state a position

Does the closing argument show the weaknesses in the opposing side's testimony and argument? The attorney

3—accurately identifies weaknesses in the opposition's case
2—notes some weaknesses but misses other key weaknesses
1—is inaccurate or fails to identify weaknesses in the opposition's case

Regarding good public-speaking skills during closing arguments, the attorney

3—speaks clearly and at an appropriate pace, using voice inflection, effective eye contact, appropriate gestures, and is able to hold the attention of the jury/judge
2—includes most of the above characteristics with omissions
1—cannot be understood, has little eye contact, and speaks too slow or too fast, with few gestures

Figure 6–2 (cont.)

and on what might be done differently next time. Debriefing is vital to the learning experience (see Figure 6–2). After the discussion ends, I ask each individual to write an opinion essay on the following questions: Do you feel this was a fair trial? Why or why not? Do you agree with the verdict? Why or why not? What would you do differently in your role to make it stronger next time? Further study and discussion can involve students in reflection or debate as to whether our judicial system helps insure a defendant a fair trial. Why or why not? What changes, if any, would they recommend in the system? Why? (See Figure 6–3.)

Mock trials in the classroom can be an exciting and real experience for students. All students can find success in this experience by working as a team with classmates. Everyone participates, and no one may sit on the sidelines and let others do the work. Students are eager to play the roles of

PROMPT
MOCK TRIAL DISCUSSION QUESTIONS

1. If you win the verdict, are you therefore right?
2. Do you agree with the verdict? Explain your answer.
3. The following are some hypothetical questions:
   What if one of the attorneys had worked for the election of the judge?
   What if the judge had ruled differently on evidence?
   What if the jury had disregarded the judge's instructions?
4. Was the judge fair? Did he favor one side or the other? Cite evidence. Did he influence the outcome of the trial? Cite examples.
5. At what point (what evidence, argument, witness, etc.) did you make a decision on the outcome of the case?
6. Was a trial (by jury) the best way to resolve this conflict? What were the alternatives?
7. Can you identify any bias in the process?
8. How did the process of a trial help or hinder the achievement of justice?

Figure 6–3

attorney and witness, which demand the most prepared performance of all roles. Combining language arts with group processes, using citizenship as the vehicle, will enliven the classroom while giving students practice that they welcome and look forward to.

For over ten years, I have passionately pursued the use of mock trials in the classroom. I have mentored nearly fifty teachers who have used this exciting method in their classrooms. I have volunteered countless hours to coach teams and judge high school–level competitions. I do this year after year because I am astounded at the high level of performance as well as the commitment and enthusiasm that the students exhibit. It is very contagious.

The strongest evidence of the powerful effect that this experience has on students is the seemingly magical boost in self-confidence that I see in the students. They amaze me year after year at how high they rise to the occasion in their thought processes. When I saw Chanesa, who had hardly raised her hand all year, volunteer to play a role, I held my breath. Then I watched with wonder the transformation as she performed her role to perfection. She worked diligently on this project as she had on no other all year long. She spoke clearly, distinctly, and with a confidence that I had not seen in her before.

I continue to devote valuable classroom time to this project because of students like Chanesa and Joseph. All year Joseph had chronic absenteeism and seemed to have lost interest in school altogether. Yet, while we prepared and performed the mock trial, Joseph was in my class every day. Students stand taller and speak in a more adult manner while acting in this positive adult role of our society. They write and rewrite statements and questions. They practice speaking over and over—for teachers, peers, and parents—to perfect their inflections. This all occurs through self-motivation because they enjoy the process.

I will always remember the time when I judged a small alternative school's first team in our state competition. When I commented to one of the witnesses to relax, that she seemed a bit nervous on the stand, her response was that she was nervous. This had been the first time she had been in a courtroom for positive reasons.

I have watched high school students cry at the verdict announcement because they had worked so hard and were jubilant at winning the case. I have also watched these students cry at the slightest criticism, again because they had invested everything they had into performing their best and took every comment to heart. They are extremely proud of the work they have done and feel a true satisfaction in a job well done. I can feel their pride, and it is refreshing.

The mock trial is a powerful method that has enabled me to see my students, and they to see themselves, as competent, capable contributors to society. In his evaluation of the mock trial experience, Chris wrote, "I think a trial is a good way to achieve justice because people can't judge you by what they think. They have to know what's going on." Molly reflected, "If there was a way for the prosecution and defense to get together before the actual case and talk it over more, there would be less tension between everyone." And Stacey wrote, "Before this I was not sure what I want to do in life. Now I want to be the first African-American woman on the Supreme Court." All these are powerful lessons that students synthesized for themselves and that go far beyond the goals and objectives that I had planned in the experience.

BIBLIOGRAPHY

Arbetman, Lee, and Richard Roe. 1985. *Great Trials in American History*. St. Paul, MN: West.

Danzer, Gerald, and James Lengel. 1983. *Law in American History*. Glenview, IL: Scott Foresman.

1983. *People v. Brad Stevens*. Available from the California Bar Association.

Riekes, Linda, and Sally Ackerly. 1991. *Conflict, Courts and Trials*. St. Paul, MN: West.

Chapter 7
Learners as Creators: Art and the Social Studies

LIBBY KENNEDY

> Creating is the highest form of intellectual development.
> *Linda Rief,* Seeking Diversity

When eighth graders enter my room each September, they can't help but notice the life-sized watercolor of author Mildred Taylor dressed in purple as she welcomes students to the class. The stylized portrait was hand painted by Lena, a former student of mine, who donated it to me for display. Jameela's richly colored oil pastel portrait of Theseus stands guard beside Ms. Taylor. Other walls are adorned with some of my collection of art prints. The bulletin boards, however, are covered simply with deep violet, neon pink, and bold yellow fadeless paper. Within the first week though, these boards start to come alive with student artwork and writing. As I look around the classroom this day in May, student work surrounds me. Personal colored-pencil maps of places where students have lived line the chalkboard in front of the class. Conté crayon sketches of African-American authors hang beside watercolor paintings based on scenes from Ray Bradbury's short story "The Fog Horn." Illustrated game boards with names like "Kwanza," "Follow the North Star," and "Zora" are posted with typed rules on the side bulletin board. On the wall above them, hang colorful construction-paper cutout masks of characters from legends written by students. Across the back board are historical student-designed westward-expansion brochures enticing settlers to Oregon, Texas, and California. In the next week or two, these projects will come down, and new creations will take their place. Students are proud and excited to see their own work displayed, and they know that it will be viewed and taken seriously by others.

This chapter is an explanation of why and how I incorporate art into my eighth-grade social studies classroom. And I do not mean just using art as an object of study, though students can gain valuable historical perspective by looking at visual images and works of art. I do want them to further their historical understanding through art so that we scan landscapes, portraits, architecture, cultural artifacts and symbols, even maps, for what they can teach us.

More importantly, however, I want students to create their own visual images and works of art. As they study history, they are asked to produce something in visual as well as in traditional written forms about what they learn—work that will be displayed and presented to their classmates. I love art, and I learn best visually—so that is how I teach. My favorite part of teaching is the challenge of designing exciting projects that get students involved in the curriculum through the arts. I want my social studies classroom to have the same feeling as a working art studio in which students are engaged in the learning process, with the materials of the discipline, with others, and with the environment.

My inspiration for this way of teaching came from Mrs. Judy Berger. I knew little of the eighth-grade curriculum at the time that I was hired, and my fourteen-year-old niece urged me to call Mrs. Berger, her favorite teacher, who promptly invited me to visit her school in Hillsboro. Walking into her classroom was like entering a living museum. There were replicas of Conestoga wagons, models of forts, life-sized wooden stockades, pieced-quilt squares, embroidered flags, colonial costumes, and hand-drawn historical posters. Each one had been designed and created by her eighth-grade U.S. History students. After she walked me around her room, Mrs. Berger pulled several handouts from numerous labeled files and shared her project lists, letters to parents, grading policies, course outlines, and her philosophy of education with me during those couple of hours. Feeling grateful, I left her room that afternoon loaded down with handouts, old textbooks, actual student project samples, and the knowledge that I wanted to teach like her.

With Mrs. Berger as my inspiration, I ask students to transfer what they learn into something visual. They are thus continually involved in the creating of maps, illustrated time lines, historical cartoons, three-dimensional characters—the possibilities are endless. Students comment about visual assignments by saying:

They make it easier to understand what people have been through.

If you can visualize a person or event it helps you remember better.

Visual assignments require more research which helps.

Learning is less boring.

Most students enjoy creating as they learn, and I can assess their knowledge through the creative process as well as through the finished products.

Presented aloud, these projects are used to teach the rest of the class. Each student's work is displayed in the classroom, and I have found that students enter the room and look for their work and are proud to see it neatly displayed on the board. Students become accountable as they present, display, and evaluate their work. As the year progresses, the four walls act as an everchanging visual reflection of what my students are learning as their work is respectfully displayed. Thus, the walls of the classroom become like those of an art gallery.

Some students approach *doing art* with insecurity and reluctance. Some may complain at first by saying, "But I can't draw," or they may feel intimidated about a blank piece of paper in front of them. I always provide clear directions and expectations when introducing a project or assignment. Sometimes I show the students previous works created by former students, but not always. I don't want to box students in. Therefore, though I give requirements, I leave the process and final product up to the students' creativity.

After my introduction, students are free to create their own personal vision. Because some students feel inadequate about their artistic abilities to the point of immobility, one of my roles is to coax and encourage them into action. Sometimes I find I have to physically help a student. One pitfall that I avoid when using art in a content-based course is this: I never simply say, "Draw a picture." Instead, I try to strike a balance within each project to combine written, visual, and oral work. This chapter aims to provide some authentic, more complex ways to use art in a social studies classroom—avenues that encourage students to think critically in the process of creation.

I have some specific objectives in mind when I ask my students to use art in their work. I use art to

- involve students with historical content
- help students look at historical people and events visually, creatively, and critically
- introduce and develop *real-world* skills (i.e., layouts, cooperative working groups, partnerships, problem solving)
- connect students with material and content
- engage students immediately

I want my students to be creative and to think critically not just while they are in middle school, but for their entire lives. We don't live in a *one-right-answer* world, so I try to structure the physical room as well as the emotional community of the group in a way that promotes and encourages creativity—mine and theirs. Student desks are arranged in pairs or in groups of four. Sometimes students sit in one large circle so that everyone can see each other. Student and professional artwork adorn every inch of the walls. It is there to enrich and inspire all who enter the room.

It is a professional challenge to develop creative lessons that encourage critical thinking. I want my students to be creators of lessons as well. I try to develop activities and questions so that students can do their own creating and questioning, and eventually, students can develop their own project ideas.

GENERAL GUIDELINES

I design my room to be personally inviting. My students spend two and a half hours there each day in a core block (social studies, language arts, and literature). While I manage to leave most of the bulletin-board space blank, I do post a few eclectic art prints, historical posters, and photographs that represent people from numerous cultures. Students usually do not comment on the emptiness of the boards until I tell them that within a week their work will be displayed, which gives them ownership of their classroom.

When displaying student work, I (1) display and post the work of each student so that every person is represented, (2) neatly display student work to look organized and professional, (3) post work as soon as it is turned in so that it may inspire others.

Prior to posting their work, students must present their projects to the class. Initially, I set up presentation rules that encourage students and foster a nurturing environment where they feel safe to share their work with others. We discuss and model appropriate audience behavior, which includes attentiveness, good listening skills, and positive written and oral feedback. After each presentation, we applaud the speaker. Questions from the audience are encouraged and put-downs are forbidden. Many students are nervous or embarrassed at first and have the option to go up front with a partner.

We start public speaking on the first day of school with partner interviews, so that students relax and usually look forward to talking about their work as the year progresses and presentations become more frequent. Presentations broaden the students' audience from teacher to peers, and public speaking soon becomes second nature to most students.

THREE OF MY STUDENTS

My classes are heterogeneously grouped so that students' skills, abilities, and knowledge run the gamut. Holly, a student who strives for perfection in all of her work, created a giant wall-sized map of the westward expansion of the United States that was beyond my wildest imagination (see Figure 7–1). She black-lined the western states and then labeled, described, and illustrated the people, events, and places along various trails

Figure 7–1

westward from Missouri while integrating a multicultural theme. Holly had listened to our discussion of project ideas in class, but then took materials home; and after many days of work, she came to school with her detailed map. She proudly explained her project to us as well as the hours and the fun she had researching and creating it. The other students were in awe of her project, but it was an inspiring awe. After it had been displayed for some time, I asked Holly what she planned to do with her map. Secretly, I was hoping that she would decide to donate it to me for use in future classes. Instead she calmly replied, "It's going up in my room, of course." It is a good sign when eighth graders want to keep their work.

On the other hand, there was John. He was the first student I had encountered who truly seemed to be limited in his artistic development. I had believed that all students could be creative with visual arts, and yet John's art skills were like that of a primary student—primitive and unrefined. He could barely cut out a small figure of a person. John said that he didn't consider himself to be an artist; in fact, he admitted, "I can't draw." And yet he said that he was "a creative student with a good imagination." John struggled all year with many of the visual assignments; but he did feel comfortable enough to attempt each one, and he even maintained a sense of humor, often joking about his work. When I asked him which qualities creative students share, he replied, "Desire, dedication, and an imagination." John was indeed a creative student.

Travis hated school. He hated reading, writing, studying, and everything else that one associates with school—except art. He had difficulty with the physical act of writing and yet thrived on the artistic projects that we did in social studies class. I often had him work with a small group or with a partner, and he would excel in creating detailed maps and realistic portraits of historical figures. His group members were thrilled that he shared his talent with them, and I believe that his interest in art literally kept him in school that year.

These three eighth-grade students typify the range of abilities that I find each year in my daily three-period core block. It is common to have different ability levels within my eighth-grade classes, and yet all types of students share some level of success in the act of creating.

A SAMPLE PROJECT

Michael is asking how much beef cost in 1894 so that he can write an authentic sales letter to Tara's pub offering a good deal on his company's ("Bob's Cows") cattle. Nate and Katrina have Time-Life books open to illustrations of early steam engines, trying to design a logo for their railroad business. Kim writes a press release on hand-designed letterhead announcing a promotional St. Patrick's Day gathering at the "Four-Leaf Clover" tavern. Shanon types her résumé on the computer in the library. Indira jots an illustrated memo to Laura about horses for their newly created pony-express mail service. Ali sketches a blueprint for the planned expansion of her "Sweet Treats" general store. Each student is either writing, drawing, typing, designing, or discussing business deals as they portray early American entrepreneurs. I stand and observe for a moment, smiling to myself. To a middle school teacher, this is magic: Students are learning historical material through involvement and creation. They are doing things that adults do in real life: cooperating, making decisions, writing to each other, solving problems, producing quality products, and guiding others—all skills that can be transferred to other parts of their lives now and in the future.

My friend and colleague Betty Barker created this simulation called "Early American Entrepreneurs" for her U.S. History classes, and I have adapted it. Each student initially receives a handout that introduces and outlines the business project in a visually appealing way (see Figure 7–2). Together, as a class, we read through the handout, discussing the assignment's goals, objectives, and expectations. Because this project involves several informational handouts, students create a simple construction-paper folder to hold all of the paperwork. Final drafts of all business writing are then placed within the folders for evaluation at the end of the project.

For this project, students choose two or three peers with whom they want to form a small business. Their goal is to decide on a product or service that they want to provide and then to apply to the bank for a loan to get the business going. I explain specific tasks that must be completed by individuals or by groups. I love this project because, although students work in a supportive business group, each person is responsible for completing his own business writing for the folder. Students are interacting within their own groups and are also dealing with other groups. A listing of sample inventions and services during this period of American history is also provided for students to use as a springboard. They may use an actual invention as their product or may come up with an idea of their own, but it must be historically accurate to fit the 1700s to 1800s. I answer questions; and before the end of the first class period, students are forming their partnerships and brainstorming ideas for possible small business start-ups.

During the second day of this project, library resources are carted in for student reference. Groups must determine their businesses by the end of the next day, and ideally they should already be deciding upon their business name, logo, location, the partners and positions within the company, and a brief description and quick sketch of the business itself. This information is then posted on a large chart in front of the room so that students

America's Growing Years (1780s-1800s)

The U.S. is growing and prospering, and you can grow and prosper with it! The new National Bank of the United States is offering loans to enterprising citizens. You are to follow the following guidelines before submitting your proposal to the Bank's Board of Directors for your loan.

I.   Determine the type of business you own (do some research)
   * name your business
   * determine the location of the business
   * design a logo and write a slogan
   * decide upon partners and their positions within the business
   * write a brief general description of the business

II.   Write a detailed description of the product(s) and/or service(s) you will provide. Who will buy them, why? Explain why the business will be successful (ie. population growth, westward expansion, overseas markets, etc.)

III.   Fill out a job application

IV.   Write your resume

V.   Write a letter of inquiry and a sales letter

VI.   Create a press release

VII.   Write a memo

VIII. Design layouts, blueprints, illustrations for your business

IX.   Determine your assets and expenditures and create a budget

X.   Write a proposal to present to the National Bank's Board of Directors

Figure 7–2

can see what other groups are doing. It is also a reference once student entrepreneurs start interacting with each other. I sometimes provide samples on overhead transparencies of former student work to give students an idea of work quality.

At the beginning of each class, I introduce one type of business communication, such as writing a résumé, memo, press release, letter of inquiry, and so forth. I provide a general list of guidelines and the format for each. I show the students real examples as well as student-created samples. After this five- to ten-minute introduction, they go to work. This is where the fun begins. Students are actively researching, drawing illustrated maps and detailed floor plans, writing letters, and communicating with each other as they make deals and compromises in the best interest of their companies. Students continue their business discussions during their break.

Midway through the project, I stop the students for a check-in time with a short series of questions such as the following:

· What business transactions have you made with other companies?
· Why does your company need a loan?
· Where will you find information to write an accurate budget?
· What does your press release announce?
· How have you used art to help you sell your product or service and to better position your company?

Focused questions provide students with a clear idea of where they should be at this point. We generally take class time to listen to individuals within each group answer the questions, which is often helpful to others.

On the day that the projects are due, students volunteer to go up front to introduce themselves and their business groups. Using props, costumes, maps, charts, graphs, and illustrations, they then present their budgets and loan proposals to a five-member bank board of directors. Betty Barker has painted a replica of the National Bank's exterior for use during the presentations. The *volunteer* directors usually take notes, and the audience must listen to the presentation in silence, but everyone has an opportunity to ask questions at the end. The loan amount and interest rate is determined by the bank's directors, based upon the presentation of detailed data and persuasive proposals. Each company has the chance to accept or reject the loan terms. The bank's board of directors changes with each business group, and ideally it would be composed of impartial adults from the business community.

When all presentations are complete, students write self-evaluations of their individual writing, the results of the presentation, their group's process, and the project as a whole. I then display the students' folders, maps, logos, blueprints, and illustrations on the board. In this way, we try to integrate reading, writing, historical research, role-playing, and various forms of artwork in our social studies unit on the Gilded Age.

STUDENT ACTIVITIES AND CREATIONS

When developing units, I look at content objectives and what students need to learn. From there, I begin to brainstorm possible activities that facilitate the objectives and that also encourage critical thinking and artistic creativity. This is the fun part and one that stretches my own creativity. My desk at home is piled high with open history books, a copy of Bloom's taxonomy, learning-style charts, state requirements, and numerous project-idea lists. Possibilities and combinations of activities are endless.

Once students have experienced some teacher-planned units, there is no reason why they cannot plan their own. This would enable students to have ownership in their education, which is an often-heard desire these days. Here is a list of student activities that combine written, visual, and oral components:

1. Mapmaking: As an introduction to cartography, students create a personal map of the places where they have lived, which may be a world, country, region, city, or neighborhood map, or even the floor plan of a house. Students draw maps throughout the year as they study various historical periods so that they have a sense of the geography of the times. They design their own maps after reading a fictional or nonfiction account by using what they have read. Maps can be enlarged and symbolically decorated as well (see Figure 7–3).

2. Cartooning: Students use cartoon characters to illustrate and interpret historical documents. They draw political cartoons and comic strips with historical content. For example, students decipher and explain the Declaration of Independence with cartoon characters and dialogue bubbles.

3. Letter writing: Students correspond with each other as historical figures or everyday people. They put themselves in the shoes of these people to think, communicate, and relate to the events of the times. For example, students write as literate slaves who comment on their experiences with Nat Turner's rebellion, Frederick Douglass's oratories, or William Garrison's *Liberator.* They also write and send letters to present-day governmental leaders.

4. Interviewing: Students write, illustrate portraits, and perform interviews with people whose life stories, decisions, and historical events

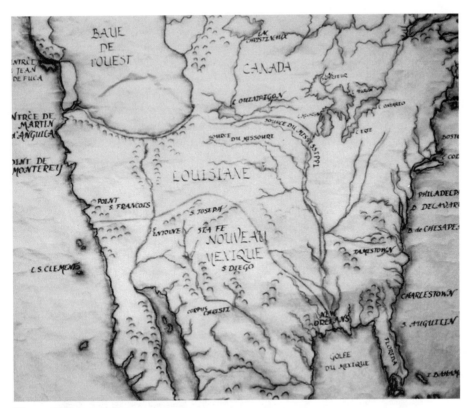

Figure 7–3

are questioned. They play the roles of interviewee and interviewer to tangle with issues of the day. Students take the role of an ordinary citizen who has the chance to meet and question a famous politician, soldier, or reformer during the Revolutionary War, for example.

5. Journal or diary writing: Again, students write and draw as if they were historical characters looking at events from a more personal perspective. Here, fiction can be combined with fact to create interest. For example, partners compile journal entries and colored-pencil illustrations as presidential assistants to Andrew Jackson, explaining his policies as well as their personal opinions as his aides (see Figure 7–4).

6. Mask making: Students design papier-mâché, clay, or paper cutout masks. Using Native American literature, students research, write, and illustrate legends and design character masks that are worn as the legends are presented aloud.

Figure 7–4

7. Magazine producing: Students write articles, letters, and advertisements as they design magazines based upon historical periods. Using actual magazines like *Time* and *National Geographic* as models, students write and illustrate their own versions by using historical content or specific subjects such as the Revolutionary War or a Native American tribe. They usually work in small groups as teams who research and create the layout and colorful artwork of the publication.

8. Newspaper producing: Student teams become newspaper staffs that produce a paper with a unique viewpoint during a historical time period. As journalists, illustrators, and editors, they report the news in

Figure 7–5

print. For example, Civil War newspapers are written from around the United States to reveal regional differences and viewpoints.

9. Portrait painting: Students paint life-sized watercolor and tempera illustrations of famous people that are displayed throughout the school. Students also create smaller portrayals of historical figures as we study them. Early portrait painters' works, such as those of Charles Wilson Peale, Gilbert Stuart, and Edward Savage, serve as models for student's portraits of presidents and other historical

figures. Figure 7–5 is a pencil portrait of James Baldwin sketched by Mike after he had researched Baldwin's life.

10. Time line constructing: Students create small, colorfully illustrated, descriptive time lines as well as giant time lines of events and peoples' lives that provide a sense of chronology. For example, students research, design, and illustrate sections of a wall-sized segmented time line of events leading to the Civil War that fit together across the back wall of the classroom (See Figure 7–6).

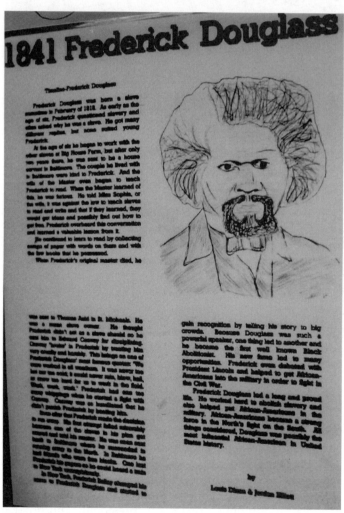

Figure 7–6

11. Historical-fiction writing: Students write stories, plays, poems, ballads, and create characters based on historical facts and then illustrate them. After reading the Ambrose Bierce story, "An Occurrence at Owl Creek Bridge," for example, students create a written and visual memento left by the main character before he lost his life.

12. Game designing: Vivid board games are designed by using novels that students have read. Rules are written, characters are created as the game's pieces, and the decorated board becomes the setting of the story. The novels come to life as students then play each others' games. Students use African-American literature, including *The Autobiography of Malcolm X, The Color Purple, Go Tell It on the Mountain,* and *Native Son,* to incorporate into meaningful games.

13. Book publishing: Students write, illustrate, and publish stories and pop-up books that cover a certain time period or event in history. With a younger audience, students must simplify the content yet include detailed illustrations.

14. Newscast producing: Students portray broadcasters and journalists as they write and design props and scenery to present their historical newscasts, interviews, talk shows, and on-the-scene reports to the class. For instance, one student acted as an eyewitness in the duel between Burr and Hamilton, and another acted as Connie Chung as she interviewed Sacajawea.

15. Poster making: All sizes of colorful posters are created as note-taking and information-gathering devices and as visual aids in presentations. For example, students design eye-catching posters that include notes, opinions, quotations, and a portrait of one framer of the Constitution and his role during the Convention of 1787.

16. Role Playing: I have found that eighth-grade students jump at any chance they have to act like adults in real-world situations. In class, students portray people in businesses, law firms, debate teams, the media. They begin to look at present-day and historical issues as they play different roles, create costumes, and design background scenery.

17. Simulation organizing: Many simulations have been published and are helpful to use. Teacher or student-created simulations can be just as effective. For example, students become small-business owners of the 1800s and present a budget and loan proposal to tne U.S. Bank.

ASSESSMENT

After each assignment, I have students evaluate their work in writing based on a list of criteria that was stated in the project's introduction and expectations. These criteria can also be student designed. Students are generally honest about the process that they followed, the amount of time that they spent, and how completely they included the requirements. I never evaluate students' artistic ability, and I reassure them of this. Instead, I evaluate neatness, legibility, and the inclusion of requirements. I spend many hours reading student work and writing comments to students about what they've created. After group projects, students individually evaluate their work and their group's process. Students have the option to be graded individually or as a member of a group, but they must explain their choice.

I also have students write about something of which they are proud and about any problems they had and how they were solved. Finally, I ask students to briefly explain what they learned and how the content relates to their lives. Students are often asked to share one part of their assessment with the rest of the class as part of their presentation. All projects are then filed in student folders that go home in June.

I want a classroom filled with lively students who, like studio artists, are constantly creating, writing, and presenting their work so that they learn from each other. Thus, I try to design assignments that challenge students to be creative as they produce something that displays their knowledge of a historical event, concept, or person. I want students to be active learners who research, design, create, chart, draw, map, read, discuss, write, listen, and share their historical understandings with each other every day in class.

Adorned with diverse student projects, our colorful classroom celebrates each person's contribution and unique vision. The work reflects a busy, respectful, creative community built upon the personalities, experiences, and knowledge that each student brings to class. From the very first week of school, our social studies classroom begins to take shape as a working studio. I watch the community grow stronger and more creative throughout the year, as my students encourage, inspire, and value each others' skills and talents.

BIBLIOGRAPHY

Baldwin, James. 1952. *Go Tell It on the Mountain*. New York: Doubleday.

Walker, Alice. 1982. *The Color Purple*. New York: Washington Square Press.

Wright, Richard. 1940. *Native Son*. New York: Harper & Row.

X, Malcolm, and Alex Haley. 1964. *The Autobiography of Malcolm X*. New York: Grove Press.

Chapter 8
A Middle Ages Potpourri

BETTY HITTLE

As a kid, I loved the stories of King Arthur and the Knights of the Round Table. As a teacher, I found most students to be negative toward any mention of the word *history.* I wanted them to share in my love of a time period that I found to be exciting, colorful, dramatic, and romantic. So, I thought, what could I do to really grab seventh graders? No problem! Give them the Middle Ages as they were—the straight stuff with all of the blood, gore, and pageantry that existed then, just what seventh graders love.

With this in the back of my mind, I began thinking about how I could create a unit that would integrate history with music, drama, art, mapping, newspaper, journal- and story-writing research, and the literature and crafts of the period. What I intended was to entice my students into learning a whole period of history and having fun throughout the process. With the premise that social studies must be much more than reading maps and lifeless textbooks, I began my medieval unit.

To really give social studies vitality, students need to experience vicariously the given time span or the lives of people of that time. Before one can understand another time and place, I believe it is necessary to know thoroughly one's own place and time.

Our study began by using the National Geographic Society's "Five Themes of Geography": location, place, human-environment interaction, movement, and region (see Figure 8–1). At first, this exercise sounded pretty awful to seventh graders from the response that I got. I wanted my students to become familiar with our school neighborhood, city, and, eventually, our county and our state. I wanted them to learn about such things as location, topography, climate, history, culture, religions, ethnic contributions, art, architecture, and other sciences, and I wanted them to learn how

National Geographic Society's Fundamental Themes of Geography*

LOCATION: Position on earth's surface

A. Absolute

    1. Map/globe

    2. Boundary sign

B. Relative

    1. Maps

    2. Landforms as markers (aerial shot)

    3. Distance markers

    4. Major landmarks that a location can be compared to (west of Mt. Hood)

PLACE: Physical and human characteristics

    1. Climate (four seasons)

    2. Monuments

    3. Lakes, Rivers, Mountains

    4. Residential areas

    5. Structures: bridges, tunnels, fountains

    6. Photos of annual events

    7. Ethnic restaurants

    8. Institutions

HUMAN-ENVIRONMENT INTERACTION: How humans have altered their environment

    1. Factories

    2. Tunnels

    3. Farms

    4. Cemeteries

    5. Churches

    6. Empty lots previously occupied

    7. Shopping malls

    8. Clear cut logging

MOVEMENT: Humans interacting on the earth

    1. River traffic

    2. Radio towers

    3. Satellite dishes

    4. Newspaper building

    5. TV Stations

    6. Airports

    7. Highways

    8. Bike paths

Figure 8–1

REGIONS: How they form and change
1. Business Area
2. Physical Characteristics
3. Residential
4. Commerce
5. Political-Government Buildings
6. Shopping Districts
7. Parks

*Contact the National Geographic Society to obtain videos and other teaching materials based on the "Five Fundamental Themes."

Figure 8-1 (cont.)

these are all interrelated to form a culture as we know it. We did learn these things as well as a lot about ourselves.

In order to bring the ideas of the five themes of geography close to now and to where we live, I borrowed slides from the Portland Tourist Bureau, copied those that fit into the five themes, and added some slides of my own. The first slide provided a map of the world for location, with Portland marked. The second slide was an aerial view of nearby rivers and hills depicting place. For human-environment interaction, I used slides of a bridge, a shopping center, and a neighborhood. Movement was probably the easiest for students to understand as I used slides of a television tower, an airport, a highway, and several ships and bridges. Students were curious about the duplication of some slides until they understood how some examples fit into more than one category. For regions, I used slides of the downtown business district, neighborhoods, parks, and several slides inside the classroom showing groups of students in the middle of an activity that we had done earlier in the year. Naturally, these were their favorite slides. I was able to go through the slides several times. We discussed each slide and why it represented a particular theme.

The students were then given a choice of working on one of five committees, each one representing one of the five themes of geography. Searching through magazines, they tore out pictures that depicted their particular theme and glued these to two-by-three sheets of railroad board. These completed collages were laminated and hung in the room for the rest of the year.

The first day of the Middle Ages unit begins with me handing out a picture of a typically dressed medieval villager or a work of architecture of the period. The remaining page is blank except for the instruction, "Write everything you know about the Middle Ages or medieval Europe." Upon completion, these papers are filed until the end of the unit, when they will be discussed and compared with new lists of what each student has learned.

After students skim through section titles in the social studies textbook, I tell the students to put away the texts for the day. I get some disbelieving, quizzical looks with this request. As I begin passing out copies of *A Proud Taste for Scarlet And Miniver* by E. L. Konigsburg, I tell my students that real people made history and that this book is a historical novel that is written much like a modern-day soap opera. I go on to explain that the book is based on real people and on the events that occurred in their lives. This novel tells the life story of a fascinating person, Eleanor of Aquitaine.

The story is unusual in that it is told from different characters' points of view from heaven, as they discuss, with Eleanor, events of her life. Eleanor lived eighty-two years (1122–1204) in medieval Europe. She lived both in France and England and traveled to Antioch (in present day Turkey) on a religious crusade. Through her eyes, and those of her contemporaries, we view life in the royal courts of England, France, and Antioch.

Eleanor had political influence in both the twelfth and thirteenth centuries: first, as the queen of France, then of England; and later, through her three sons who became kings and through her three daughters who married and were effective in other royal families of Europe. She was equally known for her guidance in the arts, literature, and music and for adopting more courtly manners than had previously existed. She is also responsible for having the tales of King Arthur and his knights written as literature. What a lady! She was under house arrest when she accomplished this final task and several others.

Discussion of place, region, and movement all fit into discussions of the events in the above paragraph.

Having introduced the novel and hooked the students into reading it, we now begin the setting of what will be an ongoing scene: We gradually change our classroom into a medieval castle. For stained-glass windows, I use some patterns that I purchased while in England some years ago. These patterns are photocopied along with a few pictures from a Middle Ages coloring book. Students select their favorite window design and choose between coloring with heavy bright crayon or using Exacto blades to cut out white parts and replace them with colored tissue paper. Both make very aesthetically pleasing pseudo–stained-glass when taped to the classroom windows. We discuss how our windows make a social comment on the art of the Middle Ages. (Stained glass windows were only found in cathedrals and castle chapels; therefore, the subjects of the windows were most frequently royalty and saints. Since our classroom fit neither category, our windows could depict any scene that we chose from the Middle Ages.)

I found it to be very important to have a variety of books in the classroom at this time for the students to look through for pictures or to use in research papers to be assigned later. Throughout the unit, I have on hand copies of everything that I have included in the bibliography at the end of this chapter, and these resources are well used.

For the construction of mosaic pictures, I use photocopies from any source of simple art of the Middle Ages, such as a coloring book or the example where the instructions are found in *The Metropolitan Museum of Art Activity Book.* We cover areas of the picture by using one-quarter-inch squares of colored construction paper glued to the picture, much as you would do to fit tiles. We hang these mosaics in the classroom to add to the castle motif.

Another popular activity in my class is the construction of castles and cathedrals. I buy a variety of castle and cathedral push-out and construction books each year. Most bookstores stock these books. I also keep on hand photocopies of cut-and-fold castles, cathedrals, and mosques from *Paper Magic.* The only other supplies that we needed for any of these constructions were scissors, tape, paper clips and large pieces of cardboard for bases.

Interspersed with the reading and discussions about Eleanor's life, the reading of the textbook chapters, and the medieval crafts that we are producing, I read chapters from *Tales of King Arthur* and excerpts from *The Canterbury Tales.* Frequently, students volunteer to read these stories to the class while everyone else works quietly on the project at hand. Sometimes a student or committee of students read from or condense information from *The Plantagenet Chronicles* or from its sequel, *Four Gothic Kings,* to check the authenticity of the information in *A Proud Taste For Scarlet and Miniver.*

Before assigning much writing, I introduce the students to different styles of writing through selected readings. Ballads were very much a part of the Middle Ages, and the best one to start with is "Bishop Hatto," by Robert Southey, because it encompasses what seventh graders like best about medieval times. The story is about Bishop Hatto, who is very selfish and unwilling to share his grain with the poor and starving citizens of his neighborhood (whom he calls "rats"). He tricks them into gathering into his barn, locks the doors, and burns the barn and contents. The bishop is then devoured by rats. This is an example of poetic justice. Student comments tell it best: "Ooh! Ick! Cool!" I use this ballad and the humorous "Get Up and Bar the Door" as an introduction to "The Song of Roland," which is much more serious and tells of the heroic deeds of Charlemagne. But each poem has a very strong moral, and the kids have no trouble interpreting that moral. Some students wrote ballads of their own, and we all enjoy the originality and companion illustrations.

A few carefully selected, quality audiovisual materials can enhance a unit. I feel quite fortunate that my school district owns a large audiovisual library. My favorite films are *The Medieval Society: The Nobility; The Medieval Society: The Villagers; Music of the Middle Ages; The Medieval Crusades;* and *Charlemagne; Unifier of Europe.* I also check out a kit of replicas of musical instruments from the Middle Ages for classroom display. Whenever we work on projects and I am not reading aloud to the pupils, we listen to the music of the period from my tape collection.

When discussing films on the Middle Ages, all represent some aspect of the National Geographic Society's "Five Themes of Geography." All five themes fit into all of the above films.

About this time, I slip in a mapping exercise, using the kinds of maps you can draw on with washable pens and then wash clean. These are wonderful because each student has a wash-off map on which to trace the course of Eleanor's crusades. Each must make a legend to distinguish between the First and the Second Crusades. This is a way to check if a student really read the book, since the starting point, stops, and end point have to be labeled. Distinguishing geographical land-forms (forests, deserts, rivers, cities, grasslands, and mountains) have to be labeled. Atlases, textbooks, or any of the reference materials in the room could be used as sources of information. All five geographic themes are represented and discussed here.

Another feature that I find helpful in creating the feeling of a medieval castle in the classroom is the design and construction of shields or banners. My students and I follow a process similar to the one used by knights to design a personal crest. Using any brand of encyclopedia, looking under the topic *heraldry,* we find a list of symbols with their specific meanings and choose which one to incorporate into a shield or banner. We hang these from the ceiling via wires. They are most effective when twenty-five to thirty adorn the center spaces of our classroom.

We carry out this project in the following ways:

1. We gather materials. Each student needs one clothes hanger, two pieces of butcher paper or heavy construction paper, masking tape, glue, colored felt pens, and a handout of a photocopy from an encyclopedia, found under the heading of *heraldry.*

2. On scratch paper, we list things about ourselves that make us unique, such as hobbies, special interests, our age, the sports we play, our place in the family (e.g. second boy), our hopes for the future. In essence and without drama, these things tell a brief story about each of us.

3. We design on another piece of scratch paper a personal shield or banner by using medieval symbols when possible to express our uniquenesses. I ask students to discuss their shields with me before going on.

4. After we have finished our designs, conferenced, and made any changes, we divide our shield-banners into four to six sections and put one symbol in each. We rearrange until we are happy with the overall design and color.

5. We make final banners in the shield shape, or a rectangle with tassels on the bottom corners. Each side displays the design. I keep samples of shields from previous years, as well as the example that I made when I started this project. I use my shield as a model for the step-by-step procedures.

6. We tape one side of the shield-banner to the hanger as shown in Figure 8–2 and then glue all around the wrong side of the second design, pressing it to the wrong side of the first design and being sure that the hook of the hanger is exposed and that the design sides are out.

7. Finally, we hang the shield-banners from the ceiling.

Small-group research projects can be selected from a variety of choices The goals for these are varied. I want students to become more comfortable with public speaking, to work cooperatively with peers, to express themselves through art, and to be exposed to the science of the twelfth century. Some of the topics that students choose from that deal with the Middle Ages: famous persons, knights and chivalry, religions, pageantry, food, games (which students design and construct), fashions of the time, manners, music, architecture (students can make a facade for the door to resemble an arched Gothic doorway made of stone), inventions, and weapons (generally a favorite for the active bunch who would rather draw and make things than read).

If two groups decide to do the same subject, it's okay as long as the final projects aren't identical. A word of warning needs to be added here. When some of these projects, especially the weapons, are demonstrated by students, be sure that everybody moves to the side of the room. You definitely would not want someone to be hit by a flying object from a catapult.

Most of these projects stay in the classroom for the remainder of the unit and make colorful bulletin boards. They are displays of importance. The art and structures become part of the ongoing redecorating project as we move back in time. This is not as fast as a time machine, but it's the next best thing to one. We begin to have information about our newly emerging time period.

The vocabulary for the unit comes predominately from *A Proud Taste for Scarlet and Miniver,* but some words are taken from the textbook.

Those students who need a little more challenge get one! I meet with this group of students to discuss the assignment and divide them into two compatible groups. The assignment is as follows:

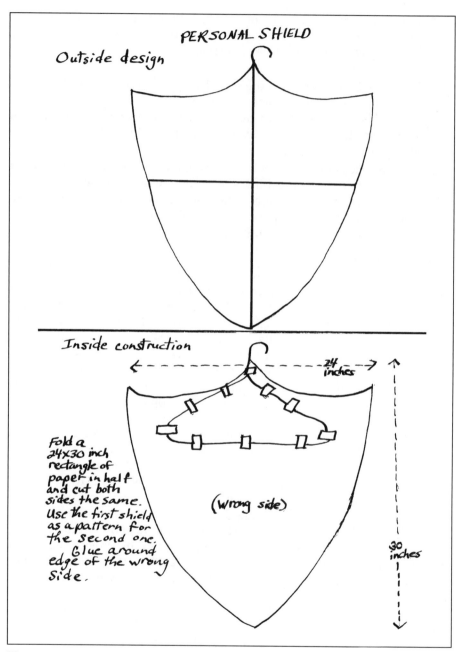

Figure 8–2

Write a simple play using a narrator (story teller). Each play is set in medieval Europe and must involve half of the class in at least walk-on roles depicting villagers going about their daily tasks. (Not everyone has to memorize lines.) There might be a scene with a farmer leading his donkey or cow to market with all kinds of action happening around him. Maybe he encounters two knights dueling in front of the manor house or a fair damsel in distress.

We can always manage to come up with some fairly authentic-looking costumes of the period. I happen to be the owner of one well-used plastic suit of armor that I share with students.They come up with the rest of the costumes that we only use on the day of our videotaping. The taping is done by whoever in my class is taking our school's video-productions class during the term when we engulf ourselves in the Middle Ages. While the writers compose, the rest of us paint student-designed scenery and listen to medieval music.

After completing the reading of Eleanor's crusade to Antioch and after sharing some of Chaucer's abridged tales (updated to modern English), it is time to assign a crusade journal written in first person but dated some time in the twelfth century.

I tell students that when I read these journals I want to feel that I am in the twelfth century and seeing and experiencing what they imagined when they created this piece of literature. We brainstorm about the sights, sounds, smells, sensations (both touch and emotional). I inquire:

> What kind of animals do you see along the way, both domestic and wild? (Remember hunting scenes from some of the reading we have done.) What are you wearing? What is your mode of transportation? What items do you carry along for food, clothing, tools, weapons, and gifts to share with people you meet along the way? Where do you sleep overnight? What kinds of social activities do you share with other people while resting? (Remember that these people did not bathe much, if at all. They did not have laundry facilities or garbage service.)

I post this information on a chart in the front of the room and ask my students to get started while all of this information is hot in their minds. I tell them to write as if they were on a ten-day crusade, traveling as far as they think they can cover in ten days. Their destinations depend on the mode and dependability of the transportation that they choose. If the mule dies along the way because of the failure to bring adequate food, then they won't get as far as someone else, but they certainly can have a very exciting story involving the death of the mule. This is not a race to see who travels the greatest distance, but a challenge to see who can help a reader experience the adventure vicariously. I invite students to illustrate their crusades and to draw maps of the routes that they followed. At this point, the students are at the starting gate and ready to go. I can almost hear the wheels turning and grinding as the writing begins and the dictionaries, thesauri, and other reference materials appear on desks. I am available to help the students who need assistance or who just wish to share. When the journals are finished, they are passed around and read. It is a wonderful way to share and compare events that impressed someone else. Every student has a partner to trade with for editing. The final copies are turned in to me for evaluation. I read them for content, grammar, spelling, and punctuation.

I usually take the students on two field trips during this unit. The first one is to the Portland Art Museum, which is a bus trip over the river and across town. This allows a lot of city viewing since it is a half hour of travel each way. I ask students to look for particular things to reinforce the five themes of geography by using a guide sheet to be checked off as we go. The second excursion happens about midway through the Middle Ages unit, when we bus again to a Gothic-style church. It is most impressive, especially when I can arrange for Gothic music to be played (live or taped) while the students and I contemplate the interior of the church. Much discussion always follows upon our return to the school.

At this point, we put together a retrieval chart comparing the present times to the Middle Ages. We start with a very long sheet of butcher paper that we extend across the front of the room and tape to the chalkboard. Then, we divide the paper in half, one half for National Geographic's "Five Themes of Geography" and the other half for cultural comparisons (see Figure 8–3). We begin by brainstorming all of the key categories that we had compiled about Portland's geographical and cultural present at the beginning of this unit. I list everything suggested by the students on the overhead projector. Duplicate suggestions are combined into one category before writing them on the paper. Ultimately, the cultural titles will be "Government," "Education," "Religion," "Food," "Occupation," "Medicine," "Dress," and "Manners." A couple of volunteers write the five geographic themes (location, place, human-environment interaction, movement, and region), count out the number of titles, divide the paper according to Figure 8–2, and write the titles as headings across the top of the blank paper.

Next, the students select a subject, divide into groups, and quickly research their chosen topic. Each group elects a leader to keep them on task and to record the information that they find in the appropriate space on the chart. This is followed by the same procedure for information on the Middle Ages to be placed in the columns for comparison.

A retrieval chart is an easy method of pulling together vast amounts of information to be assimilated and compiled into a simple, yet meaningful and organized, table. Students seem to like this because they do it all by themselves. My role during this activity is to act as the facilitator.

Middle Ages (1100s-1200s)	Portland (1994)		
		Government	Cultural Themes
		Education	
		Religion	
		Food	
		Occupations	
		Dress	
		Medicine	
		Manners	
		Inventions	
		Location	National Geographic Five Themes of Geography
		Place	
technology housing Architecture climate	Technology housing climate Architecture	Human-Environment Interaction	
		Movement	
		Region	

Figure 8-3

Our Middle Ages newspaper is always one of the most popular activities of the unit. The students divide themselves into compatible groups of their choice, usually three or four to a group. We skim through the local newspaper to make note of the sections and kinds of stories within each section. Students list various kinds of information found in the paper: news articles, society stories, sports articles, editorials, comics, human-interest stories, science-and-technology news, and advertising. A front-page news article that might be found in a Middle Ages newspaper could be about brave knights coming home from battle, but not without casualties. A society-news article could be an announcement about the coming open house, tea, and flower show to be held at the manor house or church. A sports article might be an announcement for the Sunday jousting to be held in the local field. Another sports article might inform all of the results of the previous week's jousting contest. An article about a local inventor's newest invention would be found under the science-and-technology section. An editorial could be an invitation to all citizens to attend a meeting to organize volunteer neighborhood patrols to catch the bandits who have been assaulting and stealing from local people.

Some students use hand-lettered Old English or Gothic-style lettering for headlines or draw illustrations for their articles. Most of the papers include a weather forecast. The completed newspapers are displayed for all to read and enjoy.

Sometime late in the unit, when the classroom is thoroughly redecorated as a twelfth-century castle, and preferably on the coldest day of the year (since I always teach this unit during winter term), I turn off the thermostat before going home on a given night. The next morning, the classroom is as cold as the outdoors. I make sure that I dress warmly, and I get permission from the principal before doing this activity. I place smokey candles and oil lamps around the room for lighting and a little ambiance. When everyone is seated and tired of complaining about the cold, I start a discussion about what it was like living in a twelfth-century castle with cold, damp floors and walls with no glass in the windows.

Even with all of our colorful artwork and elaborate decorations, it is still very cold. So after the students get their coats from their lockers and the thermostat is reset and the candles blown out, I pour my students some warm cocoa to thaw them out a little before they take down their creations and we begin another unit of study.

One last but important activity that I do here, while sipping cocoa and listening to medieval music, is to return to the students the papers on which they listed everything that they knew about the Middle Ages on the first day of the unit. I ask them to draw a line under the last entry and then to list everything they have learned during this unit of study. The results are never too surprising but almost always show how worthwhile this unit has been.

BIBLIOGRAPHY

Brown, Asa. 1983. *Metropolitan Museum of Art Activity Book.* New York: Metropolitan Museum of Art.

Caselli, Giovanni. 1986. *The Everyday Life of a Medieval Monk.* New York: Peter Bedrick Books in agreement with MacDonald & Co.

Chatani, Masahiro. 1988. *Paper Magic.* Tokyo: Ondorisha.

Hallam, Elizabeth, ed. 1986. *The Plantaganet Chronicles.* New York: Phoebe Phillips Editions of Weidenfeld & Nicholson.

———. 1987. *Four Gothic Kings.* New York: Phoebe Phillips Editions of Weiden & Nicholson.

Komroff, Manvel. 1964. *Charlemagne.* New York: Julianne Messner.

Konigsburg, E. L. 1973. *A Proud Taste for Scarlet and Miniver.* MA: Halliday Lithograph Corp.

Malcolmson, Anne, ed. 1964. *A Taste of Chaucer.* NY: Harcourt, Brace & World.

Riordan, James. 1982. *Tales of King Arthur.* New York: Rand, McNally & Co.

Scarry, Huck. 1984. *Looking into the Middle Ages.* New York: Harper & Row.

Chapter 9
Using Fish to Teach Geography

KRISTEL MCCUBBIN

I couldn't help thinking as I stood there on the bank of the Sandy River that *this is everything teaching is when it's at its very best*. I was watching 114 students doing the "stalking fox walk" to the salmon-spawning viewing area in Oxbow Park outside of Portland, Oregon. They were all kinds of middle schoolers: from talented and gifted students to gang wannabe's. It was a gray October day, a little chilly. It was the last week of work for the naturalist hired to answer questions for the people that came to the salmon-viewing area. The students were dressed for the weather: Daniel in all his fishing clothes and Adam in his sweats and starter jacket. They were excited even though we weren't sure we'd see any salmon.

When the students arrived at the viewing area, they continued to watch quietly, patiently waiting for a pair of binoculars, pointing out to one another the few spawning salmon that they saw. There weren't as many salmon as there could have been since it was the end of the spawning season; this wasn't hot Wild Kingdom footage. But the students had been prepared for this journey, and they cared about what they were looking for. They had studied the life cycle of the salmon. They knew that these salmon had struggled hard to return to the river to lay eggs and then to die. They understood that in the river was the beginning and end of the salmon life cycle and that they were fortunate to see this since more and more salmon habitats are disappearing.

After ten minutes, I lost four students who went to sit on the hillside. Not bad odds when you have 114 and are trying to share ten pairs of fishing glasses and four pairs of binoculars.And what brought on this phenomenon? Good lessons that had a purpose: lessons on a topic that the students cared about. The students had enough knowledge of what they were see-ing to assume ownership of the topic. They were ready to have an experi-ence that would be the reality of what they had learned in the classroom. This field trip came in the middle of the unit in which the students were learning about salmon habitats and the reasons that the habitats were dis-appearing. Now they were getting to see a healthy, protected habitat in action.

The topic had been chosen as part of a thematic unit on community. It represented a current community issue that paralleled the spotted-owl is-sue without being the hot political issue that the spotted owl was in the state of Oregon at that time. I wanted a topic that would have the same components that the spotted-owl issue had: conflict between people's needs, on the one hand, and the natural habitat, on the other, and an issue that would have to bring together different private groups and public agencies to make final decisions. Little did I know that Spring Chinook would be added to the endangered species list less than a year later. And that this issue would be covered extensively in the local media. The salmon issue is even more far reaching than the spotted-owl issue because its envi-ronmental effects cover a larger land area as well as water rights and laws. It also involves Native American rights and treaties and hydroelectric-energy issues.

This unit of study also came out of an advanced geography institute I had taken doing field studies of water and watershed management (through my state geography alliance)and several conversations with a friend of mine who was an avid salmon and steelhead fisherman. How often do we find as teachers that as we start talking to people about what we are doing, we find more and more connections and resources?

The conversations with my friend led me to organizations active in the field, such as the Northwest Steelheaders Association, Oregon Trout, Ore-gon Fish and Wildlife, U.S. Fish and Wildlife, The Army Corps of Engi-neers, and the Columbia River Intertribal Council. One thing that I have learned when I work with current public issues is that many of my best re-sources are public and nonprofit agencies. They will send materials and speakers. This can require a lot of legwork for teachers, but it makes the topic come alive for students.

Many of my students enjoyed becoming experts on an issue that was be-ing extensively covered in our local media. I often overheard conversations about how they had taught something to their parents or their adult friends about the salmon issue. So what does this have to do with geography? Everything!!!! Thanks to the work of the National Geographic Society and the National Council for Geographic Education, teachers are being taught to teach geography by using the "Five Themes of Geography": location, place, human-environment interaction, movement, and region. (See a further description of these themes in the preceding chapter.)

These five themes serve as a template for any unit that teachers might want to put together. They give teachers a structured way to infuse geography into their existing curriculum. Students are woefully illiterate when it comes to geography. Students need to learn geography in order to understand their neighborhoods, their town, their country, the world. If they understand physical geography, then they know where places and people are and how the place affects the people. If they understand cultural geography, they understand why people choose to live in a particular place and how they might affect the place. Everything comes back to geography, whether it is how to get to the store and find the fruit or what is needed for salmon to spawn and how people are affecting the salmon's habitat. The themes are an easy way for teachers to incorporate the teaching of geography into any subject area.Using the salmon unit, I will explain how the five themes can be woven into a unit of study that is also interdisciplinary in scope.

Location teaches students that a place can be identified by absolute location and relative location. Examples of absolute location are address and latitude and longitude. Relative location means how location can be described in relation to other physical or cultural features. This part of location came into play with the salmon study. Students learned that salmon are associated with the northwestern part of North America because this is where the salmon's habitat is present and where salmon have been a part of natural history for thousands of years. The students learned that salmon need the right water temperature and river conditions in order to reproduce. Anadromous fish need the right conditions to get out to sea and back since that's what anadromous fish do—and salmon are anadromous fish.

The theme of *Place* takes location one step further. The theme of place asks, What's unique about this place? It includes both physical characteristics and human characteristics of a particular place. Sometimes, it is simple: If I say, "Eiffel Tower," people know immediately that I am talking about Paris. Or it can be more complicated: If we talk about something like the "Trail of Tears," we are talking about both a physical route and a devastating human and cultural event for the Cherokee, Seminole, Chickasaw, Choctaw, and Cree peoples. In the case of the salmon, it can be said that salmon are associated with the Northwest and are a totem or symbol of this area. In our unit, we studied Native American legends and Native American art about the salmon, and we heard from Native Americans who came in to speak to our classes.

Students began to understand that salmon have been a part of the Northwest long before humans were. They came to understand the sacredness of salmon for the native peoples.

Human-Environmental Interaction refers to the way in which people affect their environment and the way in which the environment has affected human development. In the salmon study, we examined statistics on salmon counts over the years and the various changes in habitat that have caused the decline in salmon populations. Students also put together their own plan for saving the salmon and then compared it the Canadian plan, which has been in place since the 1970s.

Students were held accountable for consideration of displaced workers and other economic hardships created by their plan. Not all the students' solutions were realistic, and they were often frustrated by this limitation. This frustration gave them a taste of why the salmon problem is a hard issue to resolve in the real world. Students would simply stop fishing and get rid of or alter dams. These things may eventually happen, but part of the reality of these ideas is the economic effect.

Movement includes the movement of goods, services, and ideas that affect cultural and physical geography. Transportation of people and goods has brought ideas and materials that have changed landscapes and cultures. The Conestoga wagon and the idea of "Manifest Destiny" both fit under the theme of movement and were both instrumental in the forming of the continental United States. In the salmon study, we looked at how barge movement on the Columbia River works in tandem with the building of dams. We also learned that most of the dams on the Columbia River were built in the 1930s when the idea of harnessing nature was thought to be a statement of human progress. We looked at the building of the Dalles Dam on the Columbia River that flooded Celilo Falls, an area that native people had fished for generations. We contemplated whether the dam would be built today with our current societal values.

The last theme that my students and I discussed was *Region*. Regions are determined in a number of different ways. They can be imposed boundaries, as with countries, states, and counties. They can be geographic areas determined by climate and land-forms, such as the Rocky Mountain region of the United States and Canada. Or they can be cultural regions, like Little Italy in New York City. In the case of the salmon, we looked at how salmon have affected and continue to affect the northwestern region of North America. Salmon contribute to the economy and to the culture of our area. The federal government's policy to save the threatened and endangered species of salmon will affect my student's lives directly as the citizenry of this region.

While I have tried to use the salmon unit as a way to illustrate the five themes of geography, please note that they are not laid out as lesson plans.

There are many activities I do in the classroom that I have not discussed here. My purpose is to discuss the five themes of geography and to show how easily they can be incorporated into the classroom.

Most people see geography as only physical geography. They see it as rote learning—boring to learn and boring to teach. Teachers can also become frustrated with a world where borders and the names of countries change on an increasingly rapid basis. What is so exciting about using the five themes of geography in teaching is that they can make geography interesting and real for students and teachers. If we must "Think globally and act locally," as one popular bumper sticker asks us to do, we must find a way to make the world outside of students' local areas real places for students. Using the five themes of geography can help to do this.

In this information age in which television brings us the latest news from around the world and computer satellite hookups are the "ham radio" of the next century, we have to face the idea that the world is becoming a global village. More and more decisions are being made by groups of countries such as the United Nations (UN) and the North Atlantic Treaty Organization (NATO) rather than by one or two superpower nations. Students have to understand geography if they are to understand why things are happening the way they are and why countries make the decisions that they do. They need to know what the five themes can help us to learn about different areas of the world and how those themes are woven together to create a whole tapestry of an area of the world, not just its name, continent, and capitol.

The best thing about studying the salmon issue is that my students have continued to talk about this issue in the context of their new unit, the future, as it was discussed and as decisions were being made by our local government. When my students contemplate the future of Portland, they want the Willamette River that runs through the city to be clean enough so that there can be salmon in it. When the Yakima Indian Nation started to fish the Willamette to reclaim native fishing rights, the students reported having seen this on the news. When the local paper ran an article on the salmon issue, students showed me the news in our classroom copy of the paper and even cut it out of their newspaper at home and brought it in.

I believe that students have truly internalized this issue as demonstrated in the following piece of writing by Brian, a seventh grader.

Soul of the River

It is said that the salmon are the basis of reality and that their souls bind the universe and our lives together.

So it is also said that we must keep the salmon happy, maintain the water temperature and help them on their journey through the rivers and seas.

Because the salmon are such kingly animals, they leave their souls in the rivers where they are born. The souls give lessons to live by, and are the fabric of creation for everyone. The salmon travel down the rivers, guided by their own goodness.

They then live their lives in the ocean as predators and prey. Finally when they are old, they return to the rivers as kings.

They come to collect their souls from the gravel of the river bank. Their souls were a sign of the promise that they made as youths. With these souls they can journey to heaven in harmony with the earth.

So if you ever catch a salmon, release it. For it is loaning its soul to you, and the soul without the salmon is corrupt. We must save the salmon's soul for other things.

Most exciting for me is the empowerment that I see in my students as they discuss this public issue intelligently and thoroughly. Knowledge is power. My students understand that power; and in a democratic society, I can think of nothing more important for its children to understand.

This was most clear to me when my students did their culminating project. I started by putting them into special-interest groups that would be affected by decisions relating to the salmon: loggers, fisherman, hydroelectric power, industry, and environmentalists. Each group came up with a position statement for their group. The groups were then reshuffled so that the new groups each had one representative from each special-interest group. Each of these groups put together a salmon plan for the Northwest. The best elements of each plan were put into a final letter to Oregon's United States Senators and Representatives shown here:

Dear

Our class of sixth, seventh, and eighth graders have been studying the salmon for many months. We have studied the situation thoroughly, and feel that we are experts on the problem.

We have traveled to Oxbow Park to observe the salmon in their habitat. We have created paper salmon that are now hanging from our ceiling. We have done many current event activities. Finally, three guest speakers have talked to us, each expressing different points of view.

As a class, we have come up with a plan concerning the main industries that directly affect the salmon life cycle. Here is a summarization of our plan:

For the loggers, we have come up with A Burlap Plan. [See Figure 9–1]. We also thought they would be willing to stop logging near the streams. They will lose money and will have to fire workers. These workers, along with any others that volunteer, will be retrained by a program set up by the environmentalists.

We have decided that the Bonneville Power Administration should shut off turbines during the salmon runs. We agree that

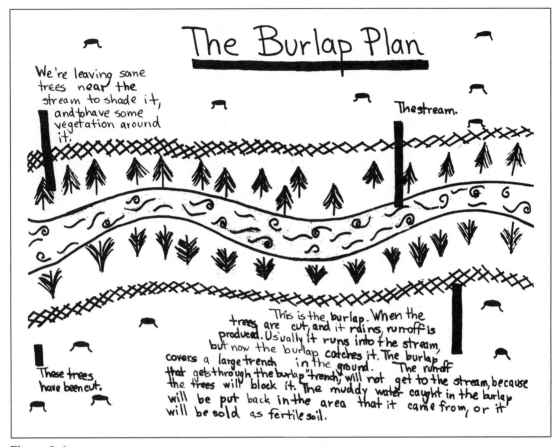

The Burlap Plan

We're leaving some trees near the stream to shade it, and to have some vegetation around it.

The stream.

These trees have been cut.

This is the burlap. When the trees are cut, and it rains, runoff is produced. Usually it runs into the stream, but now the burlap catches it. The burlap covers a large trench in the ground. The runoff that gets through the burlap "trench" will not get to the stream, because the trees will block it. The muddy water caught in the burlap will be put back in the area that it came from, or it will be sold as fertile soil.

Figure 9–1

every dam should have a fish ladder. We want to put screens or nets around the turbines.

The sports and commercial fishermen should make smaller fishing nets. We also think that the salmon catch limit should be lowered.

For the aluminum industry we propose to raise the deposit to ten cents for recyclables. We think that there should be a federal incentive to use recycled aluminum. We should increase technology!

Finally, the environmentalists are going to set up a program to retrain the loggers and fishermen who have lost their jobs. The environmentalists will also create an adopt-a-fish program to raise money.

We hope you will give our plan careful consideration. Please let us know what you think of our ideas on the salmon issue. We invite you to come and talk with us directly if you have time.

Sincerely,
Ms. McCubbin's Class

The issue of salmon habitat provided a useful entry point for teaching geography in my classroom. Public issues can be at the heart of geography instruction in middle school social studies classrooms.

Part Three

CHANGING AND REFLECTING

Chapter 10
Chance Favors the Prepared Mind: An Administrator Reflects on Change

MICHELANN ORTLOFF

T he I-Team (Interdisciplinary Team)—a radical and progressive, teacher-designed and -implemented program—is the end product of a five-year process that started slowly with the integration of language arts and social studies into three-period instructional blocks. It is the end result of five years of change that was and continues to be both exhilarating and painful. It is the end result of many hours of staff discussions that sometimes disintegrated and sometimes continues to disintegrate into arguments, punctuated with a constant and wrenching soul search about what is best for children and their families.

It is the also the end result of five years of my learning, as an administrator, about what change does and what it means and how it works and doesn't work. I had to let go of some things and embrace others, like letting go of control and embracing the power of teachers who exemplify what happens when there is a firm connection between heart and mind. I had to learn the balance between my own wishes, hopes, and dreams, on the one hand, and those of others who form the tiny culture of a school.

Two years ago, I left the school where I was part of a complex process of restructuring two programs. The early years were spent adopting whole language principles and detracking reading instruction. It was not nearly as difficult as the year before I left, which was spent helping to launch the Interdisciplinary Team. This team was to be composed of four teachers and four classrooms of heterogeneous, mixed age groups of sixth through eighth graders. Students would stay with their teachers for all three years of middle school.

The teachers designed the curriculum as interdisciplinary units based on broad themes that integrated the language arts, science, math, and social studies. The teachers' plan included students' designing their own courses of study with a particular emphasis on interdisciplinary projects. Active research would reach into the community, so that students could study issues that affect them and the world outside of the classroom. Students would be expected to function in teams: The weaker members would be coached by the stronger, and the stronger would learn to articulate their ideas to a wider audience. Each lesson would integrate social skills into its content, so that intellectual goals were meshed with social and emotional ones. Cooperation rather than competition would be the implicit message contained in all work of the group. Students in this volatile, peer-oriented age team would have the chance to learn not only how to work together but also how to include the often excluded and celebrate the strengths of collaborative thinking.

Evaluation would be a combination of student self-assessment through self-reflective essays, narrative evaluations written by the teachers, video records of students' growth over time, parent assessment of their children's learning, as well as portfolio and performance assessment. The teachers planned to design curriculum throughout the year by meeting during the day in double-planning periods. The students would leave the I-Team for two periods so that they could take elective classes and their teachers could plan.

These four teachers had hammered out a new structure for middle school that was based on everything they knew of young adolescents, based on their analysis of research on the development of language and literacy and state of the art assessment and evaluation. They had also engaged in a continuing process of asking themselves the essential questions that should direct all planning for the classroom: What are we doing, and why are we doing it?

I thought of the past, of my part in helping change a middle school from one model to another and my part in creating the present model. What had I learned about the processs of nurturing growth in an institution, in people, in myself? How could I take what I'd learned and use it in a new role, continuing to change and grow in my own understanding of leadership? My questions frame my story.

In August 1987, I became an assistant principal at a middle school in Portland, Oregon. I had been a classroom teacher for thirteen years, teaching children in grades kindergarten through eight as well as adults. Sellwood Middle School had been a school with a bad reputation. People said that the school had created two programs: one program for the bright, college-bound children of middle-class parents, another program for students who were wise in the ways of the streets but not successful in school. People even said that was the way some parents wanted it. Those who could not obtain transfers for their children to attend a middle school in another part of the city did not want their children to be in heterogeneous classes.

I found the school an interesting mix of students from a variety of socioeconomic backgrounds. The structure of the school was another common thing: a junior high frame forced onto the wacky, changing forms of adolescent youngsters. Not a middle school, but a high school clone where students moved to different teachers, different classes every forty-two minutes. The students' energy and suspension between adulthood and childhood came screaming out of those bell-defined periods into the hallways. Some of the students managed to manipulate the system, so that the hallways became their real school; the class periods captured only the already successful and school socialized or the merely fearful.

I was selected because of my background in whole language and because of the desire of the principal and the "Director of Instruction" (who is responsible for all of the schools that feed into one of the many high schools in Portland) to make programmatic changes. Whole language had been adopted as the philosophical foundation of Portland Public School's language arts program. The progressive Director of Instruction wanted no more ability grouping in her cluster of eight elementary and two middle schools. Children in grades one through eight would no longer be divided for reading and math into separate tracks, the Blue Birds and the Buzzards, *the haves* and *the have-nots*.

"Chance favors the prepared mind," said Louis Pasteur, and I believe it. I had to acknowledge that this change in my status was a desired one, this favoring of chance. It was an acknowledgment of the serendipitous combination of my professional and personal experiences.

Sellwood was forced to change from the top, perhaps the worst way to change anything. The top, in this case, was a powerful Director of Instruction with a deep concern for the academic success of all children. She read everything she could find about the development of language in children and argued the points of literacy development with teachers, principals, and curriculum specialists. She knew that perpetuating a system that tracked young children was to perpetuate the chains of inequity. This did not forgive her the criticism of teachers who had no say in what they were supposed to carry out.

The old way of bringing about curricular change is to pronounce, "You either do it or else." But in this change, I had to agree, the Director of Instruction was right. Sometimes, change comes from the radical altering of what is known and comfortable and even right by abstract ethical and moral standards. When this happens, it takes someone who acts like a wave that rocks the boat and arouses the sleepy passengers from the lull of the status quo.

Prior to this mandated, boat-rocking change, Sellwood Middle School teachers had been divided into teams by subject matter. Teachers referred to themselves as the "Math Department" and the "Health and Science Department" or as an "Elective" or "Block Teacher." The language arts teachers were the "Block Teachers." This meant that students spent two periods with the same teacher. This plan represented the best thinking at the time about a middle school program.

Students were grouped by ability into one period of reading and regrouped for two periods of language arts and social studies. The idea was to group students heterogeneously for language arts and social studies. However, with the difficulties of scheduling, these combined periods were not truly heterogeneous. No one questioned the odd grouping of subjects. Reading was isolated from language arts. Social studies was integrated with language arts only because the same students sat in the same classroom with the same teacher. But subjects were rigidly separated by sections in teachers' lesson-plan and grade books.

The Chapter One program, a pull-out program for remedial instruction in reading and math, dwindled to nothing by my second year at Sellwood. It relied heavily on computer-assisted, skill-based instruction. Teachers complained about the scheduling for their Chapter One students. Some Chapter One students had to be pulled out of social studies rather than language arts for their trip to the computer lab on the lower floor. This caused a great deal of bickering about scheduling for "pull-out" programs such as Chapter One. Since reading was ability grouped already, this was not a problem; however, students received little or no direct reading instruction in the Chapter One lab.

Assessment beyond standardized tests was minimal. Teacher observation, so crucial to a student's learning profile, was marginal. In fact, students were mostly grouped by socioeconomic status. This was exemplified by my discovery that Shawn, a sixth grader with a bad attitude, a giant skateboard, and several earrings, was scheduled into the lowest sections of math and reading although he had the highest standardized test score for his grade level in math, and the second highest in reading.

Students who were not eligible for Chapter One but were still considered "low" by teacher assessment stayed with the classroom teacher during reading. They received direct instruction from a basal text that served as an alternate to the "regular" district reading text. Predictably, the alternate text had controlled vocabulary and mangled replications of "high-interest" stories. Just as predictably, these stories had little or nothing to do with the lives of the students reading them. If students in these classes—the "low" students and the identified Chapter One students—were ever in a group together, they managed to receive double and even triple doses of the same skill-and-drill approach. All of the strategies that independent readers use—semantics, syntax, background knowledge, and graphophonemics—were not taught to students. The old "read the story and answer the comprehension questions at the end" was virtually the only approach to teaching literary analysis. Students did not select their own novels to read because, according to teachers, they couldn't or wouldn't read. Lost was the notion of reading as a habit and skill to practice and refine as well as a passion developed through choice and connection. "Low" students had to master a virtual mechanics toolbox of skills before they could ever, in fact, simply read for pleasure. Teachers did not connect their own excitement about reading and their own analytical strategies to what students could learn about reading. These teachers might not have considered that motive and engagement are the single most important ingredients in learning.

The "high" students read novels, short stories from a district collection, and the basal text for their grade level. The district's adoption of whole language as the philosophical foundation of language arts instruction meant a renewed interest in literature. But Sellwood's literature-based technique was "basalized" by the skill packages that accompanied the novel sets provided by the district.

Two teachers, both past participants in the Oregon Writing Project, had incorporated role plays and "quickwrite" responses into their "high" and "average" readers' instruction. But most of the teachers continued to rely on the recipe of instructional tasks in the basal sets: introduce the vocabulary for the story, read the story silently, answer the comprehension questions at the end, and participate in a class discussion to see where students had erred in their answers. Skill sheets from workbooks or teachers' guides dominated the students' independent work. Reading novels together presented some difficult challenges of how to read a book as a group, how to keep the students from going ahead or lagging behind, and how to teach the "skills" that teachers insisted were necessary.

One of my tasks was to build on this renewed interest in moving from the basal reader and creating a literature-based reading program. Another was to talk to teachers about integrating social studies content into literary themes. There was little, if any, consideration of literature as a nest for current social themes or as a pathway to enrich and enlarge a child's moral life, creating empathy for diversity. If we are to develop critically-literate citizens, able to sift through mountains of information and make informed decisions, then we have to find a way to connect students to the world. I wanted teachers to look out the window and see the world instead of being so conscientious about following the table of contents in the social studies textbook.

All of this new talk about integration of language arts and social studies sparked debates. Teachers asked how they could do this. Teachers saw novels as an add-on. They were concerned that they couldn't cover the social studies curriculum as it was and have time to read novels. In addition, teachers could see why *Johnny Tremain* related to social studies content, but thought that *Roll of Thunder, Hear My Cry* was a stretch. And there simply were no novels for the "low" readers.

The language arts program at that time contained virtually no writing, except for that dusty dinosaur, "The Five-Paragraph Essay," complete with stacks of index cards with research cribbed from the *Encyclopedia Brittanica*. I do not mean to imply that the program was universally poor. Some students had an opportunity to write their autobiography with photographs and interviews of relatives. Some students were assigned a social studies research paper, the form of which looked exactly like my own eighth-grade research paper. The content, like mine, was completely unoriginal. It represented a subtle altering of an encyclopedia text. Students rarely if ever participated in a writing workshop or selected their own topics, shared their writing or engaged in active research about social issues. They rarely read as writers or collaborated on pieces or offered support to their peers. Reading and writing were barely holding hands.

Teachers were not intentionally ignorant about instructional strategies to teach a wide range of levels or unwilling to examine ways to connect reading, writing, and social studies. Teachers were receptive, at first, to different views of instruction. I think they had never been offered different information by administrators, most of whom probably formed their ideas about curriculum and instruction from their own junior high experiences. What these teachers had gathered to construct their programs was a mishmash of beliefs derived from personal experience, the odd workshop or two, and devotion to packaged programs. They were required to form an instructional program based on "keeping parents happy" and "maintaining high standards." But an open discussion among the entire faculty of what, or whose, high standards had never occurred. Teachers had not been given the opportunity to discuss the learning outcomes that they wanted for all students. They had not been engaged as professionals who had opportunities to construct curriculum, question practices, and not be professionally assaulted every time they tried something new and different. The teachers at Sellwood had simply never been asked what they wanted to know and had never discussed what was important to teach. They certainly didn't feel free to ask questions about what they didn't know. Not surprisingly, a climate of fear about weaknesses in instruction and beliefs had seeped into this school. I sensed a great hunkering down behind barriers and a curious hoarding of knowledge.

I wondered if this fear that teachers felt had been transmitted to students. I thought hard about the importance of classroom experience to administrators and how instructional leadership had to come both from teachers and principals. The only way that a community could be built was by creating a safe place where people could ask questions, take risks, try things, fail, try new things, succeed, and continue to reflect on practices. This required a strong collaboration between teachers and administrators, not to mention a clear explanation to parents of goals and expectations, with reasons why. These necessary ingredients of learning were important for the adults in the community as well as the children.

Our first time together set the tone for how change would or would not occur. I asked this group to write about their doubts and beliefs about whole language and interdisciplinary teaching. As it turned out, this writing activity would set the tone for our years together. I looked at this group and realized the enormity of the change in my professional life.

The prior year at the same time, I had been creating a community for reading and writing with my third graders in an elementary school in Portland. I had been struggling with my own doubts and beliefs about developing literacy. I did the same thing every year as a classroom teacher. I met my students, I mined my heart, and I thought hard about what we would or would not be together. I had met the doubts of parents whose own success had been in traditional classrooms, but I also felt stronger than ever about my beliefs.

Daily, I saw these third grade children developing their own inner voices as writers, broadening their reading choices, and connecting with their city and the world as sources for exploration, discovery, and power. Their questions came from their reading and writing, from our discussions, and from a broader view of the powers and responsibilities of citizenship.

Writing in my third grade had been the center of our process of coming to know the world. We read as writers, we related as writers, and we learned the power of words to change the world. When we studied the environment, we were obliged to write letters to local agencies, neighborhood activists, and the federal government. When we studied the City of

Portland, we were moved to write to city commissioners, the mayor, and the Park Bureau. When we studied genres of literature, we wrote to our favorite authors and received cherished, handwritten letters from Roald Dahl, Beverly Cleary, and Ursula LeGuin. Our classroom visitors were an odd lot of city bureaucrats, writers, an architect, district instructional specialists, high school teachers, a friend who was a cook and caterer, and the principal. They all talked about the importance of writing to their lives and to their jobs. One day in May, as I wrote the daily schedule of subjects and activities on the board, Gabe, without a whiff of sarcasm, said, "Ms. Ortloff, why don't you just put down 'Writing: 9:00 to 3:30?' "

Now, I looked at these middle school teachers, and I felt a curious combination of the ghosts of past and present. I wondered which of these specters would finally inhabit our souls. I asked myself: How can I move from being a teacher of children to being a teacher of men and women? How can I be an agent for change and still demonstrate for the collective experience of these people? What obstacles might await me? Would we doubt, or would we believe?

We wrote about our doubts and beliefs for our new instructional plan. Before I had finished writing a sentence, the teachers' rustling told me that they were done. I asked them to share their writing. They said nothing. I read my beliefs. One teacher volunteered her doubts about whole language practices in general. Another joined with her belief that skills were the foundation of language arts. Students, she said, should not write until they knew how to spell, capitalize, punctuate, or paragraph. Students should memorize a large set of phonograms before reading for pleasure. One teacher talked about how she couldn't possibly use the novels with social themes in her classroom: They were too controversial and were offensive to her. Then there was silence. Finally, one veteran teacher read his piece. He said he'd seen it all, every "swing of the pendulum" from one new set of "standards and expectations" to another. This one, he said, looked every bit like the "language experience" push of the sixties. He was not cynical, only wary. In soft Southern syllables, he said, "But if this is right for kids, then I'm for it. What can we do?" There was an uncomfortable shifting in seats.

All of the teachers wanted what was best for kids, but they were not at all convinced that whole language and interdisciplinary teaching were the answers. They had their own belief systems, though some did not articulate what they were, and they had their own large doubts about my beliefs. But to their credit, they were willing to listen. How could I develop answers about integrating the subjects that had always been separate but equal? Did I really have the answers? If there were any, we'd have to find them together.

Over the years as a public school teacher, I had developed a set of beliefs about why we must design schools that encourage the development of critical literacy. I believe that schools have a responsibilty to engage students in the world as active participants who ask questions about what they find and to create students who learn how to research answers. I did not want to be a teacher in a system that produced people terrified of reading more than a paragraph and, therefore, terrified of wrestling with the increasingly difficult dilemmas that confront us as a nation and a culture. I wanted to help children be the agents of change in a difficult world. I believed in them; I believed in the power of people to revise their lives and, by so doing, revise the world. This was how I tried to live my life as an adult learner. Using reading and writing to research and know the world is natural to me.

Children, like all human beings, are meaning makers, and language is used for communication. The functions of language are what attach children to the world. Their mastery of it is a lifelong thing. Reading and writing are the core practices of human beings who are trying to make sense of piles of information. Information is the content of the world: people, their ideas, and institutions. And information changes daily.

But I had no clear answers about how to help teachers change their beliefs about how students learn, and I certainly didn't know, at that time, how to help them break the structures that confine them and their students. The practices and structures that we mutually faced were tracking, formal grammar instruction, drill-for-skill computer programs, writing only to show learning rather than to learn, and reading stories without social context. Finally, there was also the relentless pressure of upper-middle-class parents to force the school to be like their memories, the crucible for the material success of their youngsters.

I also knew that literacy should not be confined to the powerful, to the majority. It should be available to everyone on an equal basis. I wanted all children to have access to the richness of their own language and literature. I thought that achieving this goal was necessary if we were to achieve the true goals of a democracy. I thought that students educated in this way would become citizens eager to know their world, unafraid to read, write, think, and analyze. Our job, I thought, was to help youngsters see their crucial roles in our adult world.

The fact is teachers sometimes present in their own classrooms a replication of their own education: a conservative pull toward compliance to authority and power. Most teachers were and are very successful in a traditionally-structured school, and all of us are tempted to return to this familiar design even if we chafe at the constraints once imposed upon us.

Since most of us did well, we submerge our doubting selves and comply with the power structure. We see this as the path to success. This is one of the reasons why we do not encourage our children to question authority. It is also an important reason why change in schools is slow to occur.

One of the essential components of changing the structure of schools is creating a community for adults as well as students. The daily rush of making school a proper nest for youngsters necessitates forgetting ourselves. There is little time to talk, to have a professional or personal conversation that lasts longer than it takes some hallway bell to ring. There is not time to argue for our beliefs and have our colleagues argue for theirs in a way that may lead to consensus and shared values. There is no time for settling in with your journal or a book to record the mysterious course of the day, ruminate about the general magic of the time when something really works, or puzzle through the anxiety when it doesn't. A teacher's day is a roller-coaster ride of duties, demands, creations, intrusion, and disappointments. It is trying for personal confirmation and succumbing to self-recrimination. Teachers' days allow little space for agonizing over change, professional and private. We do not have techniques to break down walls that separate us, and we rarely share the hard-won wisdom of our classroom experiences.

The answer may be creating a culture of writing and writing to learn across many disciplines. Creating a culture for writing can also create a friendly place for both adults and children. My friend, essayist Kim Stafford, says we all need to tell what we almost know. And when we do that, we almost know ourselves and others.

The first thing that I did was to ask one of the eighth-grade teachers if she would be willing to coteach a children's literature class. I suggested that we teach the students about good children's literature and then help them write and illustrate their own children's books. When they were done with their books, we'd bus them around to all of our "feeder" elementary schools to read their books aloud to kindergartners through fifth graders. There were many things we would all gain by doing this. Students would

- function as real writers writing for a specific audience
- read outstanding children's books
- study and analyze a literary form
- have a chance to draw and color and learn about bookmaking and publishing
- have to edit and proofread at a high level
- learn how to read aloud
- learn something about child development and age level profiles
- have to constantly consider their audience

These eighth graders would then have a chance to launch their fledgling writers' voices into the world and to gauge the power of their words by looking at the bored or rapt faces of the younger children in their audience.

Another result, I believed, might also occur; I might gain an ally who would help me change the practices of our middle school, a strong teacher would help to convey a message of the connections between reading and writing to colleagues. Together, we could encourage students to write about the difficult issues of their lives. Not too far from childhood themselves, our middle school students could be the messengers of remembrance and hope for younger children whose lives already held difficult issues. Furthermore, as an administrator I would have a chance to teach, to be on the line with both students and teachers. I could model my beliefs and practices. And the eighth graders would literally move out into the world.

The other issue would be that we would use these eighth graders, sometimes dreaded by younger students and their parents, as goodwill ambassadors, helping to change our spotty reputation as a nest of street-smart rather than school-smart kids. If the whole thing worked, I would teach the unit in every eighth-grade language arts/social studies Block each year. We would evaluate the whole thing together: teachers, students, and assistant principal, when the unit was completed. This teacher agreed. I wrote a plan for teaching a children's literature unit, and I got the complete support of the principal who released me from some of the administrative tasks of my job, tasks he took on so that I could be in the classroom part of each day. The Sellwood Book Brigade, named by the first group of eighth graders to go through this program, was born.

Other things were born, as well. Two conferences were on the calendar for that year: One was a local conference, sponsored by the Oregon Council of Teachers of English, and the other was a national conference, sponsored by the National Council of Teachers of English. The Director of Instruction listened to me as I asked her to send all of the Block teachers of Sellwood to these conferences. She paid the registration of all members of the Block language arts team to attend the local conference and paid for six members of the team to attend the national conference. She wanted to support a change in ideas and instruction and support the professional growth of the teachers who, in all fairness, were being required to change as a result of her new policies. She believed that change occurs when teachers hear about current research and have the time and space to discuss its implications for classroom practices.

If we want to change an institution, if we demand it, then we'd better give our ideas and aspirations time and money. The Director of Instruction wanted teachers to integrate new understandings about literacy development into their classroom practices. Every Block teacher went to the local conference, and six went to the national.

In both cases, the Director of Instruction paid for all costs. This required that teachers rethink what they wanted for their teaching lives. They stamped their own doubts and beliefs on their experiences and shared them with their colleagues. Two came from the national conference eager to integrate language arts and social studies and to include more writing; four remained unconvinced.

We continued to discuss instructional strategies at weekly team meetings. Discussion sometimes turned into heated arguments about educational philosophies. Several of the teachers openly disagreed with my ideas about instruction. But our disagreements remained friendly and professional, and opened up opportunities and challenges for me to model what I meant by coming into the teachers' classrooms. Many of them invited me to do lessons, and all of the eighth-grade teachers let me take over their classrooms for three weeks to conduct the "Book Brigade." One teacher, in some ways the most traditional, was open and honest about her skepticism, but eager to try a few new things with which she felt comfortable. She became the most avid supporter of the "Book Brigade" and created a unit in which students researched a person who had made a difference and then created a *Time* magazine for this "Person of the Year."

There were other slow changes. Some of the language arts teachers, particularly at the sixth-grade level, revised their language arts programs, but made only small changes in the integration of language arts with social studies. More writing was included, but only a few had writing workshops during which students chose their own topics.

Several of them continued to have grave doubts about whole language as the philosophical underpinning of language arts instruction. These honest and appropriate concerns were sometimes fanned into rhetorical flames by content-area teachers who actively and loudly opposed the elimination of tracking students into reading and math by ability level as tested on the district's standardized test. After two years, we had two-hour language arts and social studies blocks that included reading. Chapter One was eliminated, and students of varying ability levels were together. But practices, particularly in the seventh- and eighth-grade classes, had not been radically altered in any but a few of the twelve Block teachers' classes.

Some of the teachers who opposed change in the configuration of the language arts classes talked to the parents of politically-powerful families in one section of the feeder communities of Sellwood about their grave concerns for the achievement of their "high-achieving, college-bound" youngsters. All of the fears of these upper-middle-class parents about an inclusion model of education based on strong egalitarian principles was fueled by several teachers, themselves members of the neighborhood in which our most severe critics lived. Many parents who came to me with their legitimate concerns left with, I hope, a better sense of our shared goals, not only for their children, but for all of the children in our middle school.

We maintained our momentum to change and grow, but at great cost to the emotional lives of every staff member. The differences in philosophy—exemplified by our new principal's clear articulation of a need to consider each adolescent as a separate planet, rich and ripe for success and growth—began to be battle cries. That, and his judicious hiring of several progressive, child-centered, strong whole language teachers, created the next phase of a painful growth process.

The integration of social studies and language arts, a natural blending in a strong whole language program, as well as the new administration's desire to move away from tracking with more emphasis on teaching the child and not the curriculum, emerged as the battlefields on which ideological wars were waged among teachers. We were asking ourselves essential questions about what we should do to create a child-centered school environment that supported academic success for all students. We were also concerned about creating an intellectually-rigorous curriculum because that was what some of the parents in an affluent section of the school's community demanded. However, at issue were the methods used to reach these goals. Teachers armed themselves with research data supportive of their ideological camps. The tents were unfurled, and the battle began.

On one side stood the progressive teachers, in favor of zero tracking, an integrated curriculum, alternative assessment strategies, a literature-based reading program, and the whole language philosophy. On the other side stood the traditionalists, in favor of ability grouping, discrete subject areas, letter grades, controlled reading of the "great" books, and formal English grammar instruction. And in the not-so-precise middle, I stood. Every teacher knew where I stood on the educational issues. At great personal and professional issue was where I stood as an instructional leader and as an administrator.

The new principal and I created a voluntary committee of teachers whose task it would be to analyze our instructional program and make recommendations for changes. Several of the more progressive teachers volunteered. One of the staunch traditionalists also joined the committee, whose members met first to generate a list of concerns and questions. Some of the committee members wanted to attend conferences and seminars on restructuring middle schools. It quickly became apparent that this committee would have to face the difficult dilemma of bringing a staff together, a staff that seemed daily more polarized along ideological lines. The committee members conducted a series of staff meetings at which they encouraged staff to air the positives and negatives about working at Sellwood. It became clear that a small vocal minority did not support the new administrator's direction for a child-centered school. The majority of teachers were open to ideas, even if they had myriad questions. Several members of the restructuring committee took a bold step. They invited members of the staff to form a new group to study interdisciplinary teaching with an eye toward completely and radically altering the structure of a portion of the school. Four of them decided to work together to design a program. I met with them, and we talked for a year about what they wanted to create.

They wanted to create a multi-age middle school program devoted to developing critical literacy through service learning and engagement in real-world tasks. They wanted to stay with their students for three years and replace letter grades with alternative assessment models that more thoroughly engaged both parent and child. Thus, the I-Team was born.

Sellwood's I-Team is entering its third year. Parents and students who have been on the team for two years are powerful supporters for this multi-age program. It is the first of its kind in the district, though other middle schools have implemented similar programs after doing their own research and visiting the team. Many of the parents originally critical of the I-Team have become allies. There is a waiting list of students whose parents want them to enter middle school as sixth graders attached to the I-Team for three years. In spite of the dire predictions of the traditional teachers and parents that high-achieving students would not do well, students made remarkable growth on the standardized district achievement tests. Math performance, which was the biggest worry for parents of high-achieving students, was markedly stronger for I-Team students going to high school than for students in the regular "high" math classes that are still ability grouped. And the I-Team students have learned the skills of research, analysis, and self-reflection and assessment. They have studied difficult social issues, asked questions, and felt that they had a voice in the world. They have had the support of adult mentors, parents and teachers, as they ask questions about the world, and they have acknowledged the different talents that all people bring to a problem. Students who have struggled in more traditional classroom settings are successful, because as I-Team teacher Mark Oldani says, "If a student isn't successful in my classroom, then I will find a way to make her successful. That, quite simply, is my job."

The I-Team is a school within a school, formed through the collaborative efforts of four outstanding, reflective teachers. To create their program, they had to answer a hundred questions from the principal and me; they had to attend countless workshops and spend hours designing curricula, reshaping instruction, and doing assessment; they had to stand tough for their educational beliefs through a barrage of criticism from the community and from their colleagues, criticism which flew through the air as thickly as flak. But they did it, and they created a program that has the highest standards for critical literacy and engagement that I've ever seen.

Our efforts to link language arts and social studies must be more than a convenient marriage. It must be at the heart of a commitment to create schools that develop literate, committed citizens. It must be the nest for the development in young adolescents of the desire to know their world, to know the difficult social issues that confront all of us, and to be unafraid to tackle these issues. This requires that they be communicators, and it requires that they be empathetic to the concerns of a wide variety of people. It requires deep literacy for all, not just the college bound. And it requires people who are respectful of individual differences, talents, and intellectual ability. If we create schools that force hierarchical structures onto children, making their differences weaknesses instead of strengths; if we determine that schools are responsible only to the few and not the many; and if we encourage isolated individualism and extreme competition, what are we giving to our world?

I am now the principal of a small inner-city elementary school. I left Sellwood Middle School knowing that I had helped begin the process of change. Ability grouping in reading was eliminated. Teachers were comfortable with a wider variety of instructional materials and did not rely so heavily on textbooks. Writing became an important part of all subjects. Teachers were doing more active projects with students. Many of these projects naturally linked social studies and language arts. I also believe that people were beginning to ask themselves what they were doing and why they were doing it.

But I learned some things. Change is a long, slow, sometimes excruciatingly painful process. I learned that there are strategies for making this difficult process less personally damaging.

I believe that we all have to start with talking openly about our beliefs about teaching and learning. This requires tolerance, patience, and time. There has to be shared reading of research and shared reflections on how the ideas that we gather from research might inform our practices. Then we have to support each other as we implement these practices and critique our results. There has to be time explicitly given to adults in schools to do what we ask of students. If this is not the vision for change that administrators and teachers hold dear, then it will never happen. There must be human resources available for teachers to ask questions or gather new ideas, but these resources can come from within our own school. The personal talents and expertise of teachers and administrators must be used to build a shared knowledge base. There must be constant discussion among all involved in the school community, during which conflicting ideas are not seen as personal attacks. And finally, there has to be forgiveness, more patience, and perseverance.

Whole language is a philosophy that requires long-term change. The embracing of this different way of looking at instruction requires more than redesigning the master schedule or buying new books. Teachers have to become learners with their students and respect what students bring from their own lives into the classroom. Teachers have to see the natural connections between subjects and allow students to explore their own process for making these connections. They have to remain constantly open to evolving theories of literacy development. And they have to be committed to the idea that all students can succeed; it is our job to find a way to create the conditions for this to occur. Unless teachers live out whole language philosophy in their professional lives, it will never happen in the classroom. Living this philosophy demands that teachers, students, and administrators, create schools that are active learning communities devoted to encouraging growth in a place fertile with new ideas, collaboration, analysis, and reflection. School needs to be a place where we challenge each other to be learners and support the process of taking risks that learning new things demands. A place where we devote ourselves to reading research and to writing and talking about our beliefs and how we formed them. A place where we create for our peers the same community of learning that we ask our students to form. Living this philosophy demands the recognition that the school community needs everyone involved—students, teachers, administrators, and parents. We must create these places with the powerful knowledge that we are forming our future and do this with commitment and joy.

Chapter 11
The I-Team

MARK OLDANI

JOURNAL ENTRY, FEBRUARY 23, 1992

"We just finished introducing our program to parents from the Local School Advisory Committee (L.S.A.C.) right on the heels of a meeting with the faculty. The same questions keep coming up: Will my child be ready for high school? Will they be challenged in math? How can you teach kids of different ages in the same room? What textbooks will they use? Is this program only for problem kids? What if my child doesn't want to stay with the same teacher for three years? Don't you need grades to motivate students?

These questions won't go away, but neither will the nagging feeling in me that the issues raised by these questions mean very little to middle school students. At the same parent meeting, I asked parents what was memorable about their sixth, seventh, and eighth grade years. Not one of them mentioned any fact or formula. What they remembered were their relationships with adults and other students, and their accomplishments like completing projects and winning baseball championships.

Parents and fellow teachers started to get a glimpse of our thinking when Anne, Jim, Barb, and I talked about our students. Anne told about the students she knows who can hide or waste time through any forty-five minute class period. Jim spoke about some of his A students who were the best at getting by with the least work. I spoke about the numerous times my social studies students balked at doing statistics because they didn't believe math was part of social studies. Barb said that she felt bad about not getting to know her 150 math students better, and a veteran teacher *consoled* her by telling her she would forget about them in a couple of weeks.

Right now Allan (principal Allan Luethe) and Michelann (vice-principal Michelann Ortloff) are behind us. I just hope it works out, because what we are doing now isn't working.

I often look back at that journal entry. It helps me to focus on what I believe to be important for middle school kids—namely, that they have a safe place to be successful.

I plan, teach, and write curricula with three other teachers—Barbara Currier, Jim Keiter, and Anne Williams—on what we call the Interdisciplinary Team, or I-Team. We have 110 students out of the 650 that go to Sellwood Middle School in Portland, Oregon. We are responsible for teaching language arts, social studies, math, and advisory, a home room guide program. Our students—roughly an equal number of sixth, seventh, and eighth graders in each classroom—create the themes and questions that they want to study. The purpose of the program is to create a child-responsive environment where middle school students can grow intellectually, socially, and physically. The features of the program are to

- create a strong bond between students, parents, and teachers by keeping the student with the same teacher for three years
- develop an academic program based on the students'questions and concerns about themselves and the world around them
- integrate the teaching of reading, writing, social studies, math, science, health and art, to let students explore topics of interest to them
- develop self-esteem and a sense of belonging to a community by encouraging responsibility for helping others
- celebrate diversity by eliminating ability grouping and stressing multiculturalism
- invite internal motivation for learning through goal setting, ongoing self-reflection, ongoing teacher assessment, and elimination of letter grades.

This chapter is about what we do to create a child-responsive curiculum.

EXPERT PROJECTS

We believe that studying topics that personally interest middle school students is essential for their social, psychological, and intellectual development. In order to encourage individual interests, we have students do *expert projects*. Each student does two to three expert projects a year. Through their expert projects, students show their classmates and their teacher that they know more than the average person. I received the following note from a parent about the expert projects: "The Gene Kelly idea is spiriting all of us, what fun! I hope she [Kathleen] will take the tap dance lessons she wants. Life is a whole-world education."

I thought about the presentations: Kathleen's enthusiasm for Gene Kelly, JJ's surfing demonstration, Glyness's mummies, Ariel's martial arts lesson, James's Boston Terrier, Eric's hamster, and, most of all, Larry's devotion and love for his grandfather that brought spontaneous applause from the class.

And I see that when my students are recognized as individuals, they take the responsibility to be productive members of their classroom community.

The project mentioned above gives each student the opportunity to stand out, but focusing on individual interests alone is not enough. My students also see themselves making connections with the world around them. It is essential that they be given the opportunity to construct their own understanding of how things work in the world community. All 110 students and the four teachers on I-Team work together to develop our yearlong course of study. As one student put it, "I think it's pretty cool that you [the teachers]are letting us take the time to learn what we want to learn instead of having to take the time doing just what you want us to do."

DEVELOPING THE CURRICULUM

The steps that we use to develop the topics and questions for study are based on a student-responsive curriculum model that we learned from James Beane in workshops and from his book, *A Middle School Curriculum: From Rhetoric to Reality* (1990). Before using the student-responsive curriculum model, we spun our wheels for three months teaching units that we invented and hoped students would like. This was a waste of time because the students had no stake in what they were being taught, and we found ourselves in the familiar but uncomfortable position of controllers of the curriculum. We have found that the participation of students in the curriculum-development process, the group decision making and problem-solving skills practiced, as well as the commitment by the students and teachers to making the yearlong study significant, make spending many hours of class time well worth it.

Step 1: Getting Started/Writing Questions

The purpose of this activity is for individual students to write about their personal concerns (the things that affect them, their families and their friends) and their social concerns (the things beyond their families that they care about). These lists of student-generated issues are what our yearlong study is based on. The key for a successful start is for me to make sure that my students have the opportunity to independently think and write about their concerns. When my students are feeling uncomfortable with an assignment, it is easy for them to wait for their more secure classmates to tell them the *right thing to do*. In this case, the *right thing* is for each student to have his or her own questions.

In each class, students spend about an hour (not in one sitting) brainstorming and then listing questions about their personal and social concerns.

A typical student list would contain about twenty questions about family, friends, world peace, environmental problems, as well as gangs, drugs, and crime. The students try to make distinctions between what is personal and what is social. Some of the problems that students face in this activity are their perceived or real inabilities to write meaningful questions, their insecurities about the importance of their questions ("will my cat die?"), or their inabilities to distinguish between personal and social issues.

This activity went smoother in the second year because the returning students were enthusiastic, and they also helped the new students understand the purpose of the activity.

Step 2: Small Groups Compiling Lists of Social and Personal Concerns

After I play a major role in helping students to work alone on the first day, students work in their groups during the second session with little teacher supervision. Students share their lists of questions with members of their small groups. Then each group's job is to combine their unedited individual lists into two long lists of personal and social concerns. Each list will have from 80 to 100 questions. Then the students select about 40 questions that they believe are the most important to study.

Even questions that seem silly at first (e.g., "Will the Portland Trailblazers win the championship?") are taken seriously and their implications discussed. Students talk about what it actually takes to win an N.B.A. championship. They will raise further questions like, "Is it only the players that win championships? What else is involved?" Finally, they decide if this is the kind of issue that they want to study.

A couple of positive tendencies begin to emerge in the class. Students become more secure about their questions. They notice that their concerns, hopes, and fears are similar to those of other students. They are proud of their own original contributions to the group. At this point, students start to see the significance of their thinking. Their questions cover weighty material, and they realize that they will be studying important topics.

Each group develops its own method for selecting and eliminating questions. Student Sara C. explained her group's method of choosing questions:

> "We went around in a circle and each person said what they wanted to use. One person said, "How long am I going to live?" Our table group had some discussion, "Do we want to use this?" We agreed to write the question down because it was similar to something we all had. Or we used other questions just because they were good questions.

Here are ten of the many personal concerns from a group made up of Tanita, Tynette, Marco, Larry, Ariel, John, Adam, and Wes:

1. How will my family start acting when I get older?
2. Will I use drugs in the future?
3. Will anyone in my family die from sickle-cell anemia?
4. Will high school be all I hope it to be? Will I graduate from high school?
5. What kind of career will I have?
6. Are my friends really my friends?
7. How will I react to a bully? Will I get beat up?
8. How do I get along with other people? How can I be a better person?
9. How do I get people to respect me?
10. What is my purpose in life?

This group and the other groups write their questions on butcher paper and display them around the room. Individuals circulate and add questions to their group's lists. This process is going on in all four classrooms. Intense discussion occurs as the groups of students revise their lists of questions. The same process continues on the next day with the social concerns. Here are nine of the same group's social concerns:

1. Will violence/gangs stop?
2. Will there be less pollution in the world?
3. Will I be killed off by my own race?
4. Will discrimination stop?
5. Will there be enough education in the future?
6. Will our ozone be depleted?
7. What will we do if we can't stop hate crimes?
8. Will we have World War III? Will we ever have peace?
9. How will they find a cure for AIDS? Will AIDS be the number one killer?

In each group, interesting side conversations emerge that touch on how the students try to construct meaning out of the world they live in.

A STUDENT:	"Where will I live in the future?"
JOE:	"Well, you know, eventually our planet won't do OK so we might have to live on Mars or the Moon or something."
IN THE DISTANCE:	"That sucks!"
JOE:	"Well, we still might have to."

Step 3: Categorizing

We arrange for adults to act as facilitators for each student group. For the last two years we have been fortunate to get help from adults who are from a local college's education program and who are studying to be school teachers. The students' responsibility in their group is to determine how their personal concerns are similar to their social concerns. The adult helps the students find connections between their personal and their social concerns. The adult does not find the connections for the students.

Once the students find links between their personal and social questions, they put the questions in categories. They also discard questions. The group described above came up with four categories and nineteen questions. Here is one of the categories with their questions:

Life and Friends in the Future

1. Will there be enough education? How will I achieve my goals?
2. Will discrimination stop? How do I get along with others?
3. Will violence stop? How do I react to a bully?
4. Will certain jobs/laws cause us to forfeit our lives and homes? Will I get a good job?
5. Are my friends really my friends? Will we be killed off by our own race?
6. What is my purpose in life?

Each of the four classes has four to six groups, and each group has a similar number of categories and questions. To complete their categories, the students make decisions about what is most important to them. Questions get weeded out, and the group reaches consensus about their categories and questions.

One of the adults who was helping the students explained her thoughts on the days events:

> I liked it. It's the same kinds of things you do later on in life, like when you are in college. High school kids are not prepared for college, that is why so many of them drop out. They don't know how to think when they get into the college system. And, when they get a job they have to know how to work with other people.

Step 4: Whole Class Debate and Reaching Consensus

The activity moves from small groups to a whole class activity. Each I-Team class must decide which fifteen or twenty questions to use and how to fit them into three or four categories. I sit in the back of the room and let student leaders emerge to direct the discussions. It isn't easy for them or me. The students periodically glance toward me, looking for leadership, but I opt out of this process because the students need to make their own choices without being influenced by the teacher.

In my class, Ben was the first to take the lead. He tried to focus the debate. This offended many students who felt he was showing off. He was criticized mercilessly and was replaced by a succession of short-lived leaders. Finally, the students realized that they needed a strong leader in order to make progress. It was gratifying for Ben to help conclude the debate by reemerging as a leader.

This activity helped students learn how to conduct a debate, make decisions, lead whole group discussions, and write meaningful questions. The discussions over how to word the questions were lively. Many of the original questions could be answered with a yes or no answer. Some students wanted to write questions that involved them personally, others didn't. John M. led the class in transforming a mundane question, "Will there be world peace?" to a stronger, "How can we change to create world peace?" His position was that world peace would mean nothing unless each of us did our part to change.

Step 5: Class Representatives

Once the themes are chosen in each classroom, students in each class elect representatives to debate and then decide on the final five themes. Nils explained how he felt:

> I took a lot of care selecting the questions. I was excited because I was there with fifteen other students deciding what we were going to study. I wish we had more time to debate the issues before us.

Sarah R. added:

> When I was in there choosing questions and categories, I had to remember that I was speaking for the whole I-Team, so I needed to have an open mind. That's hard, especially when you want to study something that isn't of interest to everyone else. You have to put aside your personal thoughts. When we were finished, I recall saying, "I have never used my brain so much!"

Natalie advised us on how we could make improvements: "I think we need to take it a step farther and have students involved in how we can answer the questions so we will have more control."

After many hours of discussion, the representatives decided on the following areas to study:

Our Environment

1. How can we save our rivers, oceans, and air from the effects of pollution?
2. How will global warming affect the environment?

3. How will our future technology affect our natural resources?
4. How long will the rain forests last?
5. What will happen to endangered species?

War and Conflict and our Global Society

1. How can we make our streets safer from gangs, crime, and drugs?
2. What influences us to be violent?
3. If crime increases, will the punishment increase to reduce crime?
4. How do some people's insecurities affect equal treatment?
5. How will we change to create world peace?

Education, Schools, Jobs

1. What will happen to high school sports? If they're cut, will kids drop out, and how will that affect the community?
2. How will we fund our education in the future?
3. Will everyone be able to get a good job that they are happy with and make enough money to support himself or herself?
4. How can I prepare now for my education in the future?
5. Will there be a woman or minority president?

Technology

1. Will we live in space?
2. What will our future transportation be like?
3. How will technology improve our lives?
4. What will happen to nuclear power and will we find an alternate energy source?

Health

1. Will there be a cure for AIDS, cancer, STD's, and other diseases?
2. What are the economic, physical, and social costs of drug abuse?
3. Will teen sex and pregnancy increase or decrease?
4. How will Clinton's health plan work?

The students' questions reflect the three features that J. Arnold (1993) says a middle school curriculum must possess:

First, and quite obviously, it deals with material which is genuinely important and worth knowing. Second, [it] deals with values. Third, for curriculum to be rich in meaning, both its content and methodology must relate substantively to the needs and interests of young adolescents." (pp. 66–68)

An education student visited my class one day. At forty-five, she has grown children. When I asked her how she felt about the issues that the students were working on, she said, "My life would have been different if I did this in school."

People often use stereotypes, like *hormones with feet,* to describe middle school students. Our students' questions attest to their serious nature, their desire to make sense of the world, and their desire to make the world a better place. Exploring student-generated issues is a powerful way to bring out the best in all students. Tanita is usually quiet and shy, but she plays a leading role in shaping and studying these questions. Adam, used to accepting teacher direction without question, is now analyzing data and finding huge inconsistencies in the world around him. Sarah R. is using the knowledge and organizational skills that she has learned to start an environmental awareness club. Kyleigh and Ryan take the initiative to invite guest speakers to their other classes. Tawny, Kelly, Jenna, Erin, James, Kathleen, Dede, Nils, Jacob, Mary, Stacey, Brianna, and Adrienne are following up on our team's work on the "Names Project" to make quilt panels for AIDS victims.

This curriculum could not have been developed without a strong community based on respect for individuals. In order to build this kind of community, we mix grade levels; we do not track by ability, and we integrate the study of subjects. We are committed to developing meaningful activities that ensure the success of all students, we work together to make our classrooms meaningful and comfortable places to be, and we develop activities that relate to the interests of our students.

MIXED AGE GROUPING

We combined sixth, seventh, and eighth graders in each classroom so that we can keep a stable group of students over three years. According to the Carnegie Council on Adolescent Development, in *Turning Points: Preparing Youth for the 21st Century* (1989),

> To foster continuity of relations and to create the learning climate students need to delve deeply into complex ideas, teams of students and teachers would preferably remain together for the students' entire middle grade experience. (p. 40)

This community has both the stability of the returning seventh and eighth graders and new blood represented by the new students.

ABILITY GROUPING

We do not track students by ability. We believe that all students have exceptional abilities in some areas and that they all have weaknesses in other areas. In *The Middle School and Beyond* (1992), the authors state:

> As individual differences are accounted for in the everyday work of the group, such arrangements as gifted and talented and special education programs would no longer be necessary. In fact, a general education curriculum in which democracy and diversity are prized would insist that young people, in all their diversity, be brought together, not separated out. (p. 101)

Our students need to understand that they have a lot to offer each other and that they have a lot to learn from each other. This happens in a stable classroom where improvement and risk taking are noted and valued by everyone in the classroom and where the teacher serves as a facilitator of learning and a mentor to each student.

INTEGRATED CURRICULUM

The study of language arts, social studies, math, and other subjects must be integrated in order for the students to get a realistic understanding of the world around them. An integrated approach to study fits the real-life situations of the students and of the people whom they know and see everyday. James Beane said it best in *The Middle School Curriculum: From Rhetoric to Reality* (1990):

> When we encounter life situations or problems, we do not ask which part is science, which is mathematics, which is history, and so on? Rather, we use whatever information or skills the situation itself calls for and we integrate these in problem-solving. Certainly such information and skills may often be found within subject areas, but in real life the problem itself is at the center and the information and skills are defined around the problem. In other words, the subject approach is alien to life itself. Put simply, it is "bad" learning theory. (p. 29)

MEANINGFUL ACTIVITIES

It is essential for students to value learning. As I look at students in our program, I see many who will be successful in their future educational pursuits. I also see many who used to see school as a waste of time and energy. Tynette spoke eloquently for this group:

> I didn't even care about school. I felt that I wasn't doing good, so I shouldn't have to do anything. This year I have really changed. Being on the I-Team helps a lot. It helps you understand, and they give you time to do your work.

It is very important to us that our program reaches all students, not just the college bound. Our students are making vital decisions about their lives and their future. In a letter dated November 30, 1993, Conrad Toepfer, Professor of Education at State University of New York at Buffalo, states:

> Building upon their childhood experiences, most people largely fashion their attitudes about learning, work, and enduring adult values during early adolescence. Relatively few individuals (less than ten percent) substantially change those attributes after their middle-level school years. Hopes to increase high school completion rates hinge upon how prior school experiences respond to changing conditions in our society. While most students reach legal school-leaving age during high school, most make the emotional decision to drop-out between third and eighth grades.

Students will be engaged in learning by a course of study that honors the necessity for adolescents to understand themselves and their connection to the world around them, and that respects the seriousness of their concerns.

TEAM PLANNING

The teachers Anne, Barbara, Jim, and myself work together to make our classrooms communities. We work well together because of our mutual respect for each other as teachers and as friends. Working on the I-Team has made each of us a better teacher. At our daily team planning period, we share teaching methods, we share our strengths in different subject areas, we teach each other new things about how the world works, and we question what we are doing and why we are doing it. We discuss and debate educational philosophy, and we help each other capture the essence of our students' behavior and thinking. We also seek advice from students and parents about the activities and resources that will help answer the questions. Anne, Barbara, Jim, and myself are a small community, and the positive features of our community rub off in our classrooms.

INTEGRATING THE CURRICULUM

Once the students determine what is to be studied, the teachers figure out which skills the students will need to answer the questions. Then we devise activities that will help the students gain the skills necessary to make sense of their questions.

Teaching a unit involves planning activities, deciding how to assess students, and gathering resources. We supplement normal classroom activities with guest speakers, field trips, and discussions of our responsibility to the community. For example, when we studied the environment, we read many articles about timber issues in the Northwest, and we learned about the ecology and habitats of old-growth forests. We had a lumber broker, an environmentalist, and a scientist from the state's Oregon Fish and Wildlife Division speak to our classes. We went to an old-growth forest. Based on a conversation with a student, Anne Williams developed a project that truly integrated subject matter. The students worked on this particular assignment in groups, and presented their conclusions to their class. Here is the project:

Congratulations, you have just received some valuable timberland in the Williams Wilderness Area. You have:
- 300 acres of seventy-year-old second-growth trees.
- 200 acres of two-hundred-fifty-year-old growth trees.
- a river at the west end of your land.
- a stream through the land that runs to the river.
- a spring run of steelhead.

Draw a Map to Scale of the Area. Include a Key and Compass Rose.

Helpful information (We learned this from the lumber broker.):
- one acre = 43,000 sq. ft.
- one seventy-year-old tree needs 100 sq. ft. and earns $1,000 if cut down.
- one old-growth tree needs 625 sq. ft. and earns $13,000 if cut down.
- The land value is $5,000 an acre.
- The tax rate is 1 percent per $1,000 of value of land.

Problem One: Your objective is to make as much money as possible. Describe in detail how you plan to do this.
Problem Two: Your objective is to preserve the land as much as possible, but you must make enough money to pay the taxes and live. Describe in detail how you plan to do this.
Problem Three: You want to balance business (the harvest of timber and fish) with environmental concerns. How can you make money and protect the environment?"

This project gets to the heart of our program: involving students in real issues that affect the community around them and the community in the classroom. This project required that students cooperate to complete it. In addition, students had to answer the same questions that President Clinton responded to at the Timber Summit that took place in Portland in April, 1993. Anne Williams remembered hearing students say, "This is hard because the timber workers don't have a common view and neither do the environmentalists." Students quickly learn that there are no easy answers and that working together enhances their understanding of an issue or a problem.

A parent, Shirley H., recently wrote:

There are so many things I appreciate about the I-Team! Lately, I've been thinking about how great it is that you use speaking and writing for math. Skills used to clarify relationships in reading and writing do the same job in math. Thank you for seeing clearly and offering my daughter such opportunities to think!

Another parent, Jim R., said, "Our daughter comes home with such interesting ideas to discuss. The I-Team enriches our family."

We have been able to establish communities in our classrooms because we allow students to take the initiative in understanding themselves and the world around them. Given these opportunities, our students take control of their learning and help to make their classroom an exciting place to be.

BIBLIOGRAPHY

Arnold, J. 1993. "Toward a Middle Level Curriculum Rich in Meaning." In *Reading in Middle School Curriculum: A Continuing Conversation,* ed. T. Dickinson. Columbus, OH: National Middle School Association.

Beane, James A. 1990. *A Middle School Curriculum: From Rhetoric to Reality.* Columbus, OH: National Middle School Association.

Carnegie Council on Adolescent Development, 1989. *Turning Points: Preparing American Youth for the 21st Century.* New York: Carnegie Corporation of New York.

George, Paul S., Chris Stevenson, Julia Thomason, and James Beane. 1992. *The Middle School and Beyond.* Columbus, OH: National Middle School Association.

Toepfer, Conrad F., Jr. 1993. "The Changing Needs of Youth: Preparing for Life in Tomorrow's World." Unpublished.

Chapter 12
Students Develop Portfolios

WINNIE CHARLEY

C hairs scrape across the floor of the seventh-grade commons as students lead their parents to a conference area. Families pull their chairs around one of the many student desks sprinkled around the room to accommodate privacy. Then the bustle is quickly replaced by quiet conversations and the opening of portfolios.

The seventh graders at Jackson Middle School are in conference with their parents. Each student's job is to demonstrate the learning that has taken place in their combined reading, language arts, and social studies block class by showing samples of work from their portfolios. The cover letter that each student writes supplies the lead and puts the student in charge:

> *Dear Mom and Dad,*
>
> Portfolio night is a night for me to show you what I have learned this year. It is a night to show you that I know I am responsible for my learning. It is a night for me to show you how proud I am of my work.
>
> When I put my portfolio together, I only put in things that gave examples of how I am as a student. This portfolio was put together with great care. The work I put in shows where I am at the moment.
>
> *Your daughter,*
> *Rebecca*

I stand at the perimeter of the room and witness the involvement, wondering, Is this evening going to work? Do the students have enough to say

Thank you to my friend and colleague, Dorothy Geary. Many of the ideas mentioned in this chapter resulted from our conversations.

173

about what they have learned this year? *Have* they learned enough this year? Are the parents going to be upset because the portfolios contain imperfect products that have not been *touched up* by me—the teacher, editor and coach? I begin to make my way around the room and listen:

> This is my first-quarter reading journal. Mrs. Charley and I both write in it. It's kind of like a conversation.
> And here are some of the ways I've changed as a learner this year.
> This historical dialogue was a struggle for me because I had trouble finding enough information, but I like the way it turned out. It's got a good "Show, don't tell". . . . Here, let me read you an example.

The portfolios that the students display contain work from their three core classes: reading, language arts, and social studies, which we integrate to produce poetry, historical dialogues, interior monologues, diary entries, political cartoons, and snips of historical fiction. The portfolios provide evidence of academic growth and involve the students in their own assessments.

Some of the selections are chosen by the students while I choose other pieces that demonstrate movement toward goals. However, if a student feels that a piece of writing is too personal for his portfolio, then, of course, another piece will be selected in its place. The portfolio is divided into sections: "Reading," "Writing," "Student Selected Work," "Thinking About Myself," "Thank Yous and Compliments," and "Parents' Page."

The first section contains reading information. When school begins in September, students choose the first of a series of novels to read during "Silent Sustained Reading" and as a fifteen-minute homework assignment each night.

Once a week, they write a message in their reading journal about the book they are reading: how the author is developing the characters, conflicts, and themes or using the setting and establishing the tone. They write about their involvement in the story and about questions that have emerged for them. Once a week, I respond, and a correspondence develops between us. Student reading journals and a list that describes changes in the student as a reader this year are contained in the reading section.

When we organize the portfolio for the student-parent conferences, students each search their reading journals and their writings for evidence of their growth as readers. They use number coded stick-ons to mark spots where they find this evidence.

Ray became more aware of the conflicts developed in a novel. His list describing himself as a seventh-grade reader states this: "Now I realize that the author developed a conflict. See stick-on R8."

Here is the entry from Ray's reading journal where he put the stick-on so that he could easily find it and share it with his parents during the evening conference:

The book I read was *Children of the River* by Linda Crew. It's about an Asian girl who, because of the war in her country, had to move to the United States, leaving behind her family. She didn't know whether they were dead or alive. The story tells about how rough it was for her to move, and how she adjusts to American life. It tells of her conflict between her beliefs and those of Americans. It also tells about her getting to know an American boy.

Brandon writes about his change as a reader: "I notice how authors develop main characters, mood and setting. See stick-on R3."
Here's where he put stick-on R3, an entry from his reading journal:

I'm reading the book *Fallen Angels* by Walter Dean Myers. It's about the War in Vietnam.
I think the way the author develops the main character is to write more detailed things about what he says and does. Walter Dean Myers does a good job of that.
I think the mood for this story is sad and serious. He wrote sad, serious scenes.

Julie's list contains the following self-assessments:

I enjoy reading books of real life and its problems.
In the beginning of the year, I just retold the story. Now I am able to understand the elements of literature.
I can relate books to real life.
I find myself getting personally involved in the story.
I am able to identify where the author uses "Show don't tell."
I can tell you what the character is like.
I am able to identify the mood of the story.

For every one of these self-assessment statements, Julie used a stick-on to cross-reference a journal entry that offers evidence. For example, she wrote on her list, "I have learned lessons about life through reading biographies. See stick-on R14."
Stick-on R14 marked this entry from Julie's reading journal:

Now I'm reading *Ryan White: My Own Story*. It's really good. I'm much more interested in this than in *Malcolm X*. I don't see how Ryan could live on. He was a hemophiliac and contracted AIDS. It would be so hard, especially for the mom and the sister, to know that a son or brother was going to die soon. Life would be so difficult to be sick all the time. I wouldn't have been able to stand it.

The portfolios also have a writing section. This section contains a list of changes that students have identified in their seventh-grade writing, some teacher-selected writings, a goal sheet, and a student research paper.
Natalie's list of changes include the following:

I use dialogue in my stories. See stick-on W4.
I use correct punctuation for my dialogue. See stick-on W5.

Stick-ons W4 and W5 label a piece of Natalie's writing that begins this way:

"Excuse me. Are you Siddharta Gautama?" questioned Shie with an interesting look on her face. She walked faster trying to catch up with the familiar looking man in front of her.

"Well yes, I am. Why?" replied Gautama. He turned around to look down at the small young girl. With a happy look on his face, he knelt down to the young girl's level.

"Can you please tell me a little about your past?" asked Shie.

"Well, I am a Hindu Prince . . ."

I am better at sentence combining and varying my sentence patterns. See stick-on W14.

Stick-on W14 labels this piece of writing:

Dear Jenny,

My name is Constantine. I was an unknown general until I became the emperor of Rome in 312 A.D. I promoted Christianity. I once had a dream that Jesus appeared and told me to make a cross to carry into battle. I ordered artisans to build a cross, the symbol of Christianity, and to paint a cross on my soldiers' shields. As a result, my army won a mighty victory, and I was made Emperor of Rome. A great arch was built to celebrate my victories.

I paragraph well. See stick-on W11.

I know how to develop ideas by telling how, telling why, describing and giving examples. See stick-on W12.

Stick-ons 11 and 12 label this excerpt from Natalie's paper on Ireland:

Many of Ireland's tourists are from the United States and Great Britain. Some want to find out about their family roots. They also are attracted by Ireland's natural beauty and historical sites.

Many cultural events attract travelers, too. There are musical performances, horse races, and theatrical plays.

There are many different ways to get around Ireland. People usually arrive by air. Then there are about 60,00 miles of roads connecting Ireland's cities and towns. The nation's bus system reaches every population center on the island. A state owned railway system also serves all the main population centers and links many smaller towns as well.

Now I prewrite before I write a story. See stick-on W1.

I now set goals for my writing, and I try my hardest to accomplish the goals I set. See stick-on W2.

I try to visualize the moment before I begin writing a story. This helps make my story more interesting. See stick-on W3.

I used to ramble, but now I start at the moment. See stick-on W9.

I try to eliminate weak verbs in my writing. See stick-on W10.

The writing goal sheet (see Figure 12–1) is a help in keeping goals alive. The left column contains the date and the goals. In the adjacent column, the students explain what they did to meet the goals on their most recent paper. The goal sheet is handed in with each major assignment. When the paper is returned to the student, the student and I confer to determine whether to continue working on the goal or whether to set a new goal.

Natalie's goal sheet (Figure 12–1) is evidence of her struggle and growth.

Returned papers and projects are kept in a holding file in a classroom cabinet until a "portfolio pull day" that is scheduled twice a quarter.

At that time, students search through their folders and their dialectic notebooks (daily notebooks to record responses to readings, poetry, informational articles, and discussions and to list questions that emerge from

Name			
Date	I need to work on	date	What I did to accomplish my goal:
6/13	Eliminating more "ands" Fix runon sentences	10/27	I tried to use commas and different words to fill in for the "ands." I read over my paper several times to see if I could change or fix the runon sentences. I think using less "ands" helped.
11/10	There are too many words in some sentences that can be divided into different sentences. Keep editing to eliminate runons. Keep working on show don't tell.	11/10	I tried to get rid of the "ands," but I didn't get rid of all of them. I am struggling with finding spots to use show don't tell, but once I find them, I can develop them easily.

Figure 12–1

these various stimuli.) Their task is to find work that fits one of three categories. First, they search through these to find work that they think is best. They label it "Best" and attach a paragraph explaining why they gave it that label. Second, the same process is used to find work that they feel an attachment to, which is labeled "Like." Again, an explanatory paragraph is attached. Finally, work that represents an effort that has resulted in an increase of understanding is labeled "Struggle," and that struggle is explained on the attached note. Once a paper is labeled, students can move it from the holding folder to the portfolio folder.

For social studies, Julie interviewed her mom and dad. She asked them to name people who had changed the course of history. She chose the write-up of her interview as her "Best"work and explained why:

> This interview took me all afternoon. It is five pages long, and the quality of the writing is high. The handwriting is good, and I think it is my best work. My parents enjoyed being interviewed.

One of Julie's papers was selected to represent "Like," "Best," *and* "Struggle." She wrote:

> I like my theme project. I worked very hard on it and stayed up late to finish it. I feel that the dialogue is written well and that the visual turned out nicely. I feel that the visual represents the theme nicely, too.
> I also think that this same piece of work is my best. It looks nice and sounds good. The appearance of it is just very pretty. It's just the best overall!
> I struggled with this piece because I had a hard time with punctuation, although it turned out well. I struggle with punctuation and spelling all the time.

Natalie labeled a political cartoon she had drawn "Struggle." She wrote:

> I think I struggled with this one the most because it was hard for me to really relate an opinion to a picture as I did in this cartoon. It was hard to think of a good idea that people could understand through a picture.

Self-reflection is key to the portfolio. Early in September, each student writes a description of himself as a reader, a writer, a learner, and a cooperative group member. This activity I repeat at the midpoint and end of each quarter. These records of growth are kept in a "Thinking about Myself" section of the portfolio.

In September, Ray wrote:

> When I write, I like to write with some description, but I like to get on with the story. I like to write in all kinds of styles necessary, but I always feel that I could do more to the story.

At the end of the first quarter he wrote:

> The new things I have done are writing dialogues, "Show don't tell," self assessments, working in groups, and some writing in the dialectic notebook. I have learned a lot in this class, but mostly about "Show don't tell," dialogue, and story writing.
>
> I also think this class is just about right, not too hard, not too easy.

Ray expressed some reservations about clustering when he wrote later on in the year.

> When I cluster, I'm not that comfortable because I never did it before and to me it's not much needed, but I'm sure I'll get used to it. Having a power conclusion is another difficulty, but I'm learning to make them better.

The classroom program is set up to encourage self-reflection. For example, students fill out evaluations and hand them in with many assignments. Figure 12–2 contains one of Brandon's evaluations of a writing assignment.

The students also place the block assessments that they fill out each Friday in the "Thinking About Myself" section. These self-assessments help students evaluate their behaviors in three areas: content, attitude, and striving for excellence. To give themselves a *C*, students must block in all behaviors listed under any one of the three categories. To give themselves a *B*, all behaviors under any two of the categories must be blocked in. To give themselves an *A*, students must block in all behaviors listed under all three categories. See Figure 12–3 at the end of this chapter for the block assessment.

Still another form of self-reflection is the process diary that students keep while working on a research project. Some of the learning objectives of the project include: to question; to draw inferences from pictures, maps, charts, and graphs as well as written text; to be able to use library and community resources in the process of research; to recognize main ideas; and to organize expository writing.

The process begins when each student examines various maps of a country and comes up with lists of questions regarding how the geography affects the economy, how it may have affected the history of the civilization, and how it affects the customs and lifestyle of the people. The list serves as a prewriting exercise, for not all of the questions will be answered. The student is searching for one question to start a *question chain*. For example, a question about the geography and its link to the economy may be selected, and the search will be initiated there. Once students find the answer to their first question, they look at the answer for a new question that has emerged, and then search for the answers to the new question. This process continues, resulting in a chain of questions and answers.

After looking at a resource distribution map, for example, Natalie began her research chain with the following question: "Do Ireland's resources

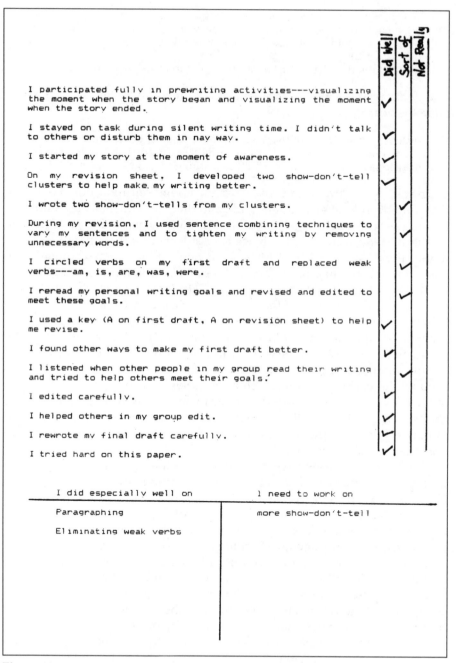

I participated fully in prewriting activities---visualizing the moment when the story began and visualizing the moment when the story ended.

I stayed on task during silent writing time. I didn't talk to others or disturb them in nay way.

I started my story at the moment of awareness.

On my revision sheet, I developed two show-don't-tell clusters to help make my writing better.

I wrote two show-don't-tells from my clusters.

During my revision, I used sentence combining techniques to vary my sentences and to tighten my writing by removing unnecessary words.

I circled verbs on my first draft and replaced weak verbs---am, is, are, was, were.

I reread my personal writing goals and revised and edited to meet these goals.

I used a key (A on first draft, A on revision sheet) to help me revise.

I found other ways to make my first draft better.

I listened when other people in my group read their writing and tried to help others meet their goals.

I edited carefully.

I helped others in my group edit.

I rewrote my final draft carefully.

I tried hard on this paper.

I did especially well on	I need to work on
Paragraphing	more show-don't-tell
Eliminating weak verbs	

Figure 12–2

make her a rich or a poor country?" She found that Ireland is a poor country and that many of its people are unemployed.

Her next question was, "Why is Ireland a poor country?" It took a while for Natalie to figure out that wealthy countries have a lot of industries and that Ireland does not have many big industries.

She continued this line of questioning: "Why don't they have big industries?" She asked questions about what big industries need and realized that they need a source of energy. The resource distribution map showed her that Ireland doesn't have much coal or oil.

Next she asked, "Before there was a lot of importing and exporting, how did the Irish people heat their homes?" Natalie found that Ireland has poor-quality coal, but peat was widely used as fuel. The follow-up question was: "What is peat?" She discovered that peat comes from peat moss, which consists of partially decomposed plant matter.

"Where do the Irish get the peat?" Natalie learned that peat is usually found at or near the surface of bogs or swamps. It forms over a long period of time when decayed vegetation becomes packed down in swamps or marshes.

"How much peat do the Irish produce a year?" Four million tons annually in the early 1980s, she found.

"Do the Irish still use peat today?" Yes. It's used for heating homes, but it's no good for industry.

The search for answers soon stretches students to all corners of the library; and before long, most have outgrown the resources available in a middle school. This encourages the students to use other community resources.

In their process diaries, students write about their successes, frustrations and changes in understanding. The following are excerpts from Julie's process diary:

> January 15: I think that research is harder and more complicated (than traditional reports). It's very confusing for me.
> January 19: Today I'm figuring out how to do question chains. They're easy once you get the hang of it.
> January 22: I am having difficulty finding a very important book for my research project. . . . I finished up one chain today and started a chain of five. I'm getting the hang!!
> January 25: Today when we did the paragraphing, I finally understood it.
> January 26: One way that I'm clarifying research from report is that research is definitely harder. Research is more extensive. Maybe we're learning more, but it is sure more frustrating.
> January 27: The chaining has clicked in and is flowing.
> February 1: Today when we were grouping our cards and trying to find the main idea, it finally clicked in that main ideas are just what the paragraph is mainly about. It's rather easy.

Ours is a cooperative group classroom in which students are individually accountable for their part in many assignments and also accountable to their group. Participation in group projects is evident in a section of the portfolio entitled "Thank You's and Compliments." When a group member is especially helpful or supportive, one of his peers may write a compliment or a thank you. The receiving student keeps his compliments in an envelope until the portfolio is put together. Then they are added to the portfolio. Some I've seen include:

> You helped keep the group on task and explained your thoughts very well.
> You had some excellent questions, and you helped me find some questions, too.
> You stayed on task and always encouraged my ideas.
> You helped me notice that I was wrong on my inference.

About six weeks before the student-parent portfolio conference, the students bring their soft-covered three-ring binders to school. The papers in the portfolio folder are arranged chronologically in the various sections of the binder: "Reading," "Writing," "Student-Selected Work," "Thinking About Myself," "Thank Yous and Compliments," and "Parents' Page." Then lists are updated.

Three weeks before the conferences, I write a letter to the parents telling them about the upcoming portfolio evening and asking them to reserve the date. Three days before the event, students bring home an invitation that they have designed.

All students sign up for one of four committees needed to actuate the evening: decorating, hospitality, physical setup, or skit. Everyone has an investment in the outcome of the event, and enthusiasm is high.

Everyone works. The decorating committee takes charge of changing the bulletin boards and displaying student projects. The hospitality committee takes charge of invitations and refreshments. The setup committee works to figure out how the space available can supply areas for private conferences, and also works to provide a system for distributing and collecting the portfolios. The skit committee writes and enacts a skit that sets the tone of the evening. Their message tells parents that the portfolios are like pictures of where the students are at that moment in their learning. They explain that while the work might not be perfect, parents can expect to see changes in understanding between work done in the first quarter and work done in the third quarter. The evening rolls.

The parents are warmly supportive of the students' efforts. The "Two Stars and a Wish" page gives the parents an opportunity to notice two exceptional spots in the portfolio and make a wish for their child. Here are some of the comments on this page from the parents of my students:

Rebecca, my darling, you have poetry in your soul, and my jealous eyes are peering over your shoulder. Know that you have powerful talents, and learn not to let formidable obstacles scare you.

Wow, Julie, I'm very impressed with all your effort. It's exciting to see how you take pride in your work. I especially like the way you explained everything to us. I like the learning process, your ideas, and the thought that went into writing your stories. Thank you, honey, for taking the time to share your work with us.

And there was a wish for Natalie that "you be successful at whatever you desire, and always be happy with lots of self esteem."

Ray's mother wrote:

The portfolio was a wonderful idea. It really helped in showing my son's progress and writing abilities. The portfolio was laid out very nicely. It was nice to see not only the teacher's comments, but the student's as well.

Brandon's mother commented:

Brandon's improvement and increased interest in writing and reading are wonderful. He has an interesting and exciting imagination. It is good to see it nourished and encouraged. I wish that all of Brandon's enthusiasm and energy help him attain his dreams.

The fears that I had of student-parent portfolio conferences didn't materialize. Some of the portfolios were beautiful displays of accomplishments. Almost all showed evidence of learning, but there were a few that I was concerned about. One of these was Emmett's.

Emmett's mother had expressed a concern earlier in the school year that the teachers didn't seem to require much homework and that the assignments seemed to lack challenge. In checking the records, I found that Emmett hadn't been handing in most of his homework and that, although he was a highly intelligent student, most of his projects were at a minimal level. Emmett, his mother, and I had a conference, but there were no significant changes in the quality of his output. When Emmett organized his portfolio, it looked pretty shabby to me.

The first time that I passed by Emmett's conference center, I noticed that there wasn't a lot of conversation going on. When I passed by again, I asked how the conference was going, and Emmett's mother commented that Emmett didn't seem to have much to say. The third time around, Emmett's dad invited me to sit down. "This portfolio speaks for itself," he said. "Emmett hasn't been working up to his potential this year." The evidence was before us and opened a dialogue about where to go from that point.

The evening provided a forum for academic conferences, provided an appreciative audience for students' work, and opened avenues for family communication. Artie and his dad had a positive experience.

Artie carries a lot of anger, and it often gets in his way. I was pleased that he had become so involved in the opening skit, and I watched with interest as he began to talk to his dad. He seemed to have a lot to say. When the conferences were over, the students served refreshments, and Artie and his dad made a point of telling me how much they had enjoyed the evening. According to Artie's dad, "Every day I ask Artie, 'How was school today?' He tells me, 'Fine.' Tonight I got my question answered." Artie added, "I like this portfolio evening better than parent-teacher conferences because when parents about teachers talk about you, you just sit there like a thing. Tonight I felt like what I had to say was important."

We schedule our portfolio night for the end of the third quarter, a point in the year when we have a lot to show. We continue our portfolio pulls to the end of the year. We also update our "What I Have Learned This Year" list before the students take their portfolios home a few days before school closes. Happily, the students' interest in their portfolios continues throughout the school year.

My own interest in portfolios has evolved over five or six years. Each year, I began by setting up a writing portfolio. Until I started the student-led portfolio conferences, I couldn't clearly establish whom the portfolio was for. Each year, it fizzled out some time in January. However, I continued to read books and articles, took courses, and talked to my colleagues about portfolios. The student-led portfolio conference seemed like a great idea, but I worried about the risk. What if the academic growth wasn't evident enough?

The thing that set these last three years apart from the others was the commitment I made early in the year to do the parent-student conferences. The commitment was key. I had to make the portfolios work.

The sharing of refreshments after the conferences are over is a celebration. Then, with the spirit of community that we have developed, I work with my students and their parents to put the classroom back in order for the next day. There is a glow of success in the faces around me, and the glow is alive in me, too. Desks are returned to their places in the classroom, and chairs once again scrape across the floor. Then the bustle is replaced by quiet as we turn out the lights and head for home. The light inside of us, though, burns on.

Now that three successful years of student-led portfolio conferences are behind me, I want to do it again and do it better. My experience with the activities involved in portfolio development have strengthened my belief that students need to have more voice in the curriculum, in their goal setting, and in their assessment. My personal goal is to work toward this objective. Why not?

Grade Yourself

One block filled in is equal to a "C."
Two blocks filled in is equal to a "B."
Three blocks filled in is equal to an "A."

BLOCK I: ATTITUDE AND RESPONSIBILITY

To fill in 100% of this block, I must:

Weeks 1 2 3 4 5 6 7 8 9

1. make up work when absent.
2. be in my seat and reading when the bell rings.
3. help, cooperate and participate in group work.
4. practice reciprocal respect with the teacher and with
    other students.
5. volunteer ideas and questions in discussions.
6. take responsibility for my own papers and materials.
7. complete assignments on time.
8. focus on silent reading during entire SSR period.
9. listen.
10. try on all work.

BLOCK II: CONTENT

To fill in 100% of this block, I must:

1. demonstrate understanding of literative elements in
    individual and group work.
2. communicate my interpretation of literature verbally
    so that others can understand my thinking.
3. communicate in writing my interpretation of literature
    so that others can understand my thinking.
4. demonstrate that I have become involved in the text.
5. revise and edit key papers to a quality level.
6. read a minimum of fifteen minutes for homework each
    night.
7. demonstrate growth in vocabulary.

BLOCK III: STRIVE FOR EXCELLENCE

To fill in 100% of this block, I must:

1. interact with books and demonstrate involvement
    through high quality reading journal entries and
    discussions.
2. make an obvious extra effort in class and with
    homework assignments.
3. revise key papers and presentations to an exceptional
    level.
4. share my creativity and insight generously.
5. demonstrate a high level attitude.
6. demonstrate a high level of content.

Figure 12–3

BIBLIOGRAPHY

Atwell, Nancie. 1987. *In the Middle*. Portsmouth, NH: Heinemann.

Crew, Linda. 1989. *Children of the River*. New York: Dell.

Graves, Donald. 1992. *Portfolio Portraits*. Portsmouth, NH: Heinemann.

Hartman, Sandra. "Two Stars and a Wish" statement as part of a video done by the Wyoming Public Schools in Wyoming, Michigan.

Myers, Walter Dean. 1988. *Fallen Angels*. New York: Scholastic.

Rummel, Jack. 1989. *Malcolm X*. New York: Chelsea House.

Van Allsburg, Chris. 1985. *The Polar Express*. Boston: Houghton Mifflin.

White, Ryan, and Ann Marie Cunningham. 1991. *Ryan White: My Own Story*. New York: Dial Books.

Chapter 13
Community Service Learning: A Bridge to Meaning

MARK A. WOOLLEY

> Our culture is at a critical cusp—a time that requires that we define what it means to be a citizen in a democracy. Within our nation we need to foster a greater sense of collective responsibility.   Robert Bellah, *Habits of the Heart*

Defining what it means to be an engaged citizen in a democracy, or what it takes to be a *whole person* or *lifelong learner,* is difficult. But once in a great while, the ability to see clearly and define compellingly arrives in a simple act, the act of reaching out to make a difference. This chapter is about bridges, real and figurative, and how to make crossing them to find deeper meaning part of a teacher's journey.

Working for the last two decades as a social studies educator, specifically in the area of government and citizenship, I have long sought in my own way to help create citizens who care. Whatever one teaches, the connection of students to the community and to real issues has a powerful effect upon the knowledge, skills, and attitudes required of engaged citizens in a pluralistic society. Having visited schools in Denmark and Japan that openly teach virtues such as honesty and personal responsibility, I find recent attempts in the United States to forge school-community relationships and to consider benefits of character education heartening trends.

Engendering what the founders and framers called *civic virtue,* a powerful and personal commitment to the common welfare of all citizens in a free society, is our collective responsibility. Longtime educator Dr. Isidore Starr, considered the father of law-related education in the United States, often shares his deep conviction that *citizen* should be an action verb instead of a noun. *To citizen* effectively requires knowledge, reason, commitment to the value of law in a free society, and personal involvement in national and community life.

I have found that community service learning, the integration of meaningful youth service into the curriculum and culture of a school, is a powerful tool to facilitate the type of citizenship envisioned by Dr. Starr. Such involvement reaps tremendous educational rewards in terms of student feelings of self-worth, skills in critical and creative thinking, cooperative learning, written and oral communication, and introducing students to the real world of work. To me this is a WIN WIN WIN situation: students who care with the skills to make productive changes in their communities, schools with fewer discipline problems as students find meaning and purpose in their education, and communities with serious problems being addressed by well-informed, committed young adults.

Community service to many has a punitive meaning—it's what we *do* to those who have broken the rules. By putting the *learning* into community service, we are simply refining and extending a practice used by master teachers since at least the time of Confucius: learning by doing. Educators have taken many paths to the realization of the transformative power of meaningful service on student knowledge, skills, and attitudes. This chapter is a description of my own path to this realization and what I have learned are key elements of successful community service learning initiatives that nurture caring, skillful, and engaged learners.

My predisposition to community service learning was formed in a quietly activist family. I say *quietly activist*, because at the time I was in high school during the height of the Vietnam conflict, we were not marching or wearing black armbands like students John and Mary Beth Tinker of Iowa, who took their claim of protected free speech for students all the way to the U.S. Supreme Court. However, my formative years were spent in groups built upon an ethic of service to others. Our church youth group provided twice-weekly physical therapy to a brain-damaged girl our own age who could not speak or move, and my Boy Scout troop restored a pioneer cemetery through two years of careful research and hard work. Later, watching the Vietnam war in color every night on television, seeing students shot down at Kent State by our own National Guardsmen, witnessing the violent deaths of Martin Luther King, Jr. and Robert Kennedy in short succession, and living through the low jinks and high crimes of Watergate, I did practice more overt activism in my college years.

Following my graduation in political science and education from Lewis and Clark College in Portland, Oregon, in 1974, I accepted a middle school social studies teaching job in the small farming community of Scio ("SY-oh"), population 550, in the mid–Willamette Valley. Scio's claim to fame, I soon discovered, was the ten intact covered bridges surrounding the town, the reason for its self-proclaimed title of "Covered Bridge Capital of the West" (or "of the Universe," depending on who was advancing civic pride). I was hired three days before the start of school. In one short weekend, I went from working as a waiter in a European restaurant in Portland and living in a house with college friends to renting my own small cottage on a dairy farm, surrounded by the pungent aroma of rotting silage, with the joys of covered bridges that were a short bike ride away.

As any teacher knows, the world intrudes, whether we invite it in or not. For me, in that spring of 1975, the chaotic end of the Vietnam conflict and the fall of Saigon to the North Vietnamese became much more than an occasion for classroom discussions of current events and an analysis of the policies (or lack thereof) that resulted in our eventual retreat. The brother of a sensitive eighth-grade girl was blown apart in a military exercise on a U.S. base shortly after learning that because of the U.S. withdrawal he would not be going to Vietnam. Students were captivated and horrified by images on television of the "baby lifts" from Saigon, during which anxious parents literally pushed or threw their children onto cargo planes to escape what many believed would be a bloodbath for the South Vietnamese most closely associated with the United States. Although the unfortunate military-base accident made students realize that even training for war is dangerous, the television images still seemed of a place far away—a tortured place that we tried to forget, at least to get to sleep.

It wasn't until a phone call to a parent from a nun in the small nearby convent town of Mt. Angel that the events in Vietnam became real for my students. For me, the powerful, positive connection of service and learning was about to become strikingly apparent. A retired Army captain residing in Mt. Angel had volunteered to find temporary housing, clothing, food, sponsors, and specialized medical care for *sixteen* disabled children and some parents who had escaped in one of the last airlifts from Saigon. They had been living in a special school in Saigon run by the Catholic Church, and school officials were convinced that the disabled children would be killed outright because of their "minimal" value in rebuilding a devastated society. The captain received a call from Seattle that the *160* handicapped children and a few adults that he had agreed to sponsor had just landed and would be traveling to Mt. Angel in a bus convoy, expecting their first American meal and a comfortable place to rest!

The small-town network of churches began sending out the "ALL CALL," with the caveat that perhaps children would not want to be directly involved with the unexpected guests because of the severity of some of the conditions and because certain tropical diseases from Asia might be present. For my classes and some others in the area, this was a compelling challenge to become involved, to help provide directly for the many needs of this group, and to relate on a one-on-one basis with these children who had survived against great odds. After the appropriate phone calls, parent permission slips, collections of clothing, blankets, toys, books, and names of possible long-term sponsors, a dozen students and I were given permission to personally deliver the items.

The Vietnamese group had been given temporary shelter in a public beer hall on grounds used annually for a community Oktoberfest celebration and surrounded by a tall metal fence topped by barbed wire. After recent units on the Japanese-American internment and the Holocaust, the irony of refugees successfully surviving a harrowing flight to freedom from a burning city only to be deposited in a barbed wire enclosure in a small town in America was not lost on the students. None of us will forget the hours that we spent inside that compound, playing games with the children and realizing that in reaching out to meet a human need, we were also a part of the American policy of standing by our allies.

Our ongoing efforts to see that our new friends' stay behind barbed wire was short-lived, even though the gates were open, provided a purposeful focus for the remainder of the school year, a time usually spent thinking about baseball and track season. Through service activities designed and carried out by the students and throughout detailed study of American history, politics, and policy regarding Southeast Asia, the students gained insight into the many cause-and-effect connections between our government's actions and people on both sides of the world.

The experience of integrating service to unexpected Vietnamese guests into my classroom activities and content provided the spark for me to continue to seek ways to enable students to become more involved in their own learning. The creation of the Scio Bridge Brigade cemented it.

In the late 1970s, Linn County officials in our county seat of Albany, Oregon, voiced opposition to a State of Oregon plan to place at least five of the county's ten remaining covered bridges on the National Register of Historic Places. Such a national designation would not guarantee that all bridges with protected status would never face demolition, only that there would be many more opportunities for public input should the county attempt to replace them with new steel and concrete spans.

As a suburbanite, I had never seen a covered bridge until moving to Scio and was fascinated by the differences in their style and construction. As a teacher, I saw that this issue had all the elements of a truly integrated course of study: Oregon and U.S. history; engineering; public policy at the local, state, and national levels; writing and research; and the creative arts. Yet as a newcomer, I had no idea whether my enthusiasm for the bridges was truly shared by the locals, specifically by my students who had grown up with them just as I had grown up with the many sleek steel spans crossing the Willamette River in downtown Portland.

As an initial exercise to gauge interest in the topic and to generally spur creativity among students who hadn't had much exposure to free writing and drawing, I took several rolls of slides of the bridges from various perspectives and at different times of the day, provided students with paper and colored pencils, put on some soft jazz, slowly showed the slides, and asked them to write or draw anything at all about covered bridges or about anything else which came to mind. What occurred has never happened quite the same way before or since on any other issue that I've introduced in a classroom. After some initial questions ("Where did you get this weird music, Mr. Woolley? Is this what they listen to in college?") and a few comments ("That's where Jubal jumped off last summer!"), there was silence, broken only by the sound of pencils and pens writing, shuffling papers, and incidental requests. ("Mr. Woolley, I *really* need green. Can you get me a green, Mr. Woolley?")

What I had intended as an activity for one class session extended to three, as students asked to view the slides again and again, continuously refining or adding to what they drew and wrote about the covered bridges that were so much a part of their lives. The results spilled over desks, filled the counters and bulletin boards: poems of every length and description, three-dimensional drawings in exacting detail by students with no specialized art training, stories and memories and recollections composed with care and love. Students with spelling deficits and other learning difficulties pored over their work, changing a word here, a color there. Often students combined poems and images on the same large sheets of paper, filling every corner with emotion. The power of their words and images, notwithstanding a few spelling errors or awkward syntax, was stunning. To pull out a red pen (or even a friendly lavender one) and *correct* what were one-of-a-kind art pieces would have been unthinkable.

I deferred my next lesson plan to have the students compose and refine business letters to the county commissioners that would outline their feelings about the covered bridges and explore options for their preservation. Knowing that an important hearing regarding the covered bridges and the federal designation was coming up, I asked the students whether we should send some or all of their work to the commissioners so that they could get a better idea of local feeling about the bridges. After all, noted

some of the students, the county commissioners lived in the much larger town of Albany and may not have understood the role of the bridges in the lives and struggling tourist businesses of the little town of Scio. It was unanimous: We would send our creative work in all its spontaneity and colorful glory, with a cover letter inviting the commissioners to come to the school to explain their viewpoints as well as to return the original artwork. Surely, the elected leaders of the county would not only appreciate the time, effort, and creativity contained in the large package of citizen opinion, but the sentiments expressed would go a long way toward convincing them to do everything in their power to save the bridges.

Two days later, I got a phone call in the evening from a teaching colleague who lived in Albany and who received its daily newspaper, the *Albany Democrat-Herald.*

"You don't get the Albany paper, do you?" she asked.
"No, why?"
"Well, why don't you sit down and I'll tell you."

I quickly envisioned a possible headline: "STUDENT WRITING SWAYS COMMISSIONER OPINION ON BRIDGE PRESERVATION." As I sat listening, first in confusion and then in growing anger, this is what my colleague read from the front page of the *Albany Democrat-Herald* of March 11, 1978:

"BAD SPELLING MARKS KIDS' APPEALS FOR COVERED BRIDGES"

Scio Middle School youngsters did what they thought they could do to support saving Linn County's covered bridges. But the response wasn't all it could have been.

The Linn County commissioners Friday read through some of the more than 100 letters, poems, essays, and drawings the students sent. But instead of being challenged to do more about preserving the county's 10 covered bridges, the commissioners said maybe they should do something about offering some English classes.

The spelling was bad, the grammar bad and the letters seemed to miss the whole point, the commissioners said. The point, said Vernon Schrock, commission chairman, is that Linn County wouldn't have any covered bridges now if the county wasn't already doing all it can to save the bridges.

Commissioner Ian Timm, noting a line in one of the letters about slaughter of our bridges, said the only way he could figure that a bridge could be slaughtered would be for a loaded log truck to try to cross some of the narrow, weak covered bridges the county wants to replace.

Commissioner Mary Keenan, a former teacher and county school administrator, said she was disappointed that the students' teacher hadn't taken more care on spelling and grammar.

They will be included in hearings such as the one set for 7:30 p.m. Wednesday in the county's armory building to review the effects of a state proposal to place the bridges on the National Register of Historic Places.

The front-page public rebuff of my students' sincere attempt to share with public officials their deeply held views about a public policy matter resulted in a quick succession of feelings in students, parents, teachers, and residents of Scio, not dissimilar to the stages that individuals go through who experience a death in the family: initial denial and disbelief, confusion and anger, and a final determination to channel one's feelings about the incident into long-term, positive actions designed to move beyond the sense of loss. In this case, students were determined to share their feelings face-to-face with the commissioners at an upcoming hearing regarding the fate of the covered bridges. In addition to a flood of letters to the editor and the commissioners, the chronology of subsequent headlines in the *Albany Democrat-Herald* tells the story of the creation of the "Scio Bridge Brigade," a committed group of sixth through eighth graders who ultimately changed Oregon history regarding the preservation of covered bridges:

"Snubbed Students to Visit Commissioners" (3/15/78)
"Covered Bridges, Kids, Win Support" (3/16/78)
"Scio Group Fails to 'Cover' Feelings: Scio Bridge Brigade Born" (3/23/78)

In the course of the next two years, approximately forty student members of the "Scio Bridge Brigade" lived out a lesson in civic participation and meaningful youth service. Combined with classroom study about the political system, bridge design, media campaigns, historical research, and persuasive writing, the students organized a comprehensive program dedicated to covered bridge preservation of covered bridges that had some amazing results.

The County Commissioners, after initial foot-dragging about placing any of the remaining ten bridges on the National Register of Historic Places, agreed to place five bridges on the list for added protection. The students organized intensive public campaigns regarding two bridges slated for complete demolition. Using a self-published "Guide to Bridge Saving in Linn County," students presented petitions signed by many Linn County residents at public hearings.

One of the doomed bridges was bypassed by a new span and left open for pedestrians and another stands today at a completely new location,

SCIO BRIDGE BRIGADE
save our bridges!

painstakingly reconstructed piece by piece by the Oregon National Guard. The students were also instrumental in forming the "Covered Bridge Society of Oregon" in 1979, which remains to this day active in the study and preservation of covered bridges.

Honored with a cash award and citation in Washington, D.C.'s Renwick Gallery by the National Trust for Historic Preservation, the story of the "Scio Bridge Brigade" is chronicled in the *American Civics* textbook by

Harcourt Brace as an example of *Citizenship in Action*. As a teacher, I was convinced by the experience of the "Scio Bridge Brigade" convinced me that the combination of service and learning is a powerful bridge to meaning that creates a multitude of potential benefits for learners and communities. In addition to its transformative power over students' self-confidence and feelings of efficacy, community service learning develops and refines specific skills in critical thinking and analysis, oral and written communication, cooperative learning, and retention of purposeful and interrelated data.

With the passage of the National and Community Service Act of 1990 and its "Serve America" program, which provides millions of dollars for community service learning programs sponsored by schools or community-based agencies, and an aggressively proservice administration in the White House, it is tempting to rush headlong into almost any initiative or program with the term "youth service" attached to it. Luckily, principles of good practice for combining service and learning have been incorporated into the competitive process in many state programs participating in "Serve America." These principles reflect grassroots experience and the thinking and research of thousands of people in hundreds of programs. Many of these principles have long been a part of effective programs in community service learning in some of America's private schools as well as in the classrooms of teachers committed to *outcome-based education* and *performance-based assessments* well before the terms were attached to the notion that integrated, demonstrated learning contributes directly to the creation of curious and engaged lifelong learners and citizens.

If not all programs are created equal, what are some key elements for effective community service learning initiatives? From my own classroom experience as well as programs I've evaluated in rural, urban, and suburban settings, there are a number of factors that seem to be present in the creation and refinement of programs that achieve positive results in terms of learning and that provide ongoing, meaningful service to the community. My own list would include the following principles:

- Successful programs begin with a thoughtful, collective student examination and analysis of the community to determine real community needs. Methods for such examination and analysis abound: "drawing one's community" with subsequent oral presentations and additional research, community-needs assessments utilizing surveys and structured interviews with community leaders and agency personnel, and creative projects employing video, taped interviews, slide/tape presentations, and mixed-media art presentations.

- Central to programs that successfully tie learning to service is a focus on policy. Essentially, policy can be described to students as an agreed-upon course of action created, adopted, and followed by individuals, institutions, and government to attempt to solve a problem or achieve a goal. Helping in a soup kitchen may give a student feelings of empathy and warmth in serving others. For such a student to comment, as some have, "That was incredible! I hope my children and grandchildren get to do this," shows that such a student has not made the connection between the specific action of serving food and understanding and seeking to ameliorate the serious social problems of homelessness and hunger in our society. To examine possible causes of these problems and various effects of social and governmental policy regarding them offers a much more powerful lesson in cause-and-effect as well as government's potential and limitations in facing a multitude of social issues.

· Effective community service learning projects and initiatives reflect student ownership and individual or collective preference. I believe that the sequence of events that resulted in the student creation of the Scio Bridge Brigade, with its clear mission and broad student and community support, was a rare occurrence. More often, the design and implementation of effective student service initiatives are more individualized, reflecting the diversity of issues and policy alternatives in most communities. While the issue at hand and plan of action to deal with it may vary, the connection with careful policy analysis and a clear student voice is essential.

· Programs that are built around the enthusiasms and dedication of one faculty member and result in extracurricular clubs may be exciting, but are often short-lived. When I left Scio, the School District, City of Scio, and an adult covered-bridge group based in another city vied for the appropriation of the popular logo of the "Scio Bridge Brigade." Although certain students and adults carried on the effort individually, it did not remain an ongoing part of the curriculum. Faculties that explore together the many benefits of community service learning, refine models for interdisciplinary collaboration, and integrate initiatives into existing required and elective courses reap the long-term benefits of student engagement, critical thinking, and enhanced oral and written communication skills.

· Successful programs provide for frequent, structured reflection and evaluation and well-defined learning goals and tasks. Tools for individual and collective reflection include diaries and journals, interdisciplinary writing projects, and simply time set aside to thoughtfully compare results to initial goals. Specific rubrics and instruments to evaluate projects are as numerous as the projects themselves, but most seek to answer some key questions:

- Did the project address a genuine need? Describe how.
- Did the project reflect clear service and learning goals?
- Did the project engender genuine, active, and sustained organizational commitment?
- Was the project flexible enough to provide for changing circumstances and individual and group needs?
- Did the overall program reflect a thoughtful attempt to reach diverse populations, whether through intergenerational aspects or cross-race, collaborative projects?
- Did the project truly link service learning to the curriculum and enrich student understanding of the curriculum? Did it reflect interdisciplinary collaboration?
- Did the individuals involved in the project deal positively and creatively with obstacles?
- Did the overall program enhance connections and partnerships with business and community groups?

Not all of the questions above have easy or easily quantifiable answers, but a thoughtful response to each one by students, teachers, community members, and other individuals impacted by community service learning initiatives provides valuable input in the refinement of ongoing programs. Successful programs become part of the culture of schools, crossing the bridge to meaning offered by the marriage of meaningful service and purposeful learning.

Many reference materials are available that provide direction in answering the multitude of questions raised by this approach to education regarding funding, liability, scheduling, educational credit, and whether to require or simply encourage the development of such programs. Many of these resources are listed at the end of this chapter. I invite you to explore the richness and transformative power of community service learning for learner-citizens of all ages, a value so well expressed by Dr. Martin Luther King, Jr.:

> Everyone can be great because anyone can serve. You don't have to have a college degree to serve. You don't have to make your subject and your verb agree to serve. . . . You only need a heart full of grace. A soul generated by love.

SERVICE LEARNING RESOURCES

Active Citizenship Today (ACT). Close-Up Foundation, 44 Canal Center Plaza, Alexandria, VA 22314. Attention: Frank Dirks, Project Co-Director. 1-800-336-5479, ext. 350.

Changing Our World. Zephyr Press, PO Box 113488-F, Tuscon, AZ 85732-3448. (602) 322-5090.

Civic Achievement Award Proram. Close Up Foundation. 44 Canal Center Plaza, Alexandria, VA 22314.

Combining Service and Learning: An Annotated Bibliography. National Society for Experiential Education, 3509 Haworth Drive, Suite 207, Raleigh, NC 27609-7229. (919) 787-3263. Two volumes.

Connections: Service Learning in the Middle Grades. National Center for Service Learning in Early Adolescence, Center for Advanced Study in Education, Graduate School and University Center of the City University of New York, 25 West 43rd St., Suite 612, New York, NY 10036-8099. (212) 642-2946.

Conrad, Dan, and Diane Hedin. *Youth Service: A Guidebook for Developing and Operating Effective Programs.* Independent Sector, 1828 L Street NW, Washington, DC 20036. (202) 223-8100.

Coordinator's Handbook. The Thomas Jefferson Forum, Inc., 131 State Street, Suite 628, Boston, MA 02109. (617) 523-6699.

Effective Participation in Government. Effective Participation in Government Program, Box 632, Fayetteville, NY 13066.

Facts and Faith. National Youth Leadership Council, 1910 West County Road B, St. Paul, MN 55113-1337.

Kielsmeier, James, and Rich Willits, eds. *Growing Hope.* National Youth Leadership Council, 1910 West County Road B, St. Paul, MN 55113-1337.

Learning By Giving. National Youth Leadership Council, 1910 West County Road B., St. Paul, MN 55113-1337.

Lewis, Barbara. *Kid's Guide to Social Action.* Free Spirit Publishing, 400 First Avenue North, Suite 616, Minneapolis, MN 55401-1724. 1-800-735-7323.

Making a Difference. Washington Leadership Institute, 310 Campion Tower, Seattle University, Seattle, WA 98122. (206) 296-5630.

McPherson, Kate. *Developing Caring Children.* Project Service Leadership, 12703 N.W. 20th Avenue, Vancouver, WA 98685.

————. *Enriching Learning Through Service.* Project Service Leadership, 12703 N.W. 20th Avenue, Vancouver, WA 98685. (206) 576-5070.

————. *Learning Through Service.* Project Service Leadership, 12703 N.W. 20th Avenue, Vancouver, WA 98685.

Melcher, Joseph. *Caring Is the Key: Building a School-Based Intergenerational Service Program.* PennSERVE: The Governor's Office of Citizen Service, 1304 Labor and Industry Building, Harrisburg, PA 17120. (717) 787-1971.

Middle School Curriculum. Maryland Student Service Alliance, 200 West Baltimore Street, Baltimore, MD 21201. (410) 333-2427.

The National Indian Youth Leadership Model: A Manual for Program Leaders: National Youth Leadership Council, 1910 West County Road B., St. Paul, MN 55113-1337.

No Kiddin Around. Activism 2000 Project, Information USA, Inc., PO Box E, Kensington, MD 20895. (301) 942-6303.

Our Only Earth: A Curriculum for Global Problem Solving. Zephyr Press. 1-800-350-0851.

Parsons, Cynthia. *SerVermont and the U.S.A.* National Youth Leadership Council, 1910 West County Road B., St. Paul, MN 55113-1337.

Principles of Good Practice. The Johnson Foundation, Inc., 33 East Four Mile Road, Racine, WI 53401-0547. (414) 681-3344.

Reaching Out: School-Based Prorams for Community Service. National Crime Prevention Council, 1700 K Street NW, Second Floor, Washington, DC 20006-3817. (202) 446-6272.

Reflection: The Key to Service Learning. National Center for Service Learning in Early Adolescence, Center for Advanced Study in Education, Graduate School and University Center of the City University of New York, 25 West 43rd St., Suite 612, New York, NY 10036-8099, (212) 642-2946.

Reflective Teaching. Pennsylvania Institute for Environmental and Community Service Learning, Pennsylvania State University (Ogontz Campus), Sutherland Building, 4th Floor, 1600 Woodland Road, Abingdon, PA 19001.

Rolzinski, Catherine A. *Adventure of Adolescence.* Youth Service America, 1319 F Street NW, Suite 900, Washington, DC 20004.

Salzman, Mariam, and Teresa Reisgies. *150 Ways Teens Can Make a Difference.* Peterson's Guides, 1-800-338-3282.

Skills for Adolescence. Quest International, 1-800-837-2801.

StarServe Resource Directory & Packet. StarServe, 701 Santa Monica Boulevard, Suite 220, Santa Monica, CA 90401. (310) 452-STAR.

Teen Power! Volunteer Centre of Metropolitan Toronto, 344 Bloor Street West No. 207, Toronto, Ontario MSS 3A7. (416) 961-6888.

Valued Youth Partnership: Programs in Caring. Coca-Cola Valued Youth Program, Intercultural Development Research Association (IDRA), 5835 Callaghan, Suite 350, San Antonio, TX 78228-1190. (512) 684-8180.

VYTAL (Volunteer Youth Training and Leadership). Volunteer Action Center, 730 River Avenue, Pittsburgh, PA 15212. (412) 261-6010.

Special Education

Special Education Curriculum. Maryland State Department of Education, 200 West Baltimore Street, Baltimore, MD 21201. (301) 333-2427.

Peer Assistance

Myrick Robert D., and Robert P. Bowman. *Becoming a Friendly Helper: A Handbook for Student Facilitators.* Educational Media Corporation, PO Box 21311, Minneapolis, MN 55421.

Myrick Robert D., and Tom Erney. *Youth Helping Youth: A Handbook for Training Peer Facilitators.* Educational Media Corporation, PO Box 21311, Minneapolis, MN.

Videos

Citizen Stories: Democracy and Responsibility in American Life. CloseUp Foundation, 44 Canal Center Plaza, Alexandria, VA 22314. 1-800-765-3131.

Coming Across. The Right Channel, 21 Ozone Avenue No. 5, Venice, CA 90291.

The Courage to Care, The Strength to Serve. Maryland State Department of Education, 200 West Baltimore Street, Baltimore, MD 21201. (301) 333-2427.

Today's Heroes. Today's Heroes, PO Box 19247, Washington, DC, 20036.

Databases

K-12 School-Based Programs. Contact: Ingrid Sausjord, Program Director, Ford National Expansion Project, Constitutional Rights Foundation, 601 S, Kingsley Drive, Los Angeles, CA 90005. (213) 487-5590.

Service Learning Program Descriptions. Contact: Felicia George, Clearinghouse Coordinator, National Center for Service Learning in Early Adolescence, Center for Advanced Study in Education, Graduate School and University Center of the City University of New York, 25 West 43rd Street, Suite 612, New York, NY 10036-8099. (212) 642-2306.

Chapter 14
A Conversation
on Assessment

*O*n June 3, 1994, a Friday evening at the end of a long school week, a group
of friends gathered for potluck supper and conversation. Twelve Portland
public school teachers, many of whom have written chapters in this book,
took part in the discussion: Mary Burke-Hengen, Winnie Charley, Tim Gillespie,
Libby Kennedy, Toni Kennedy, Cher Laughlin, Kristel McCubbin, Marilyn Man-
chester, Theresa Murray, Jackie O'Connor, Mark Oldani, and Michelann Ortloff.
All were veteran middle school teachers, though by the time of the conversation
Mary had moved to a high school position, Theresa to an elementary school, Tim to
a district curriculum job, and Michelann to an elementary principalship. The others came straight from their middle school classrooms. All knew ahead of time that
the conversation was to be about assessment in the social studies; but, as will become quickly apparent, the talk ranged over many fields. We met high up in Mary
Burke-Hengen's condo in downtown Portland, enjoying a view of the thickly
wooded hills that rise west of the city and the Willamette River as it angles north-
ward toward its confluence with the Columbia River. We filled plates, sat down in
a circle, turned on two tape-recorders, and began to talk. Over the next two hours,
the conversation drew the circle tighter as night settled on the city.

Later, a typed transcript of the tape was mailed to the participants in the discussion. All were given an opportunity to review the transcript and edit their remarks, adding or subtracting for clarity. The following is thus an edited version of
our discussion about assessment.

TIM: Our topic of conversation today is assessment in the
social studies. By assessment, we usually mean a process
by which we evaluate how we are doing, students and
teachers. Evaluation has, at its heart, *valuing*. So the first
question is, what do you value in your teaching of social

studies? What is it that you want your students to know
or be able to do? What learning or behavior are you looking for, from your students and from yourself?

KRISTEL: I want students to understand that history is fluid. A lot of
times students think it's a given, cut and dried. I remember a moment I had with my "J.D." social studies class—
that's juvenile delinquent, all the kids had been in and out
of trouble with the law. We were studying Lewis and Clark
and their Shoshone guide, Sacajawea, and we were talking
about how Sacajawea might have gotten connected up
with her husband, the French trapper Charbonneau. It is a
historical speculation; there is no definitive answer. We'd
read a novel, Scott O'Dell's *Streams to the River, River to the
Sea*, and we read the textbook, and some students looked
in the encyclopedia. All have different versions of Sacajawea's story.

TIM: In O'Dell's book, Sacajawea is won in a bones game, like a
piece of property, right?

KRISTEL: Exactly, that story has her won in a gambling game. Another version is, "Oh, they fell in love." Personally, I doubt
that one the most. And there are others. So we were talking about that, and there was this moment when someone
said, "So they don't *know*? But it's history, they're supposed to *know*!" That's when the class *got it* about the tentative and fluid nature of history.

MICHELANN: So you want students to know that there are alternate versions of the truth, different people's stories?

KRISTEL: A lot of times, I think, in rote teaching of history, we lose
the fluidness, the stories, and the people's voices that are
important.

MARY: One of the things I think we want to teach about history is
to pay attention to whose voices are heard and whose are
not. The writers of the story have the power to tell it in
their own ways. Helping our students to develop their
abilities to consider differing viewpoints about historical
facts and ideas is one of the most important teacher responsibilities. Meantime, we live and work in a system
where the time it takes to acquire knowledge and skill is
divided into quarters and semesters and years. How can
we retain and maintain our sense of what is important for

us to attend to and yet evaluate the knowledge you believe students need to learn?

KRISTEL: I look for examples in the students' writing. The students wrote a reaction piece at the end of the novel, and I
looked to see if they had put in there somewhere this idea
of alternate versions. I wanted them to express some
sense that history is, in part, a series of questions and that
there's not always an exact definitive answer, or there
may be different historical perspectives that reflect different biases.

THERESA: Tying into that, I want my students to be able to take different theories and perspectives and make sense of it all
for themselves, to use their own critical thinking and make
some sense that means something to them and has value
to them.

MICHELANN: I agree that an important learning for students is to become critical analyzers of the barrage of information they
receive so they don't accept just one perspective. We had
recently a very bad experience with a child bringing a gun
to our school. It got extensive coverage on TV and in the
newspapers. I talked with our fifth graders, and they realized that what was presented in the press was very different from what the reality was for the child and his family.
They were very upset about that. Our task, then, is to help
children become critical readers and thinkers and analyzers, not content with reading one source, but able to go to
other sources and to form opinions that reflect different
and varying perspectives.

TONI: My hope is that my students understand that all events
arise out of a specific time and place, that the social conditions and economics of one era are not the same for another. In the specific historical era we study, I want the students to know that society shapes events and events shape
society and there's this dialectic going on all the time. Last
year, we learned that up until the late nineteenth century,
laws considered women as chattel, like a good cow or a
herd of sheep. One of my girls said, "That would never
have happened to me," and another student responded,
"Oh, yes, it would have." These comments led to a discussion of what people accept at one time they may find re-

pulsive at another. Why do students need to know this? So they can bring to their study the realization that we don't have to repeat our mistakes of the past.

WINNIE: One of the things I value is the recognition by my students of recurring themes in history, like the idea that civilizations often develop along rivers, or the idea that many times the abuses by a ruler of his own people have led to the ruler's demise. I'd like them to make connections between themes, too.

MARK: What I try for in my teaching of social studies is what I value in myself and in my students—that they *do* something about something when they learn, that they make a change in behavior, do an action, empower themselves in some way, accomplish something. Right now, my students are cleaning the school the last period of the day. They go around and pick up paper in the halls and in the bathroom. There are a lot of problems at my middle school in terms of how people treat each other, and my students decided that was something they could do right now to make it a better place. It's a little thing, but it's the kind of thing I look for, that truly spontaneous action—initiating a letter to someone, trying to solve a problem with someone by talking things out. So, one thing I look for when I evaluate students is how they change and how they act to make their school, their home, or their community a better place.

MICHELANN: That's the kind of building community and connecting to the world I value, students recognizing that they have an essential connection with the world, and *demonstrating* it.

JACKIE: I want students to understand history as stories. If they can get a sense of the stories of people, and feel for them and understand them, you've got your history. I still remember seventh-grade Texas history. Mr. Little, the teacher I remember, told history through stories.

TIM: Maybe that's the final assessment for us all, whether years later students remember our classes as fondly as you do Mr. Little's class, Jackie.

MARK: Stories are important not only for empathy but for understanding. I heard a speaker talking about scientists who work with advanced computers that are broken. The speaker discovered that these high-caliber computer technicians would sit around and start telling stories: "Well, when I fixed this similar machine one time. . . ." or "When I had this other problem with this thing . . . ." They'd go through their background and dredge up information, and it helped them come up with ways to repair the computers. For students, too, to find a personal story helps them get meaning for themselves and their understanding of a problem or issue. Because we're talking about eleven- to fourteen-year-olds, and when you take big historical issues, in my experience, very few students will make great intellectual analyses. Most of them rely on a personal way of reacting and try to relate their thinking to their lives somehow and how the world works. It's great when students make generalizations such as, "Tyrants will always fall," but it's more likely students will construct their own meaning from a historical abstraction by saying, "Yeah, I remember this guy who was a playground bully, and he got his comeuppance."

MARILYN: I want students to find relevance in studying history by making personal connections, whether it be through a new insight or observation or by finding a familiar place on the map or a person in history they find fascinating or a relative with a story. That personal connection is what I want.

KRISTEL: I don't want students to just make personal connections, to focus on themselves. I want them also to understand others. I've always liked that term "historical empathy," which I try to cultivate using writing. I've often used "An Incident in Little Rock," about the difficult desegregation of schools there. After the students have learned what happened, then they write from a cop's perspective, the Black children's perspective, and the White children's perspective of that incident. I ask my kids to write from roles other than what they're already sympathetic to, so they can try to step outside themselves.

MARY: Understanding point of view is a big part of what we're trying to accomplish. We all need opportunities to have our assumptions and beliefs challenged, to reevaluate the way we look at the world. John Dewey, for one, defined education as change. Just learning dates and times, stuffing students with information, is not going to change anybody, but if you come to understand another person's point of view, you are changed, altered in your thinking and in your behavior. You have become a different person. It's a tall order, but I think that's what we want, to bring change. If students come into my classroom as bigots, they shouldn't leave as bigots. For example, some kids tend to be homophobic, but I won't give up on trying to challenge their thinking about this. One student said on the last day of school last year, "You just never let up, do you?" And I said, "Well, this is the last day and this is my last chance!" As the other students were working on their final test, he and I continued our dialogue. Finally, he said, "Okay, I get it. I don't have to like them, I don't have to be one, but I need to have respect that they have the same legal and human rights that I have." That's change. He was changed. I wish I could say that always happens. It doesn't, but I never give up. And that's why an important part of how I view assessment is the answers we can give to ourselves about how we as individuals and as a group are changed.

TONI: Of course, that's at the heart of our task. But I'd like to make a slight detour to ask a question of the group. I've heard some criticism of information, but I stress dates and facts in my class. I can't imagine studying history without doing so. I want to know how the rest of you feel about that.

KRISTEL: Facts are a part of the study of history, but not the focus. How can you eliminate data? Details provide context.

MARY: I often use essay questions for assessment and draw many of the questions from the kids. Each question will ask students to speak to an issue, whatever it is, but I also ask the students to give a context, saying, "If you come within five to ten years of the correct date, most of the time that's good enough." I agree with you, Toni, that it is important that students know World War II didn't happen in 1890. Maybe you start with that personal connection again. Sometimes in the classroom kids will ask me, "Did they have refrigerators when you were little?" Actually, my family didn't have one in my very early childhood. So I tell them, "I'm a living historical time line, ask me anything about 1939 on, you got it!" And once in a while I'll bring in people, like two women who work in our school library. They come up and they do the Charleston for the kids, because they were alive when the Charleston was the dance, and they tell them about the speakeasies, and they tell them about what they did in the war, and they tell them about coupon books; and the kids then begin to build a time line. But, I agree, they ought to know World War I came before World War II.

MARK: Yeah, in 1963 and 1965, wasn't it? *(Laughter)*

TIM: It seems to me that facts, in and of themselves—names, dates—they don't have meaning, and they don't stick in students' minds just by being presented. Students need larger understandings, conceptual frameworks, theories, ways to use information. But theories have no weight without data; they have to be supported by examples. So students need it all: dates and names, stories, personal connections, concepts and themes, intellectual frameworks. Maybe dates and times have gotten a bad reputation from experiences we've all had when we weren't called on to consider the meanings of events but just had to do a lot of memorizing for a test, when the assessments didn't go much deeper than, "What year was the Battle of Hastings?"

TONI: 1066!

MICHELANN: See! Toni knows! *(Laughter)*

TIM: Let's keep talking about what we value in the teaching of social studies, and how we then assess those learnings of our students and ourselves.

THERESA: Social studies is an action, as Mark was saying, that requires reading and writing and speaking and performance. Citizenship is just a portion of the social studies curriculum, but it's my passion and why I've always taught American history. The picture I want my students to get at a young age is that citizenship is active and that part of a citizen's responsibilities, linked with all those wonderful rights, is that we have to do something to protect our rights, we have to speak up, and we have to vote. If they see that in the classroom, then it becomes natural in their life.

MICHELANN: The responsibility of citizenship is to become a critical analyzer and an actor. Much of the empowerment of people, it seems to me, comes through words: writing and speaking. Somehow I want to give kids the notion of the power of words to shape the events of history, to shape personal events, to craft stories to share, and to connect.

TONI: Jean Vanier, who established the L'Arche communities for the mentally handicapped, has spoken about the power of words. He says that our *words* will always be way ahead of where we are in our moral development. But if we speak the words, and we believe in them, their power will thrust us forward. So I try to provide opportunities for the students to write and speak about what they value so that their words can move them forward morally.

MARY: My goal is that my students will become adults who live in society in a just and honorable way.

LIBBY: I want students to have a sense of hope in their future and in their role in it. I had a speaker come this week to talk about Native American history, and many students—it was a mostly white class—left feeling guilty and terrible about themselves, without a sense of hope. They need to note the realities, but they also need to feel that there's some hope, that there's something they can do now, in their own lives, to change things for the better. I also think kids can be real negative, cutting things down, tearing the program apart. They can have their opinions, but I want them to also come up with some solutions and alternatives, ideas of their own, positive ways things can be changed.

TIM: I recently read an interesting remark by Kathy Acker, the writer. She said that we've done a great job of deconstruction the last twenty years in society; we've refined our skills at pricking pomposity, attacking oppressive institutions, being skeptical, and questioning authority and old myths. But what are we left with, besides cynicism? We still need new visions and ideals and ways of working that can bring us together and give us hope. Our students can't only be critics of the world; they have to be creators of it. So maybe the final assessment will be the world we see them making when we're retired in our rocking chairs!

(At this point, we took a break in our conversation, stretched, reprovisioned ourselves, then began to talk again.)

TIM: We've talked about many qualities we value and learning we want to occur in our social studies classes, from an ability to see multiple perspectives to a willingness to engage in civic activity to a capacity for hope. But the question is, How do we evaluate all that, how do we assess it? We have these very high ambitions that we've collectively expressed. How is it that we know we're getting where we want to go? How do we let students know they're getting somewhere, and how do we let parents know, and the tax-paying citizenry? What sorts of assessments are you doing in your classrooms?

JACKIE: Well, I was really curious about what I do, so I made a list: Students do written work, they make visuals, they discuss, they keep learning logs, they do tests, they do self-evaluations, they do projects, they do presentations, they do homework. It's like a little bit of everything. There's not just one way to assess growth and achievement.

TIM: So you have multiple measures of progress. Okay, then what do you *do* with all that stuff, all that varied data from all those different kinds of activities?

JACKIE: Well, *(in bemused voice)* you just grade them and put them in the grade book. Isn't that what *you* do? *(Laughter)*

MARY: Okay, so how *do* you grade, how do you decide?

JACKIE: It depends on what I'm doing, it depends on what I want.

TIM: Let me check on something. We all work at different schools. Is everyone here responsible for giving letter grades? Who's not? Okay, just Kristel and Mark. Looks like everyone else has a traditional report card on which you're required by your school to give letter grades. How do any of you make sense of that antiquated system?

CHER: What I like to do is let the kids in on my criteria for grading by showing them what an A looks like.

TIM: By showing them excellent sample papers or projects, you mean?

CHER: Yes, like say we're doing a visual project about the Constitution. It has to have rich, accurate content, but it also has a visual quality to it. I put the A's in a pile and share and discuss them with the class. When the kids see that, there are less arguments about, "How come you graded mine this way?"

TONI: I also try not to let students' grades ever be a surprise to them to the extent that they'd have to ask me why they got a certain grade. I try to work with them so that they and I have both somehow had a share in their grade. I conference with students regularly, once a week if I can. When my projects fail and I'm left with grades that don't seem to match my experience with a particular student, often it is because I have asked them to do something that I have not attempted myself. I cannot share with them what I found to be pitfalls, challenges, or successes. In these cases, for me, learning is not mutual, and neither is the evaluation. I want to remember that through true dialogue, my students and I both share in an evaluation process that's fair.

MARILYN: I have another way of involving students. Sometimes I take a paper or project and say, "Now, *this*, . . . what kind of a grade would you give this?" And I have the kids look at it, and make evaluative decisions.

WINNIE: I like using student models, because it works terrifically. But I'm having more of a problem now because I ask students to select what they consider their best works for their portfolios, and they own the portfolios. It used to be that I'd have all kinds of student examples. Now they take that portfolio home in June!

CHER: Then what you miss, Winnie, is a target for kids to shoot at. I think they need to see quality models, to spur them on, to see how to take an idea farther.

LIBBY: I don't often show kids' work, because sometimes students get intimidated or their creativity is stifled or funneled in the direction of the models. My way of getting quality work is letting the kids know that their products are going to be seen and that everything they do will be presented to the class. That makes them accountable and makes them want to do well.

CHER: Tell me about how you have students present their work, Libby.

LIBBY: Well, they get up and talk about what they've done. They show it to their classmates and pass things around. Then it goes up on display. I grade it months later, and often they've forgotten that it's going to be graded. The motive for doing a good job is the presentation. The grade is not why they're doing it; it's a separate thing.

MICHELANN: How about building more complex performances into this notion of assessment? I don't want us to limit ourselves to just products—papers or projects or tests—but to look at how students can act through a situation, how they can connect with other people using social studies themes and ideas. Now that I'm working as an elementary school principal with younger children, what I would see as a performance assessment in social studies is whether a child who has a conflict with another child can come to me, sit down with that other child, articulate the problem, come to a solution using words, write that solution out, agree to act on it, then act on it. So, I want to see us get off the paper a little bit and think of the notion of assessment as something being . . .

THERESA: Practical in the big world.

MICHELANN: Right, but also complex, and something using listening and speaking and reading and writing *connected* as a demonstration of the acquisition of social studies content.

JACKIE: I have kids do a lot of their own grading. They have to justify their grade. It's real interesting, they usually are tougher on themselves than I generally would be. And any time we do group work, they all have to privately grade each other, and they have to give reasons for the grades they give other group members. They are so specific, and generally the grades they give the others are pretty much right on with what I would give. I think students are pretty aware of who their classmates are and what they can do. They understand that this low kid who really belongs in special education can't do what this talented kid can, and they grade him based on that. I think we need to use them more, focus on them more.

TIM: Yet I just had some graduate school students in a writing class I teach at night do self-evaluations the week before report cards, and they *all* gave themselves A's, those who had done exceptional work as well as those who had missed class periods and assignments. It seemed more an opportunity for self-promotion than honest self-assessment. Of course, how can you feel free to give yourself an honest evaluation when the teacher ultimately has all the power and that darn final grade determines whether you can stay in graduate school, whether your district will reimburse the tuition you paid, all that stuff? Maybe this is just an issue for adults, but I sure hate those reductive little letter grades.

WINNIE: I've had that experience with middle school kids, too. There are kids who say it's an A paper and you look at it and you know it's not close.

JACKIE: They should have to back it up, that's the difference. If you're going to give yourself an A, you're going to have to prove it to me.

WINNIE: For some students, just doing an assignment and minimally meeting the requirements is an A or a B. Their work may have no exceptional points, but in their experience, if you just *did* it, then it deserves a high grade.

JACKIE: Part of it is training them at the beginning of the year, holding up a piece from a past class that is not so great. "Okay," I ask, "what grade do you think that would be?" When I did this last week with a sample of a project, the consensus was, "Well, that's about a B book." The important thing is the follow-up discussion: "Well, why is that? How could you make it better?" The key is to consider what could be done to improve it.

MARILYN: I also always tell kids that if they are able to justify a grade they think they should have gotten, and if they can either show me facts or give me some reasons why . . . hey, I'm willing to change it.

MARY: How can we connect grading and the different reasons for assessment? Most of us are required to record grades, whether we assign them or invite students to assign them for themselves. We know that there are different kinds of assessments going on simultaneously; there are the assessments that result in grades for students, and there's an assessment for teachers: Have we reached the goals we set for our teaching? So it isn't just that we're assessing kids and what they've demonstrated about what they know and they can do, but we're also assessing our teaching. How well have we taught an idea or a skill? How can we grade in a way that reflects these different kinds of assessment?

TIM: I don't particularly think grades serve very well at either purpose: assessing students or assessing ourselves. A letter grade is a low-information, singular mark that is supposed to convey something about a whole complex welter of factors. It sums up and labels, but it doesn't *teach* anything. We're usually not even very clear with students and parts—or ourselves, for that matter—about what grades denote. Do they communicate students' performance in relation to others? On a bell curve? Do they reflect each individual students' personal growth related to where they started the unit or semester? Do they reflect absolute performance against a set standard? Achievement? Effort? Number of tardies? Do they reflect the quality of our teaching? Sometimes they do each of these, I suppose, but we muddle it all up and reduce it to this singular standard. I don't like them.

MARY: I heartily agree. I want my students to take risks in their learning and to realize that learning often happens after a number of trial-and-error situations. They point out to me, however, the consequences for them if I don't take their grades very seriously.

TONI: I don't use comparative grades. I talk to students about their personal best. What is your personal best? That's my criterion for grading.

KRISTEL: Can I jump in here? This year I am in a program where we don't give letter grades, and we are trying to look at some different things. One is to have assessment criteria ahead of time for any task. I almost never put the criteria, or rubrics or scoring guides or whatever we're calling them these days, together by myself. I build them with the kids, with group discussion. For example, we do "expert projects," a project they work on for two and a half months on a topic they choose that they want to become an expert on, and then they have to give a half-hour presentation to the class. So we made up a scoring guide in the fall, we put the components together. My only requirement was that they had to do some sort of class participation during their presentation, because it's too boring if they just get up there and talk for a half hour.

TIM: So you have *some* standards! (*Laughter*)

KRISTEL: When we put the rubric together, the scoring scale together, we talked about aspects of a presentation like voice quality. Then we got in this huge thing about eye contact. Should it be on our scoring guide or shouldn't it be on there? I was forceful in my opinions as to why I thought certain things should be on there, and they were forceful in theirs, such as not wanting anything on there about not using "um." It was a great discussion. But the even more important discussion to me wasn't the first one, it was after they'd done their presentations of the expert projects, and we went back and reviewed the scoring guide and changed it. "Perhaps visuals shouldn't have the same weight as content," they said. So the scoring rubric we have now, a lot of it is the same. But they went back and changed some of it, and it's better overall. It has been very exciting to me to have them involved.

LIBBY: So then you do a different one with the next group, is that right?

KRISTEL: Well, we'll look together at the one I have and ask, "Do we want to use this or do we want to use something else? Do we want to throw the whole thing out and start again?" One of the things I'm going to push for next year is I would rather they didn't use numbers to rate each other, because I would rather see them doing written feedback comments.

MARK: I think that assessment has to happen in individual ways for each individual student. I'll see some student presentation, and the kid will think it's the greatest performance in the world. And I'll think, it really wasn't that great. But it really *was* for the kids. Here's an example: Our eighth graders have to do this exit project, and these two boys did one on photography. They went to a high school photography lab and learned how to develop film, then they went to a photographer and learned about what a professional photographer does, and finally they went to a camera store and saw masses of film getting developed. I heard their presentation, and I read their report, and they were really excited about it. But it was all stuff I already knew. So I was thinking, this isn't so great. But then I thought, *they* didn't know any of this stuff. Or when a kid goes up and presents before class who has never done that before, they are just so proud of the fact that they could make a presentation. So, I am less and less likely to give assessment criteria to students before they undertake a task. I want every kid to say, "Here's what I did well and here's where I need to improve," on their own individual terms. I don't want to impose a rubric or a generic standard or scoring guide or anything else except kids' own view of themselves. Someone will probably say about this attitude, "Well, then, how do we know how those kids stack up against the norm?" And I'll have to say, "I don't know." I'm probably in the wrong job now. Because when it comes right down to it, I can't assess students like that anymore. Each kid is so individual, there can't be a normative standard. A generic scoring guide doesn't celebrate the accomplishment of individuals. Like today, I see a student of mine, Tanita, going up and talking about the FBI and giving her eighth-grade exit report. This is a girl who two years ago would *never* have gotten up in front of a class. When she did her first expert project, it took two minutes: She was looking at the ground, and then she was back in her seat. This year, she spent fifteen minutes giving bland information very confidently! I was very happy. She was happy. The adult she worked with was happy. We were all happy.

TIM: The question, though, is what do you do when someone's not happy, when a student is happy and you, the teacher, feels this is really poor work or that the student has slacked off from her personal best?

MARK: The solution to that is in the relationship between student, teacher, and parents.

MARY: Mark, you talk about the kids' doing well. How do they know that they're doing well, if it's all individual? What is this standard of *well?*

MARK: It's *their* impression of "well."

MARY: How do they build that, how do they know?

KRISTEL: They've been in school for six years before they get to middle school! They have a very clear idea about who they are as students and whether they do well according to what school standards are. They know that stuff backward and forward.

MARY: So there *are* standards against which they are measuring themselves?

KRISTEL: Oh, yeah, they've gotten them from every teacher they've encountered for the first eleven years of their lives!

MICHELANN: Let's talk about the child who *doesn't* have a sense of *wellness,* the child who has been held up against these arbitrary standards and already by grade three is saying, "I'm not a good learner." The question for me is, How do we build success for a child through assessment? I consider assessment to be part of curriculum and instruction, and I think of it in terms of gathering information from students about what I've done, where they are, where we need to go, and how we're going to get there. I don't see it as simply an end point, a final judgment. I see it as an ongoing process, though in most places I don't see assessment being viewed as such. The critical thing we are working on next year at my school is designing ongoing assessment so we know where each child is and where we are in relation to each child, so we can shape what we do next. What are we going to do about it when kids don't learn?

KRISTEL: In my situation, we use a written assessment form that both students and teachers fill out. There is a split column, so one side has the student's response and the other the teacher's response. First term we did this, and I had several kids whose self-assessments and my assessments were quite different. This last term, they were much closer, because they've gone through it and they know. It's that question of learning the language and understanding where they are. I don't miss grades. Kids don't need them. I have a girl this year in eighth grade that I had in traditional sixth grade, and this is a girl who would barely speak in sixth grade in front of a group. This year, she was the first runner up for giving one of the eighth-grade speeches. There's no formal assessment of it, but she can get up there and is one of the funniest kids in the room, from being a wallflower.

TIM: Now wait a minute. This all sounds almost too good to be true. Both you, Kristel, and Mark have shared inspiring stories about great successes you have had with students. But the successes can't just be because of the fact that neither of you has to give letter grades in your programs. And what about the other stories?

MARK: Well, I do have some other stories. Let me give you this one. I'm reading off the self-reflection sheet we have kids do at the end of the year: "What were your biggest accomplishments this year?" I have this great kid in sixth grade, and I just read his response today. He wrote, "My greatest accomplishment is I never goof off and I get all my work in on time." And I just wrote back to him, "Bill, that's a lie." I mean, he knows it's a lie. I know it's a lie, and I don't know what he was doing.

KRISTEL: I have kids that don't do their work. And I do all the traditional things I have always done; they have to stay after school, I call their parents, and so forth. In some ways it's more difficult to deal with, because you can't hang the old "You're gonna get an F!" threat over their heads. But on our evaluation forms, on the column that says, "Works Up to Potential," I still have those kids who wrote, "Nope, I'm lazy, I'm not working up to my potential, I'm not doing all my work." Now "lazy" is a word I'd never use to describe any kid, but they are telling the truth on these assessments.

MICHELANN: I think we've built that into kids. I do not see one five- or six-year-old who does not want to learn—who says, "I don't want to learn." But I sure see it by eighth grade. So what kind of assessment *didn't* we use to move us forward with that enthusiastic six-year-old so that we produce an enthusiastic eight grader? At *all* schools, not just at schools where you have families that are very supportive, but at *all* schools—there's your high standard—we ought to be assessing children's movement, celebrating the successes, and finding ways when they don't succeed to do something different in our program, maybe even to throw it out and start over. I think of a teacher at my school who has revised her language arts program a number of times this year to meet the needs of the children that she has in the classroom. She came in with one mind-set, did good assessment, built in student reflection, and the information she got said to her, "Whoa! I need to do something quite different here." I guess I think of that as assessment, not just an end-of-term report card grade.

WINNIE: I think if we all did more individual conferencing all the way through a student's years, we'd be better serving kids. They need to hear, "This is what you're doing really well" and "This is a goal for you to work on" or "What do *you* think you should work on?" The impediment is the *time*.

MARY: I want to go back to the notion of a standard of "doing well." There is a balance in what I'm hearing. If we do not hold up some kind of a standard, then there's a vacuum.

But it's excessive to hold up value judgments of "good" and "bad," because in an ironic way, we defeat the very thing we want, which is for students to learn. Instead, the judgments may just make them want to give up. So we need some kind of idea of a goal or standard, but then we need for students to see themselves as individuals learning in their own ways, their own styles, making progress on their own time frames.

THERESA: Our district defeats that vision over and over. We teachers do all these wonderful different assessments, and we have students perform on papers and portfolios and self-assessments, and then the only thing the parent wants to talk about—and even the kid!—is the score they got on the district achievement test! You throw up your hands and say, "What have we done all year? What have you been doing?" With all this other valuable information, that one measure is still held up as the end-all and know-all.

MICHELANN: It's because we've allowed that to become the single measure. As teachers we need to have classroom assessment that is ongoing and diagnostic in measuring a child's growth. Then we need to hold that up and say, let's not be frightened of the district achievement test, it's one very tiny slice of information, here's this other body of evidence we have. And I think we can have standards for classroom-based assessment. I believe those would emerge as we began to talk among ourselves about the ways we assess and what we do with that assessment.

TIM: To me, district achievement tests are irrelevant to the ongoing work of the classroom. I recognize that they can have weighty consequences, because low scores may send students into remedial reading classes or the low track in high school. But I don't think the test is that revealing or relevant to my classroom program. If I don't already know before that midyear achievement test that a student has a reading problem, if I haven't seen it in my class and been addressing it, something is really wrong. I'm not observing very clearly or carefully. The district test shouldn't be telling me something I don't already know.

KRISTEL: But the tests are also important to many parents. For instance, I've got this student who came down with viral meningitis, right?

MICHELANN: The test caused it! Let's get rid of the test! *(Laughter)*

KRISTEL: And he takes the district standardized test when he's not feeling well, but his illness hasn't yet been diagnosed. Then he's hospitalized in intensive care, gone for months, the whole thing. So I'm going through my class's test scores, and I notice that this boy's test scores went down from the prior year. Surprise, surprise! But what's amazing to me is how little they went down. So I'm saying to his mother on the phone today, when she's calling me, because now he's back for the first full week of school after months away, "Isn't this a cool thing? His test scores hardly went down even though he was so ill. That Jeremy, he's super!" But she freaks out because his test scores went down. She tells me, "We've got to worry about this; we've got to watch these test scores." I'm coming from a totally different perspective. But the parents in my neighborhood feel it's important.

MARK: But it *is* important, because the test directly affects kids. I think of Tanita, again. It's really sad. She's going to high school next year, and I have to send her records up. She said to me the other day, "Mr. Oldani, you aren't going to have me put in the low class, are you?" She has always been in low classes until our program, and she has always scored in the lowest percentile on the district achievement tests. However, on the Oregon State Writing Assessment she scored very well, and she did that great presentation—for her—on the FBI today. So I know her individual strengths and weaknesses make a complex picture. However, I have *no* say in anything related to high school. They will just look at her number on the reading test—205, or whatever the score is—and they'll stick her in a remedial class, say she hasn't met graduation standards, and make her take the test again and again. And this girl has done all her homework, done everything that any teacher would ever ask anyone to do, reads tons of novels a year, and has performed. I called those guys down in the Evaluation Department, and I said, "Can we talk about this?" "No," they told me, "we can't." I said, *"Well, I know her better than you."* So, even though the district achievement test may not affect our classroom every day, it does impact in a big way some of our students. Furthermore, the test can be crucially important to programs, because the school board and the newspapers certainly pay attention to those scores. Those achievement test scores are relevant to politically-motivated school boards and to the public relations success of superintendents. And a lot of parents of students in our new program were looking for what the test scores did, as part of their judgment of the program and to make sure our students' scores didn't go down.

THERESA: So then principals get pressure from the school district. You know if your scores are below the baseline, you are going to start getting rid of new programs, throwing away enjoyable stuff, and begin pounding it into students and teachers because those scores are low.

TIM: Part of our job, then, is to work at the district level and with our parents and our peers to communicate that a single measure that takes place in a couple of hours once a year ought not to carry that much weight. What adult would stand for a short-term, multiple-choice test given once a year to make ultimate judgments about their job placements? For such a narrow measure to make such a difference, to actually hurt children and programs, doesn't make sense to me.

TONI: I think we teachers are partly to blame for the fact that there's so much weight given to the district achievement tests. We have not communicated with one another enough about the other types of successful assessments that we do in our classrooms. I also think that there's a place for the district assessment. Even if we did have performance-based evaluations and portfolios, something similar to these objective, comparative tests would be a part of the student's total evaluation as a kind of snapshot, one part of a whole evaluation process.

MARK: Classroom teachers do have ideas for alternative assessments, they just aren't accepted. If you're a teacher, let's face it, you're working time and a half. Do you really want to spend a lot of time developing an assessment that no one's willing to listen to? It's a lot of work. There is this attitude in education that we want only one answer. But why not let individual teachers or schools or clusters of schools try different things? Why not say to teachers, "We want to see other forms of assessment"? The school district has to encourage us to try things, but the only place that's going to come from is teachers saying, "We want to do it."

MICHELANN: We dissipate a lot of energy in the criticism of the big test, rather than saying, "Here is something that is good, that works better, that reflects what we're doing in the class-room." We can be more creative.

Outside, the sun was down and nighttime fully drawn. The lights of downtown Portland spread across the sky. Our evaluation: It was a beautiful spring evening. In our final assessment, we agreed that teachers don't get enough time to talk to one another. Together, we can *be more creative.*

About the Authors

Bill Bigelow teaches high school history in Portland, Oregon. Parts of his article first appeared in *Rethinking Our Classrooms: Teaching for Equity and Justice,* published by Rethinking Schools, Milwaukee, WI.

Winnie Charley has been the recipient of three Impact Two grants for innovative classroom projects. A graduate of Loyola University in Chicago, Winnie has an amateur theater background, which adds a dramatic dimension to her classroom. Winnie is currently teaching a seventh-grade integrated reading, language arts, and social studies block at Jackson Middle School.

Betty Hittle is recently retired from a twenty-year middle-school teaching career in Portland. Among other things, she taught science, math, and Core (literature, language arts, and social studies). She has also taught at the Oregon Museum of Science and Industry. Currently, she teaches geography to teachers and Mother-Daughter Choices for the American Association of University Women. She also volunteers as an expert on bats and birds for the Audubon Society and assists in her teacher-daughter's classroom when needed. More frequently, she can be found at the beach, traveling, or engaged in one of her many hobbies and pursuits.

Libby Kennedy began working with middle-school students in 1981 in Portland as a teacher of social studies, reading, art, language arts, and ceramics. After teaching in a Spanish/English bilingual program in Washington, D.C., Libby returned to Portland, where she presently teaches a Core program to eighth graders at Beaumont Middle School. She has been the recipient of three Impact Grants.

Toni Kennedy has been involved in education for the past twenty years. Her experience ranges from primary to graduate level teaching. She received her B.A. from Marylhurst College and her M.A. from St. Bonaventure University. She has taught social studies, literature, and language arts to eighth-grade students at Fernwood Middle School in Portland, Oregon for the past four years. Participation in the Oregon Writing Project and the Northwest Writing Institute has deepened her commitment to the writing process for herself and her students.

Kristel McCubbin currently teaches in a multi-age, interdisciplinary program at Mt. Tabor Middle School, which is similar to the I-Team described in the piece by Mark Oldani. Kristel has been involved in the Oregon Geographic Alliance Summer Institute both as a participant and an instructor. She recently participated in the National Geographic Society's first Urban Institute for teachers.

Theresa R. Murray began working with middle-school students in 1981 in Portland as a teacher of social studies, reading, and language arts. In 1982 she became involved with the Law Related Education Project. In addition to teaching many local training sessions for mock trials, she has participated as a coach and judge in local, regional, and national mock-trial competitions. She has been a consultant for the Social Science Education Consortium in writing performance assessment tools for Law Related Education activities. She has worked as a district social-studies specialist and currently serves on the board of the Oregon Council for the Social Studies.

After a variety of work experiences, **Jackie O'Connor** entered college at the age of twenty-eight. She spent her first years as a teacher, substituting in many schools in the Portland School District. For the past seven years, she has been teaching the sixth grade at Fernwood Middle School.

Born and raised in Germany, Jackie loves to travel, especially to places in the Caribbean area.

Mark L. Oldani is forty-three years old and has been a teacher for ten years and has taught middle school children for the last nine years. Before he became a teacher, Mark worked as a janitor, a warehouseman, and a lumber and sawmill worker.

Michelann Ortloff is currently principal at Applegate Elementary School in Portland. Previously, she was vice-principal at Sellwood Middle School. She has taught every age level from preschool through college, currently serves on the editorial board of the *Oregon English Journal,* and has served as president of the Oregon Council of Teachers of English and as codirector of the Portland Writing Project. Michelann is a writer and a poet.

Mark Woolley has spent twenty years in public education in Oregon as a social science teacher, curriculum developer, staff development specialist, and writer. Through an overseas study program at Lewis and Clark College in Portland he visited schools throughout Denmark and Norway and in 1985 spent six weeks in Japan as part of a Fulbright fellowship. His poetry and artwork have been published widely in small-press publications, with eleven illustrations in the 1994 publication of U.S. Poet Laureate Rita Dove's *Darker Face of the Earth,* published by Storyline Press. He currently works as a school-community resource specialist for the Classroom Law Project in Portland and serves as board president for "Sisters of the Road Cafe," a nonprofit dining facility offering low-cost meals and other services to residents of Portland's "Old Town."